FELIX'S LIFE OF SAINT GUTHLAC

Written around 730–740, the *Life of Guthlac* by the monk Felix is an important and colourful source for the obscure early history of East Anglia and the Fens. It describes how the youthful Guthlac (674–714) won fame at the head of a Mercian warrior band fighting the British on the borders of Wales before entering the monastery at Repton at the age of twenty-four. Distinguished from the first by his piety and asceticism, Guthlac moved on around 700 to a solitary life on Crowland, an uninhabited island accessible only by boat deep in the wild and desolate fenland separating Mercia and East Anglia. Here he built a shelter cut into the side of a burial-mound in which he lived austerely, skin-clad in the manner of the Desert Fathers, for the rest of his life. Tormented by demons but at the same time consoled by visions of angels, Guthlac gained a reputation for sanctity and miraculous healing which spread far afield and continued to grow after his death. This *Life* vividly reflects the cult of St Guthlac as it existed in East Anglia only a generation later.

FELIX'S LIFE OF
SAINT GUTHLAC

INTRODUCTION, TEXT,
TRANSLATION AND NOTES BY

BERTRAM COLGRAVE
formerly Reader in English, University of Durham

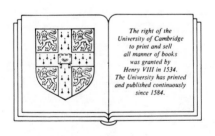

The right of the
University of Cambridge
to print and sell
all manner of books
was granted by
Henry VIII in 1534.
The University has printed
and published continuously
since 1584.

CAMBRIDGE UNIVERSITY PRESS

CAMBRIDGE

LONDON   NEW YORK   NEW ROCHELLE

MELBOURNE   SYDNEY

Published by the Press Syndicate of the University of Cambridge
The Pitt Building, Trumpington Street, Cambridge CB2 IRP
32 East 57th Street, New York, NY 10022, USA
10 Stamford Road, Oakleigh, Melbourne 3166, Australia

© Cambridge University Press 1956

First published 1956
First paperback edition 1985

Printed in Great Britain by Redwood Burn Limited, Trowbridge, Wiltshire

Library of Congress catalogue card number: 85–16620

British Library cataloguing in publication data
Felix
[Vita Sancti Guthlaci auctore Felice. *English
& Latin*] Felix's life of Saint Guthlac.
1. Guthlac, *Saint* 2. Christian saints –
England – Biography
I. [Vita Sancti Guthlaci auctore Felice. *English
& Latin*] II. Title II. Colgrave, Bertram
IV. Life of Saint Guthlac
270.2′092′4   BX4700.G95

ISBN 0 521 30926 3 hard covers
ISBN 0 521 31386 4 paperback

To the memory of
WILHELM LEVISON
and
EDWARD PACE

CONTENTS

PREFACE

FELIX's Life of St Guthlac has been printed on several occasions, the last time being by W. de Gray Birch in 1881. Admirable in many ways as his edition was, it was confined to a hundred copies, and these are now so rare as to be practically unobtainable. Though he was aware of the existence of a number of manuscripts of the Life, Birch contented himself with using the British Museum manuscripts only. It therefore came about that he failed to make use of the Douai manuscript 852 (D), originally a Crowland manuscript and of much importance both for the sake of the text itself and for the general light it throws upon the construction and use of the Life and the cult of the Saint. It therefore seemed worth while to produce a new text, with translation, critical apparatus, notes, etc., to make this important eighth-century work more easily available to scholars and others interested in the obscure early history of East Anglia and the Fens. Unfortunately the Pseudo-Ingulf's Chronicle has done so much to overlay this early history with a mass of unhistorical fabrications, that nowadays even serious scholars fall into the traps laid for the unwary by these fourteenth-century forgers, such, for instance, as the supposed foundation of a monastery at Crowland by Æthelbald.

I have followed in the main the method of editing which I have already employed in *Eddius's Life of Wilfrid* and the *Two Lives of St Cuthbert*. Though a great deal of information given in the latter might reasonably have been repeated in the *Life of St Guthlac* owing to the similarity of outlook and form of this Life with the *Vita Anonyma Cuthberti*, I have contented myself, for the most part, with a reference to the relevant notes in the *Two Lives*.

I am indebted to many friends for much help which I gladly and gratefully acknowledge: to the Librarians and staffs of the Durham University Library, the Durham Cathedral Chapter Library, the Cambridge University Library, the Library at

Corpus Christi College, Cambridge, the Bodleian Library, Oxford, the Department of Manuscripts, British Museum; and to the Librarians of the Public Libraries at Arras, Boulogne, and Douai, for allowing manuscripts to be deposited in the British Museum and photostats to be made there. I am also very grateful to Dr Dorothy Whitelock of St Hilda's College, Oxford, to Dr R. W. Hunt and Mr N. R. Ker and Professor R. A. B. Mynors of Oxford, to the late Professor Max Förster of Munich and Professor Francis Wormald of London, and the Rev. Father W. I. Meagher of Durham, for help of many kinds.

To three scholars I owe a very special tribute of grateful thanks: namely, to Professor Bruce Dickins of Corpus Christi College, Cambridge, and to Father Paul Grosjean, S.J., Bollandiste, for having read most carefully through practically the whole of my manuscript and for having made the most valuable criticisms and suggestions throughout; and to Dr Cyril Wright of the Department of Manuscripts of the British Museum from whom I obtained constant help and encouragement; his vast knowledge of palaeography and the make-up of manuscripts was always at my service. There is scarcely a page in the section devoted to a description of the manuscripts which does not owe something to him.

I am also very grateful to the Council of the Durham Colleges for generous grants towards the provision of photostats and other expenses.

The proofs were finally checked while I was teaching in the University of North Carolina, Chapel Hill, U.S.A., during the spring semester of 1956. I should like to acknowledge with gratitude the valuable help I received from members of the library staff there and also from several of my colleagues.

My thanks are also due to the Syndics of the Cambridge University Press for undertaking the publication of this volume and to the staff for their constant vigilance and unfailing patience.

This work was begun as far back as 1939, but, owing to the war, it had to be put aside for a number of years. After the war, other work, academic and literary, prevented me from making much headway with it. It is only during the last two or three years that I have been able to give my full attention to it. Through these delays I lost the assistance of two of my most valued helpers. In January 1947 Professor Wilhelm Levison died suddenly, but not before he had given me many notes and suggestions from his profound stores of learning which later proved of the greatest value. And after his death, his widow Mrs Elsa Levison allowed me to use his splendid library, a privilege which those who have visited their home in Durham will know how to appreciate. Even more suddenly, in February 1953, Edward Pace died while he was in the middle of going laboriously through my translation and making comments and suggestions of a kind which had helped me much in my other works. His knowledge of medieval Latin and his splendid sense of style made his help invaluable. It is with a deep sense of my obligation to them both that I gratefully dedicate this book to their memory.

BERTRAM COLGRAVE

DURHAM

ABBREVIATIONS

A.E.E.	G. Baldwin Brown, *The Arts in Early England*. 6 vols. London, 1903–37.
AA.SS.	*Acta Sanctorum*, ed. J. Bollandus and others. Antwerp, Brussels, 1643, etc.
A.S.C.	The Anglo-Saxon Chronicle in *Two Saxon Chronicles Parallel*, ed. J. Earle and C. Plummer, 2 vols., Oxford, 1892–9.
Aldhelm	*Aldhelmi opera*, ed. R. Ehwald. Berlin, 1919.
An. Boll.	*Analecta Bollandiana*. Brussels, 1882, etc.
Archiv	*Archiv der Gesellschaft für ältere deutsche Geschichtskunde*. Frankfurt-a.-Main und Hannover, 1820, etc.
B.h.L.	*Bibliotheca hagiographica Latina*, ed. Socii Bollandiani. Vols. 1, 2 and supp. Brussels, 1898–1911.
Bede, L.T.W.	*Bede, his Life, Times and Writings*, ed. by A. Hamilton Thompson. Oxford, 1935.
Bede, *Opp.*	*Venerabilis Bedae opera*, ed. J. Giles, 12 vols. London, 1843–4.
Bernard	E. Bernard, *Catalogi librorum manuscriptorum Angliae et Hiberniae*, 2 vols. Oxford, 1697–8.
Birch	*Memorials of Saint Guthlac of Crowland*, ed. W. de Gray Birch. Wisbech, 1881.
Bosworth-Toller	J. Bosworth and T. N. Toller, *An Anglo-Saxon Dictionary*. Oxford, 1882–98. Supplement by Toller, Oxford, 1908–21.
Cat. gén.	*Catalogue général des manuscrits des bibliothèques publiques de France*. Paris, 1849, etc.
Cath. Enc.	*Catholic Encyclopaedia*, 15 vols., index and supp. New York, 1907–22.
Catt. vett.	*Catalogi veteres librorum ecclesiae cathedralis Dunelmensis*. Surtees Society, vol. VII, 1837.
Chadwick, *O.E.N.*	H. M. Chadwick, *The Origin of the English Nation*. Cambridge, 1907.
D.C.B.	*Dictionary of Christian Biography*, ed. W. Smith and H. Wace, 4 vols. London, 1877–87.
D.N.B.	*Dictionary of National Biography*, ed. Leslie Stephen, etc., 63 vols. and 5 supps. London, 1885, etc.
Die Heiligen Englands	F. Liebermann, *Die Heiligen Englands*. Hannover, 1889.
Du Cange	C. Dufresne du Cange, *Glossarium mediae et infimae latinitatis*, ed. L. Favre, 10 vols. Niort, 1883–7.
Dugdale, *Monast. Anglic.*	Sir William Dugdale, *Monasticon Anglicanum*, 6 vols. in 8. London, 1817–30.

E.E.T.S.	Early English Text Society.
E.H.R.	*English Historical Review.* London, 1886, etc.
E.R.E.	*Encyclopædia of Religion and Ethics*, ed. J. Hastings, 13 vols. Edinburgh, 1908–26.
Eddius	*The Life of Bishop Wilfrid by Eddius Stephanus*, ed. Bertram Colgrave. Cambridge, 1927.
English Kalendars before 1100	F. Wormald, *English Benedictine Kalendars before 1100*, Henry Bradshaw Society. London, 1934.
English Kalendars after 1100	F. Wormald, *English Benedictine Kalendars after 1100*, 2 vols. Henry Bradshaw Society. London, 1938 and 1943/4.
Forstmann	H. Forstmann, *Untersuchungen zur Guthlac-Legende*, Bonner Beiträge zur Anglistik, vol. xii (1902), pp. 1–40.
Gonser	P. Gonser, *Das angelsächsische Prosa-Leben des hl. Guthlac.* Heidelberg, 1909.
Gougaud, C.C.L.	L. Gougaud, *Christianity in Celtic Lands.* London, 1932.
Greg. dial.	*Gregorii magni dialogi*, ed. U. Moricca, Fonti per la storia d'Italia. Rome, 1924.
H.A.	H. M. Chadwick, *The Heroic Age.* Cambridge, 1912.
H.ab.	*Historia abbatum auctore Beda*, ed. Plummer. See *H.ecc.*
H.B.S.	Henry Bradshaw Society.
H.ecc.	*Baedae historia ecclesiastica gentis Anglorum: venerabilis Baedae opera historica*, ed. C. Plummer, 2 vols. Oxford, 1896.
Halm	*Sulpicii Severi opera*, ed. C. Halm, Vienna Corpus, vol. i. 1866.
Hardy	*Descriptive Catalogue of MSS. relating to the History of Great Britain*, ed. T. D. Hardy, 3 vols. in 4. Rolls Series, 1862–71.
Hier. Vita Pauli	*Vita sancti Pauli auctore sancto Hieronymo.* Migne, *Patrologia latina*, vol. 23, cols. 17–30.
Historia Ingulphi	*Rerum Anglicarum scriptorum veterum tom. I.* Oxford, 1684, pp. 1–107.
Kemble, Cod. dip.	J. M. Kemble, *Codex diplomaticus aevi Saxonici*, 6 vols. London, 1839–48.
Ker, Med. Lib.	N. R. Ker, *Medieval Libraries of Great Britain.* London, 1941.
Kurz	B. P. Kurz, *From St Antony to St Guthlac.* University of California Publications in Modern Philology, vol. xii, no. 2, 1926, pp. 104–46.
L.I.S.	*Lives of Irish Saints*, ed. C. Plummer, 2 vols. Oxford, 1922.
Liber vitae	*Liber vitae ecclesiae Dunelmensis*, ed. J. Stevenson. Surtees Society, vol. xiii, 1841; and facsimile, Surtees Society, vol. cxxxvi, 1923.

Liebermann, *Neues Archiv*, XVIII	F. Liebermann, 'Über ostenglische Geschichtsquellen des 12., 13., 14. Jahrhunderts', *Neues Archiv*, XVIII (1892), pp. 225–67.
Mab. *AA.SS.*	*Acta Sanctorum ordinis sancti Benedicti*, 6 saecula in 9 vols., ed. J. Mabillon, Venice, 1733–8.
Migne	*Patrologiae cursus completus. Patrologia latina*, 221 vols. 1844–80.
N.E.D.	*A New English Dictionary on Historical Principles*, ed. J. A. H. Murray, etc. Oxford, 1888–1935.
Neues Archiv	*Neues Archiv der Gesellschaft für ältere deutsche Geschichtskunde*. Hannover, 1876, etc.
Plummer	See under *H.ecc.*
R.S.	Rolls Series.
Redin	Mats Redin, *Studies in Uncompounded Personal Names in Old English*. Uppsala Universitets Årsskrift. Uppsala, 1919.
Ryan, *Monast.*	J. Ryan, *Irish Monasticism*. Dublin, 1931.
Script. rerum Merov.	*Monumenta Germaniae historica. Scriptores rerum Merovingicarum*, 7 vols. 1885, etc.
Searle, *On. Sax.*	W. G. Searle, *Onomasticon Anglo-Saxonicum*. Cambridge, 1897.
Stenton	Sir Frank Stenton, *Anglo-Saxon England*. Oxford, 1943. Second edition, 1947.
Stubbs, *Dunstan*	*Memorials of St Dunstan*, ed. W. Stubbs. Rolls Series, 1874.
Surt. Soc.	Surtees Society Publications. Durham, 1834, etc.
Two Lives	*Two Lives of St Cuthbert*, ed. Bertram Colgrave. Cambridge, 1940.
V.a.	*Vita sancti Cuthberti auctore anonymo*, see under *Two Lives*.
V.C.H.	*Victoria History of the Counties of England*. London and Oxford, 1901, etc.
V.pr.	*Vita sancti Cuthberti prosaica auctore Beda*, see under *Two Lives*.
V.S.H.	*Vitae Sanctorum Hiberniae*, ed. C. Plummer, 2 vols. Oxford, 1910.
Vit. Ant.	*Vita sancti Antonii, auctore sancto Athanasio interprete Evagrio*. Migne, *Patrologia latina*, vol. 73, cols. 125–70.
Warner	Sir G. F. Warner, *The Guthlac Roll*. Roxburghe Club, Oxford, 1928.

INTRODUCTION

THE Fenland, that stretch of marshy land which covers some 1300 square miles of the eastern counties, has played a greater part than might have been expected in the history of Britain. It is just possible that there was some settlement in prehistoric times, seeing that Guthlac himself chose what may have been a prehistoric chamber grave as his abode. It is more probable, however, that this was a Roman rather than a prehistoric barrow,[1] for a chambered grave in this area dating from prehistoric times would be a very surprising exception to the general pattern of distribution of these monuments. During the Romano-British period, as recent research has shown, parts of the Fens were comparatively densely settled.[2] The irregularly shaped and small rectangular fields associated with the Celtic system of agriculture are found in various places throughout the area and would seem to suggest a fairly widespread occupation until somewhere about the middle of the fifth century. But by the end of the seventh century, when the Anglo-Saxon invaders had already been in the country for over two hundred years, they were thought of as typical marchlands such as the place where Grendel dwelt. He dwelt in the 'borderland, the fens and the fastnesses', and in the 'misty marshes' in 'perpetual darkness'.[3] Felix describes Guthlac's place of retreat in similar terms (c. xxiv). But whether there were any survivors of the British race is a more difficult question. It has usually been supposed that the Life provides sufficient evidence to prove this. But the passage in question (c. xxxiv)

1 G. E. Daniel, *The Prehistoric Chamber Tombs of England and Wales* (Cambridge, 1950), pp. 22–3 and notes.

2 See C. W. Phillips, 'Romano-British Times', in *The Cambridge Region*, ed. H. C. Darby (Cambridge, 1938), p. 92. See also H. C. Darby, *The Medieval Fenland* (Cambridge, 1940), pp. 3 ff., and particularly plate 2, an air photograph showing Romano-British evidence at Throckenholt, Isle of Ely.

3 See H. C. Darby, 'The Fenland frontier in Anglo-Saxon England', *Antiquity*, viii (1934), p. 185; *Beowulf*, ll. 103–4, 161–2; and D. Whitelock, *The Audience of Beowulf* (Oxford, 1951), pp. 75–6.

can hardly be interpreted in this sense.[1] Further it has been noticed that surviving place-names of Celtic origin are very few.[2] So far as the Anglo-Saxon invaders are concerned, it seems more than likely that though the Fens in Guthlac's time were wild and desolate country with a few scattered inhabitants, yet they had been explored and the more fertile lands occupied.[3] The figures in the 'Tribal Hidage', a document of presumed eighth-century date, which throws some light on the territorial divisions of the Midlands, would imply that the population was small and scattered.[4] Gradually, with the growth of the Mercian and East Anglian kingdoms, the Fenland seems to have become a frontier region, a march-land between East Anglia and Mercia, of which the southern portion including Ely was in the kingdom of East Anglia,[5] and the northern portion, the region around Crowland, Thorney and Whittlesmere, was part of Mercia.[6] It is a Mercian, Bishop Headda, who comes to ordain Guthlac and consecrate his island (c. XLVII). Crowland which is described as 'on middan Gyrwan fenne' in the 'Resting places of English Saints'[7] is described in the Life as being in the land of the Middle Angles (c. XXIV), or at least that is the reading of the two manuscripts (H and D) which are most closely connected with Crowland. The Middle Angles were a collection of peoples who by the middle of the seventh century had fallen under the domination of the Mercians.[8]

Guthlac, the subject of the Life, seems to have been born in the year 674, for Æthelred was already on the throne of Mercia (see c. 1). Felix tells us that Guthlac was of royal stock and

1 See, however, Arthur Gray's views 'On the late survival of a Celtic population in East Anglia', *Proceedings of the Cambridge Antiquarian Society* (N.S.), IX (1911), pp. 42–52; also K. Jackson, *Language and History in Early Britain* (Edinburgh, 1953), p. 236, n. 3; cf. below, p. 185.

2 Cf. O. K. Schram, 'Fenland Place Names', *The Early Cultures of Northwest Europe*, Chadwick Memorial Volume (Cambridge, 1950), p. 430.

3 C. Fox, *Archaeology of the Cambridge Region* (Cambridge, 1923), p. 274.

4 H. C. Darby, *The Medieval Fenland*, pp. 7ff.   5 *H.ecc.* IV, 19.

6 H. C. Darby, 'The Fenland frontier in Anglo-Saxon England', *loc. cit.* p. 195.

7 The 'Resting places of English Saints' is an eleventh-century document, in Latin and Old English found in several MSS. See *Liber vitae: Register and Martyrology of New Minster and Hyde Abbey*, ed. W. de Gray Birch (Hampshire Record Society, 1892), p. 88; and *Die Heiligen Englands*, p. 11.

8 Stenton, pp. 42–4.

belonged to the family of that Icel who was the great-grandson
of Offa I, king of Angel, and whose name appears in the
Mercian genealogies, five generations above Penda.[1] His father,
Penwalh, lived in the territory of the Middle Angles. The
infant is given the name of Guthlac 'after the tribe of the
Guthlacingas' (c. x). It may be that this family had descended
from the hero incidentally mentioned in the *Gesta Herewardi*[2]
who had once been celebrated in the songs of the ancients.
If so, it is not surprising that young Guthlac should have been
stirred by these songs of the ancient heroes to take up fighting.
We are told that he spent nine years in this way (c. xviii) so
that he must have begun his martial career at the age of fifteen.
Though Felix's account of these years is probably exaggerated,
yet it is clear that he must have gained some fame as a leader,
for we are told that his followers came from various races and
from all directions (c. xvii), a true indication of his military
prowess.[3] He seems to have done some, though not necessarily
all, his fighting on the Welsh marches, for the earthworks on
the Welsh border known as Wat's Dyke and Offa's Dyke[4]
remind us of the continual trouble on this Mercian border
throughout the seventh and eighth centuries. And indeed Felix
makes it quite clear that Guthlac had had much experience of
the Britons. He even states that Guthlac had been an exile
among them (c. xxxiv) and had learned their language. Is it
possible that at some time he may have been a hostage among
them, perhaps in his early youth?[5] But during a period of
temporary quiet Guthlac had time to think more seriously
about his future; the stories of the heroes which had once
stirred him to emulate their deeds, warned him of their wretched
deaths and shameful ends. So at the age of twenty-four he

1 *A.S.C.* (A) *sub anno* 626; I, p. 24.

2 'Godwin Gille who was called Godwin because he was not unequal to
that Godwine, the son of Guthlac, who was formerly celebrated in the songs
of the ancients.' *Gaimar*, ed. T. D. Hardy and C. T. Martin (R.S., 1888),
I, p. 372. See also R. M. Wilson, *The Lost Literature of Mediaeval England*
(London, 1952), p. 31.

3 Cf. *H.A.* pp. 350–1.   4 Stenton, p. 211, n. 2.

5 Dr Whitelock suggests that Guthlac's exile might, like Æthelbald's, be
connected with his royal descent and the fear of the reigning house that he
might strive for the throne.

decided to enter a monastery and took monastic vows at Repton in Derbyshire, a double monastery of monks and nuns, presided over by the Abbess Ælfthryth. There he speedily distinguished himself by his extreme piety and asceticism so that at first he gained the dislike of the brethren, especially because of his refusal to touch any intoxicating drinks. Herein he began his series of likenesses to St Cuthbert[1] which reached their climax in the death scene in which Felix borrows considerable sections from Bede's Life of that saint.

At Repton he received instruction in reading, chanting, and the usual ecclesiastical routine, and soon began to study the lives of hermits of the past and to emulate them, just as he had once emulated the deeds of earthly warriors. So, obtaining permission from the elders of the monastery, he made his way along the Roman road to Cambridge, a journey of some ninety miles, and thence by skiff to Crowland.[2] His first trip was no more than a preliminary survey, for after a few days he returned to Repton and there spent a period of ninety days, eventually returning to Crowland on St Bartholomew's Day.[3]

It was probably in the year 699 that Guthlac began his solitary life at Crowland. Æthelred of Mercia was still on the throne. Though his kingdom may have been less extensive than that of his father Penda and his brother Wulfhere, yet he seems to have ruled over a territory stretching to the west as far as the British kingdoms of Powys and Gwynedd and, in the south, towards the country about the middle and upper Thames.[4] To the north the river Humber formed the boundary once again, after the recovery of Lindsey from the Northumbrians in 678. Æthelred seems to have been a pious king, at any rate in his later days,[5] and his name is associated with the foundation of the monastery at Abingdon, while he granted lands in Wilt-

1 Cf. *V.pr.* c. 6. So far as Guthlac himself was concerned, the imitation was unconscious, for none of the Lives of St Cuthbert was written until after Guthlac's death.

2 Still in the twelfth century, Crowland could only be approached by water. H. C. Darby, *The Medieval Fenland*, p. 113.

3 25 August. See note, p. 182.   4 Stenton, p. 201.

5 Bede tells us that in 676 he made an attack on Kent and ravaged churches and monasteries there. *H.ecc.* IV, 12 and notes.

shire and south Gloucestershire to Aldhelm for the foundation of the monastery at Malmesbury.[1] He was also the benefactor of many other churches in his kingdom and the friend of Archbishop Theodore and St Wilfrid.[2] He finally retired to the monastery at Bardney in 704 and afterwards became its abbot.[3] His wife Osthryth, daughter of Oswiu, king of the Northumbrians, had been a great patroness of this monastery and had translated the bones of her kinsman St Oswald there; for some unknown reason she was murdered by the Mercians in 697.[4]

On the abdication of Æthelred, his place was taken by his nephew Cœnred who ruled until 709. He also was a pious king, but beyond that we know practically nothing of him except for Bede's story of the impenitent *gesith* whom Cœnred sought in vain to bring to repentance.[5] At the request of Æthelred he declared himself ready to receive Wilfrid on his return from his last appeal to the pope.[6] This was just after his accession. In 709 he also resigned and went to Rome where he was tonsured by Pope Constantine. It was evidently considered a great occasion, for the official historiographer of the popes duly recorded it.[7] Cœnred is mentioned only once by Felix and that casually. It was during his reign that Guthlac saw the devils who spoke British (c. xxxiv).

Cœnred was the son of Æthelred's brother and predecessor Wulfhere, but Æthelred had himself a son named Ceolred. It may be that he was passed over because he was considered too young to succeed in 704. It may equally well have been that his pious father suspected that the son might prove a bad ruler. Such indeed proved to be the case when he ascended the throne in 709, for in spite of his pious protestations to St Wilfrid,[8] he was a dissolute ruler. Boniface, in the famous joint letter he wrote with seven other bishops to Æthelbald, declares that it was from the time of Ceolred and his contemporary Osred,

---

1 Stenton, p. 68. 2 *H.ecc.* v, 19.
3 *Ibid.* v, 24; v, 19. 4 *Ibid.* v, 24.
5 *Ibid.* v, 13. 6 *Eddius*, c. 57.
7 *Liber Pontificalis, Pars Prior*, Vita Constantini, c. 9; ed. T. Mommsen (Berlin, 1898), p. 225.
8 *Eddius*, c. 64.

king of the Northumbrians, that the sacrilegious attacks on the English church could be dated.[1] Boniface speaks of his violation of nuns, his breaking into monasteries, how he was attacked by an evil spirit while sitting with his *gesithas* at a splendid banquet and how he died impenitent and unshriven. Boniface, in another letter to Eadburh, abbess of Thanet, describes how a monk of Much Wenlock had a vision of the next life and saw Ceolred being carried off by devils to the tortures of hell. Boniface declares that the monk saw the vision while Ceolred was still alive.[2] He died in 716.

Meanwhile Guthlac was pursuing his solitary life in his hermitage at Crowland. But one of his many visitors to his lonely island was none other than Æthelbald who was eventually to be Ceolred's successor. From Felix we learn that he was living as an exile because, being the grandson of Penda's brother Eowa, he was a possible rival to Ceolred. His visits to the saint during this period seem to have been numerous and on one occasion at least (c. XL) he is in the company of Wilfrid who, with Cissa, Guthlac's successor at Crowland, afterwards provided some of the material from which Felix composed the saint's Life. One of Æthelbald's retainers, Ecga, was freed from an evil spirit by the saint (c. XLII), while another *gesith*, Ofa, was cured of a poisoned foot (c. XLV). Later (c. XLIX), Felix describes how Æthelbald once came to Guthlac for comfort and was assured that, in spite of Ceolred, he would become king in due course and by peaceful means. When Æthelbald hears of the saint's death (c. LII) he hurries to the island in great distress and visits his tomb. That night, while sleeping in the saint's cell, he is visited by Guthlac in a vision and is promised that within twelve months he will have ascended the throne. And in 716 he became king, apparently soon after the elevation of the saint's relics by his sister Pega. The latter, twelve months after Guthlac's death, had placed her brother's incorrupt body in a shrine which was afterwards enriched by Æthelbald (c. LI).

---

1 *S. Bonifatii et Lulli epistolae*, ed. Tangl (Berlin, 1916), *Ep.* 73, pp. 152–3.
2 *Ibid. Ep.* 10, p. 14. See also K. Sisam, 'An Old English translation of a letter from Winfrith to Eadburga', *Studies in the History of Old English Literature* (Oxford, 1953), pp. 199 ff.

It is no wonder that the king should have honoured the holy man with whom he had so often taken refuge and from whom he had received much encouragement. Nor is it surprising that Felix should speak highly of him. When he wrote, Æthelbald still seems to have been at the height of his power (cf. c. LII). But, judging by the letter already mentioned which Boniface and his seven fellow-bishops sent to Æthelbald about the year 746, there was a gloomier side to the picture. There he is accused of leading a dissolute life and making attacks on the privileges and possessions of monasteries. It may well be that in his later life he wandered from the paths of virtue. At any rate we know that he became a powerful monarch, and in 731 according to Bede[1] all the 'provinciae' south of the Humber were subject to him and remained so in spite of various revolts until his death in 757, when after reigning for forty-one years he was murdered one night by his bodyguard at Seckington near Tamworth.[2]

Very soon after the saint's death a miracle is performed at his tomb (c. LIII) and this, so far as Felix is concerned, is the end of the story except that we have already been informed that Cissa, a converted pagan, became his successor in the island (c. XLVIII) and, when Felix was writing, he was still there. It is important to notice that there is no hint in Felix of the foundation of a monastery. One can only presume that, when Felix was writing, there was no monastery there but just the hermit's cell and the shrine of the saint.

And now occurs a blank in the history of Crowland which was later filled up by Ordericus Vitalis and still later by the fourteenth-century forger who invented the so-called Chronicle of Ingulf.[3] The account of the foundation of a monastic establishment at Crowland immediately after the death of Guthlac comes, not from Felix, but from the pen of Ordericus, and was obviously regarded by the thirteenth-century monks as the official account, for in MS. Douai 852 (D) which was certainly written at Crowland, the passage from Ordericus

1 *H.ecc.* V, 23.
2 *A.S.C. s.a.* 755 and note; II, p. 47.
3 Cf. F. Liebermann, *Neues Archiv*, XVIII, pp. 255 ff.

which contains his account of the foundation has been added to the end of Felix's Life.[1]

Some time during the abbacy of Abbot Geoffrey (1110–24), Ordericus spent five weeks at Crowland at the abbot's invitation and, while there, he put together the traditions of the monastery which he had learned from the sub-prior Ansgot. He began with a summary of Felix's Life, which he describes as being 'very long and the style somewhat obscure'. Perhaps the difficulty of the Latin led Ordericus to exaggerate the length. He confuses Felix the author with Felix who established a see at Dunwich and converted the East Angles, oblivious of the fact that Bishop Felix died twenty years before Guthlac was born. After the summary, Ordericus goes on to describe the foundation of the monastery by Æthelbald. Having already followed Felix in describing how Æthelbald had heard of the death of Guthlac while still an uncrowned exile, he nevertheless immediately afterwards tells the traditional story of the Crowland monks, how Æthelbald had visited the saint as king and how Guthlac had asked the king for a quiet abode on the island and, to ensure this, the latter had granted him a considerable piece of land free of all customary dues, which grant he later confirmed by charter. The charter, obviously a forged one, still remains.[2] Needless to say it was very much to the benefit of the monastery in the early days of the Conquest to be able to point to ancient authority for the possession of the lands. But it has often been pointed out that the charter attributed to Æthelbald offers immunities quite unknown in the eighth century.[3]

Ordericus then goes on to assert that after the foundation by Æthelbald the continuity of the monastery was never broken. But he is only able to name one abbot, 'Kenulphus', during the period between 710 and 870 and that on the extremely uncertain evidence of an inscription on a boundary

1 See p. 39, n. 2 below.

2 Dugdale, *Monast. Anglic.* II (1819), p. 107. Kemble, *Cod. dip.* no. 66, I, p. 77.

3 Liebermann, *Neues Archiv*, XVIII, pp. 247–8. Hickes, in his *Thesaurus*, as early as 1703 drew attention to the fact that the charter was probably forged. G. Hickes, *Thesaurus*, III, p. 73.

stone.[1] He goes on almost immediately to speak of the destruction of the monastery by the Danes in 870 and its refoundation under Thurketyl in the reign of Eadred (946–55). It is clear that the monastic traditions in Ordericus's time were largely based on imaginings rather than on facts.

Though the tradition of the establishment of a monastery at Crowland before the mid tenth century[2] is based on little or no evidence, yet the interest in the saint is vouched for by the appearance of Felix's Life some time before 749. But there are no facts to go upon until the second half of the tenth century when his name appears in the Old English Martyrology,[3] while by 970 the saint's name already appears in capitals in the Leofric Missal from Glastonbury under 11 April. His appearance in this calendar may be due to the fact that some relics of the saint had already by this time reached the monastery there.[4] Another late tenth-century calendar which contains his name under 11 April is also from the West Country and is now in Salisbury Cathedral library.[5]

By the beginning of the eleventh century there was to be found an Anglo-Saxon translation of Felix's Life and two Anglo-Saxon poems on him, as well as the reference in the 'Resting places of English Saints', and the entry in the *Anglo-Saxon Chronicle* under the year 714.[6] A mass for the feast of

1 There is still a base of a boundary cross known as Kenulph's stone. It stands on the old bank of the Welland where a drain called Southlake runs into the Welland. It is now surmounted by a modern block of stone marking the boundary between Kesteven and Holland with the date 1817. A. S. Canham, 'Notes on the history, charters, and ancient crosses of Crowland', *Fenland Notes and Queries*, II (1894), p. 249.

2 The date given by Ordericus Vitalis for the refoundation of the monastery by Thurketyl between 946 and 955 can hardly be correct as Dr Whitelock has shown in her article entitled, 'The conversion of the eastern Danelaw', *Saga Book of the Viking Society*, XII (1941), pp. 174–5. That there was a monastery there in the early eleventh century is proved by the reference to a monastery in the 'Resting places of English Saints'; *Die Heiligen Englands*, p. 11.

3 Ed. G. Herzfeld, E.E.T.S. 116, 1900. See below, p. 25.

4 *John of Glastonbury*, ed. T. Hearne (Oxford, 1726), I, p. 19; II, p. 446. Henry de Blois, bp of Winchester, is said to have given *a great part* of the body of St Guthlac to Glastonbury. Cf. c. 11 and p. 10 below.

5 *English Kalendars before 1100*, p. 19.

6 See below, pp. 19 ff.

St Guthlac appears under 11 April at the beginning of the famous Jumièges Missal of the mid-eleventh century now in Rouen,[1] while part of another eleventh-century mass for the feast on 11 April occurs in MS. Harl. 1117.[2] His name also appears regularly in the eleventh century in West Country and South Country calendars including Canterbury,[3] and of course figures importantly in the Crowland calendar about 1050 (MS. Oxford Bodl. Douce 296), which also gives his translation feast as 30 August, though it is not at all clear what translation this was. All this leads one to suppose that his cult was popular and widespread. But it is worth noting that Ælfric in his Homily on St Edmund (996–7) does not mention the fact that St Guthlac's body was found uncorrupt, though three of the four uncorrupt saints he mentions were connected with East Anglia (St Edmund, St Æthelthryth and 'her sister', presumably St Withburga). The fourth saint was St Cuthbert. William of Malmesbury mentions seven uncorrupt saints, adding to the above four, Fursey, Ælfheah and even Waltheof, but yet omits all mention of St Guthlac. This silence suggests that though the cult was widespread, it was not so popular as that of such saints as St Cuthbert, St Edmund, or even St Æthelthryth of Ely.[4]

In the second half of the eleventh century and during the rule of the first abbot of Crowland whose name is definitely known

1 This famous missal was written for Robert of Jumièges while he was bishop of London (1044–50). It was sometimes known as the 'Book of St Guthlac', because the mass of the saint appeared at the beginning of the book. H. A. Wilson, *The Missal of Robert of Jumièges* (H.B.S. 1896), pp. xix–xx, 3.

2 See *Two Lives*, p. 28. There is also a fragment of an office for the feast of St Guthlac, with neumes, in MS. C.C.C.C. 198 at fo. 377b. The MS., though it once belonged to Worcester, was not necessarily written there; it is a late eleventh-century book of homilies; the office, however, may well have been added at Worcester. Cf. Birch, pp. 70–1. K. Sisam, *Studies in the History of Old English Literature*, p. 155, n. 4. For references to Guthlac relics at Lincoln and Salisbury see C. Wordsworth, *Notes on Mediaeval Services in England* (London, 1898), pp. 155–6, 222–3, 257, and *idem, Ceremonies and Processions of the Cathedral Church of Salisbury* (Cambridge, 1901), p. 38.

3 *English Kalendars before 1100*, p. 173.

4 B. Thorpe, *Analecta Anglo-Saxonica* (London, 1868), p. 125. William of Malmesbury, *Gesta Pontificum*, ed. N. E. S. A. Hamilton (R.S. 1870), pp. 33, 154, 171, 266–7, 275, 322f., 337.

(Ulfcytel), the famous Earl Waltheof was executed for treason (1076). The abbot got permission to have his body reburied at Crowland. Though there is little evidence that Waltheof gave the monastery any lands, yet so great was the honour with which he was reburied, that in the twelfth century he was referred to by a chronicler, Ralph de Diceto, as the founder of Crowland monastery.[1] Ulfcytel's successor Ingulf (1085–1110), the abbot on whom the fourteenth-century forgeries were fathered, translated the body of Waltheof to the church, from the chapter house where it had originally been placed in 1076, and miracles were recorded at the shrine. The disastrous fire of 1091 only led to a great rebuilding during the abbacy of Geoffrey, formerly prior of Saint-Évroul, who was appointed by Henry I in 1110. It was while he was abbot that Ordericus came, at his invitation, to Crowland and wrote the history of the place as described above. Geoffrey, obviously an enthusiastic abbot, determined to make Crowland into a splendid and wealthy monastery. Much was made of the two local saints, for Waltheof had by this time achieved the rank of saint, and Ordericus seems to have been provided fully with the local traditions from which his pseudo-historical account is made up. It would seem as if it was all part of Geoffrey's scheme that he obtained the services of his late fellow-monk of Saint-Évroul, now well known as a historian, to provide the necessary historical justification for the cult of the two saints.

Geoffrey's successor was Waltheof, a relation of the earl, who naturally encouraged the cult of his famous kinsman. But he did not neglect St Guthlac, and on 23 August 1136 took place an elaborate translation of which an account is preserved in the D manuscript, probably written during the abbacy of Edward (1142–72). In the same manuscript also occurs the *Miracula sancti Waldevi gloriosi martyris*, probably written about the same time, though based upon an apparently earlier *Libellus de miraculis Waltheofi ex quibus probatur quod merito nomen martyris ei adscribitur*, quoted by Jocelyn of Furness about

1 *Ralph de Diceto*, ed. W. Stubbs (R.S. 1876), II, p. 211. Cf. also Forrest S. Scott, 'Earl Waltheof of Northumbria', *Archaeologia Aeliana* (4th series), XXX (1952), pp. 163–4.

1207.[1] In 1147 another disastrous fire took place, but thanks to Edward's enthusiasm, the buildings were largely restored before his death in 1172.

Thus the cult of Guthlac continued to flourish, though that of his fellow-saint, Waltheof, seems to have faded away after the end of the century. Crowland too became richer and more important owing to the gradual reclamation of Fenland which took place about this time.[2] It was some time towards the end of the century that there were drawn the eighteen or more roundels illustrating scenes from the life of the saint, which are now preserved in B.M. Harl. Roll Y. 6.[3] This is a roll measuring in its present state 9 ft. by 6½ in. containing eighteen roundels, each 6 in. in diameter. Only half of the first roundel survives and it looks as if there may have been two more. Each picture has a short explanatory inscription on it. The last represents Æthelbald and twelve other benefactors of Crowland, with the donation of each written out on a scroll which he carries in his hand. One of these, Alanus de Croun, is offering Frieston Priory to the saint. This was founded in 1141 and so we get the earliest date for the pictures. They were quite possibly intended as sketches for painted glass windows, though no evidence remains that they were ever used for this purpose.[4]

1 *AA.SS.* Aug. I, pp. 249–51. Cf. Liebermann, *Neues Archiv*, XVIII, p. 250. See also p. 41.

2 K. Major, 'Conan son of Ellis, an early inhabitant of Holbeach', *Lincs. Architect. and Archaeol. Soc. Reports and Papers*, XLII (1936), p. 1. Also H. C. Darby, *The Medieval Fenland*, pp. 43 ff.

3 This roll has often been reproduced, e.g. by J. Nichols, *History and Antiquities of the County of Leicester* (London, 1807), IV, pt. I, pp. 1–7; Jacob Schnebbelie, *The Antiquaries' Museum* (London, 1791); Birch, pp. xxxv ff.; Gonser, pp. 189 ff. But for a full account and the best reproductions of these pictures see Warner.

In the thirteenth-century catalogue of the library of Leominster is an entry *Rotula cum vita sancti Guthlaci anglice scripta*, *E.H.R.* III (1888), p. 124; and also R. M. Wilson, *The Lost Literature of Medieval England* (London, 1952), p. 98. What this was we do not know, but it is tempting to suppose that it may have been related to the Harley Roll. Perhaps it was a similar series of pictures with English captions.

4 A. S. Canham, however, writing in the nineties of last century says that 'quite recently a fragment of glass was found near the great west window with ornaments and treatment very similar to the aforesaid drawings'. *Fenland Notes and Queries*, II (1894), p. 252. See also, F. Wormald, 'Some illustrated manuscripts of the Lives of the Saints', *Bulletin of the John Rylands Library*, XXXV (1952), pp. 262 f.

Judging by the form of the name Beccelmus, which only occurs in D, it is possible that this may have been the manuscript of the Life which the artist had before him. On the other hand it may be that Beccelmus was the traditional Crowland form. The artist also had access to the history of Ordericus, or perhaps he was relying, like Ordericus, on the local tradition, for he too makes Æthelbald visit the saint, not as an uncrowned exile, as Felix does, but after he had become king, an anachronism of which Ordericus was also guilty. But, in addition, the artist makes two mistakes which do not occur in Felix or Ordericus: the abbess of Repton is called Ebba instead of Ælfthryth, while Headda of Lichfield is confused with Hæddi, bishop of Winchester, a confusion also found in the eleventh- and fifteenth-century Crowland calendars (see p. 190). He also uses two pieces of local tradition. One of these is that Bartholomew presented the saint with a scourge: in plate 8 of the roll Bartholomew is seen presenting the saint with it, which Guthlac is seen to be using effectively against a devil in the next plate.[1] The other tradition is that the saint possessed a psalter. This psalter which is recognizable by its curious shape, is seen first of all in the hands of the abbess when Guthlac is being tonsured at Repton (pl. 3). In plate 4 he holds it in his hand though its curious projection is hidden under a fold of his garment. In plate 6 he also holds it in his hand while he converses with the angel. In plate 8 Bartholomew holds it in a fold of his garment while he presents Guthlac with the scourge. In plate 9 the psalter is on the altar in his oratory while he uses his scourge upon a devil. In plate 11 where he is being ordained by Headda, a monk holds it, also in a fold of his garment, while in plate 12 Guthlac holds it as he consoles Æthelbald (who is wearing a crown and is called 'Æthelbaldus rex'). As Pega (pl. 15) enters the boat to see about the burial of her brother at Crowland, a monk

---

1 The scourge which is not mentioned in Felix is referred to in the Pseudo-Ingulf; on the seal of Henry Longchamp is a representation of St Bartholomew giving a three-lash scourge to St Guthlac. The latter seems to be holding a book, perhaps the psalter. Cf. Warner, p. 23. The same three-lash scourge appears on a shield on a medieval boundary cross between Thorney and Crowland, known as Thurketyl's Cross; *Fenland Notes and Queries*, II, p. 237; see also p. 24 below.

behind her carries it, and lastly in plate 17 when the saint appears to Æthelbald, he is still carrying the book, again holding it in a fold of the garment.[1] It is clear therefore that the psalter played an important part in the Crowland tradition.[2] It is mentioned in the poem referred to below (p. 23), written by Henry of Avranches; the Pseudo-Ingulf also knew the tradition and relates how when Pega went to elevate her brother's relics she left the psalter and scourge in the hands of Kenulph, the supposed abbot of the monastery which, according to this account, had been recently formed.[3]

Henry Longchamp, brother of William Longchamp, bishop of Ely and chancellor to Richard I, was appointed abbot in 1191 and ruled for forty-six years. During this time, owing to his enthusiasm and vigour, the abbey flourished. A new epitome of Felix's Life was made by Peter de Blois; a new poem was made at the abbot's request on the same subject by Henry of Avranches and based upon Peter's epitome.[4] The saint's body was again translated on 27 April 1196. Not content with this policy of reviving the cult of St Guthlac, Henry Longchamp also had the bones of St Neot translated from St Neots in Huntingdonshire and the bones of St Waltheof translated in 1213. It is doubtless to his time that the collection of writings associated with the three saints belongs, which is found in the manuscript D.[5]

1 This method of holding a book, especially a sacred book, is frequently seen in Christian art, from the earliest times. It is seen in England, for instance, on the coffin of St Cuthbert and on the south face of the Ruthwell Cross, in the Lindisfarne Gospels and the Book of Kells, all seventh-century work. For later English examples see Francis Wormald, *English Drawings of the Tenth and Eleventh Centuries* (London, 1952), pls. 2, 4*b*, 6*b*. See also F. Cabrol et H. Leclercq, *Dictionnaire d'archéologie chrétienne*, x, col. 1209, *s.v. mains voilées*.

2 It was this tradition which led to the belief that Guthlac had translated the Psalter into English. A certain John Lambert, who in 1538 was accused of heresy, declared that he had seen a book at Crowland Abbey called 'St Guthlac's Psalter', which was kept as a relic. He recognized that it was in Old English and took it to be King Alfred's translation of the Psalter (the Paris Psalter?). *Foxe's Acts and Monuments*, ed. G. Townsend and S. R. Catley, v (1887), p. 213. This statement led to the confused belief that the translation was Guthlac's own work. See A. S. Cook, *Biblical Quotations in Old English Prose Writers* (London, 1898), pp. xviii ff.

3 *Historia Ingulphi*, p. 5. See above, p. 8.

4 See below, pp. 22 ff.   See below, pp. 40 ff.

Of the cult of the saint during the next centuries, there is little more to say. He is mentioned in a mid twelfth-century Durham Calendar (Durham Cathedral Chapter Library, MS. B. iv. 24). There is an office for his festival in the thirteenth-century Hereford Breviary.[1] The fact that his Life appears in the great passionals, such as the late thirteenth-century passional of Jervaulx (E₂) or the West Country collection of lives from the fourteenth century recently in Gotha (G), shows that he had not been forgotten. Churches with ancient dedications to him occur in the counties of Bedford, Leicester, Lincoln, Northampton and Norfolk,[2] and there was a priory in Hereford also dedicated to him. But it is curious that there are no dedications to him in the West Country where his cult seems to have been popular. At Crowland of course his popularity remained and more particularly because of the quarrels which were constantly arising between the Fenland monasteries over the possession of lands. St Guthlac was constantly invoked in the forged charters which the Pseudo-Ingulf and the Pseudo-Peter have preserved.[3] On the whole one may say that his cult in these later centuries was largely inspired by the constant efforts of the Crowland Abbey authorities to keep his fame as widely spread as possible, not only to encourage pilgrims but also to give them a strong and early claim to the lands which they fought for so strenuously all through the Middle Ages.

AUTHORSHIP, DATE, SOURCES AND STYLE

The Life was written, as the prologue tells us, by a certain Felix who calls himself 'catholicae congregationis vernaculus', though nothing very definite can be deduced from this phrase for it is borrowed from Aldhelm's preface to his work called *De metris et enigmatibus*.[4] The Life was written at the request of King Ælfwald of the East Angles who ruled from about 713 to 749 and who addressed a letter to Boniface[5] promising him

1 W. H. Frere and L. E. G. Brown, *The Hereford Breviary* (H.B.S. 1910), II, pp. 140ff.
2 F. Arnold-Forster, *Studies in Church Dedications* (London, 1899), III, p. 365.
3 Liebermann, *Neues Archiv*, XVIII, pp. 257ff., 263.
4 *Aldhelmi Opera*, ed. R. Ehwald (Berlin, 1919), p. 61.
5 *S. Bonifatii et Lulli epistolae* (ed. Tangl), *Ep.* 81, p. 181. The widespread

the prayers of seven of the monasteries of his kingdom. Little is known of Ælfwald otherwise. It is clear that Felix was either an East Angle or at least living in East Anglia when this was written, for besides this dedication he refers to another king, Aldwulf (c. xlviii), without mentioning the fact that he was king of the East Angles. Felix was certainly a monk and perhaps he lived in one of the seven monasteries which Ælfwald spoke of to Boniface, but we do not know which one. Why Ælfwald should have asked for the Life of a Mercian saint is not clear, though possibly, because Crowland was on the borderland, it was of interest to both. And the favourable picture of King Æthelbald in the Life, and the important place he occupies, suggest that the relationship between Æthelbald and Ælfwald was good at the time when Felix was writing. It may well be that Æthelbald had taken refuge in East Anglia during the exile and so, though according to Bede all English provinces were subject to him,[1] yet he had grateful remembrances of kindnesses received during his time of exile. Of Felix's identity we know nothing. But one or two facts may be deduced about him. He was not influenced by the Celtic tradition. He states very definitely that Guthlac received the Petrine tonsure at Repton (c. xx), and, later on (c.xlvi), he makes Wigfrith speak slightingly about the 'pseudo-anachoritae' whom he had seen among the Irish.[2] He was a good scholar and familiar with Bede's writings, or at any rate with the Life of St Cuthbert which he uses very considerably. He was also familiar with some of the works of Aldhelm and of course with those lives of saints which had much influence on all writers of saints' lives of the seventh, eighth and later centuries. These were Sulpicius Severus's *Vita Martini*, his Epistles and Dialogues dealing with the same saint, Jerome's

idea that the Life was dedicated to Æthelbald of Mercia is due to a mistake on the part of Mabillon who headed the prologue 'Prologus ad regem Ethelbaldum'. This was copied by the Bollandists, though the Bollandist editor in a note equates Ethelbaldus with Ælfwaldus, king of the East Angles. Birch repeats this error (p. liii) and so do Forstmann (p. 17) and Plummer (ii, pp. xxxvi, 342).

1 *H.ecc.* v, 23.

2 It is only fair to note that Wigfrith adds that there were also true anchorites in Ireland.

Vita Pauli, Athanasius's *Vita Antonii* in Evagrius's translation, and Gregory the Great's Life of St Benedict as told in the second book of his *Dialogi*. In addition, like every other medieval writer, he was familiar with Virgil, and frequent Virgilian echoes appear throughout the text. Our writer too knew the *Vita Fursei*, as one would expect, considering his interest in visions of the next world. And needless to say he was very familiar with the Scriptures and has many biblical quotations and echoes, especially from the Psalms.

Felix's style seems to have caused difficulty from early times, for Ordericus refers to it as being 'prolixus et aliquantulum obscurus'. Nor need we be surprised when it is noticed that for nearly fifty words the only authority quoted by Du Cange is Felix.[1] In addition to that there are a number of poetical phrases borrowed particularly from Aldhelm with whose prose and metrical treatise on Virginity he seems to have been very familiar. From the metrical treatise we find *virecta* (pr.), *omnitenens* (c. IV), *luciflua* (c. IX), *forcipe* (cc. XIX, XXXIX), *torridas, tartari turmas* (c. XXVII), *caelicolae* (c. XXIX), *strofosus* (c. XXX), *buccula, flammivomo, raucisonis* (c. XXXI), *limphas* (c. XXXV), *sablone* (c. XLIV), *spiraminibus* (c. L), while from Aldhelm's prose treatise on the same subject there are: *fribulas, deliramenta* (c. XII), *libaminis* (c. XX), *roscidis* (c. XXII), *criptas, intercapedinem* (c. XXXI), *laticibus* (cc. XXIV, XXXI). All this is sufficient to show the debt of the author to Aldhelm. To him too he probably owes his fondness for alliteration, many examples of which are to be found, especially in the first few chapters. And in all likelihood he imitated Aldhelm in his use of glossaries where he would find such words as *libratim* (pr.), *spatulo* (c. XIX), *ventinulam* (c. XXXIX), *orfanitatem* and *offertoriam*

---

1 The words are: *perculserit, rivantur, volentiae, ortodemia, libratim, ortonomia* (pr.), *epidendarum, nixandi* (c. IV), *propiante* (c. VIII), *auleis* (c. XI), *bardigiosas* (c. XII), *spatulo* (c. XIX), *moderantiae, flactris, rivigarum* (c. XXIV), *vestimine, poculamento* (c. XXVIII), *venenifluam* (c. XXIX), *zabuliticum* (c. XXX), *clangisonis, sparginibus, favillantium, falsivomis* (c. XXXI), *gallicinali, strimulentas* (c. XXXIV), *tonderare, hebido* (c. XXXV), *simulaticias, axatum* (c. XXXVI), *ventinulam* (c. XXXIX), *limali, exerti* (c. XLI), *verbocinium* (c. XLIII), *notabunda, ludibri* (c. XLIV), *anximonia, medilanium, inflatico, luterio, melotinae* (c. XLV), *pseudo-sanctitatis* (c. XLVI), *pallidescere, transtolli* (c. L), *annilem* (c. LII). Some of the words occur more than once, but only the first occurrence is noted.

(c. LIII). But side by side with this he seems to have had a flair for inventing new words, such as *ignivomos* and *falsivomis* based on Aldhelm's *flammivomus*, or *clangisonis* based on Aldhelm's *raucisonus* (all in c. XXXI), or forms like *tonderare* from *tondere* (c. XXXV), or *bardigiosos* based on *bardus* (c. XII), or the curious *verbocinium* which he uses three times in three consecutive chapters (cc. XLIII, XLIV, XLV), based perhaps on *sermocinatio*. He also uses or invents a few words of Greek or partly Greek extraction, such as *ortodemia* and *ortonomia* (pr. etc.), *plasma* (c. XXX, an Hisperic borrowing),[1] *pseudo-sanctitatis, pseudo-anachoritas* (c. XLVI), and *pseudo-sodalitate* (c. XXX heading).[2] But in addition to this ornate and bombastic style, there is a tendency especially in the later chapters to model himself on Bede rather than Aldhelm, as for instance in the straightforward but none the less vivid account of the erring monks who visited the widow (c. XLIII), or the chapters dealing with the saint's death and the miracles after his death. Nor is this surprising considering the amount he has borrowed verbally from Bede's Prose Life of St Cuthbert. To sum up, it may be said that Felix stands stylistically as well as geographically between the two contemporary schools of writing, the far-fetched highly elaborate and often almost unintelligible style of Aldhelm whose influence, especially in the south, was great; and that of the north-eastern scholar whose Latin style, though by no means entirely free from rhetorical elaboration, was nevertheless clarity itself, compared with that of Aldhelm.

The date of the Life is fixed within definite limits, for the translation took place twelve months after the saint's death in 715, and the visit of Æthelbald to the saint's tomb was less than twelve months before the king's accession to the Mercian throne which was in 716. The miracle at the tomb is undated, but the

1 Felix's borrowings from the *Hisperica Famina* are small and all seem to come through Aldhelm. Examples are *forceps* (cc. XIX, XXXIX) in the sense of 'beak', *roscidus* (c. XXII), *plasma* (c. XXX) and perhaps *solatium* (c. LII) used in the sense of food based on the Hisperic and Aldhelmian *solamen*. See further A. Campbell, 'Some linguistic features of early Anglo-Latin verse', *Transactions of the Philological Soc.* (1953), pp. 1 ff.

2 This cannot be taken to mean that Felix knew Greek. They are few, and some of them may well have been borrowed from a glossary, the rest being hybrid compositions of his own.

tone suggests that it happened very soon after the saint's death and even before the translation. A closer dating is possible in view of the fact that Felix makes much use of Bede's Prose Life of St Cuthbert, which was not written earlier than 721. But the reference to Æthelbald in c. LII shows that he was well established on the throne and apparently at the height of his power and popularity. Cissa and Wilfrid, contemporaries and friends of Guthlac, are apparently still alive (pr. and cc. XXVIII, XLVIII). Cissa is still inhabiting Guthlac's cell. The latest date is provided by the fact that Felix addressed his prologue to Ælfwald, king of the East Angles who died in 749. Bede nowhere mentions Guthlac in his *Ecclesiastical History*. In view of Bede's interest in East Anglian and Mercian affairs, it would be surprising if he had not come across Felix's Life, supposing it had been written before his *Ecclesiastical History* which appeared in 731. Bearing all these facts in mind, one might suggest a date somewhere between 730 and 740.

OTHER GUTHLAC MATERIAL

In MS. B.M. Cott. Vespasian D xxi,[1] an eleventh-century manuscript, is an Old English translation of the Latin Life. Two chapters of this same Life also occur in the eleventh-century Vercelli Book,[2] one of the most important of the surviving collections of Old English poetry. It also contains some prose pieces, one of which is the fragment referred to. This Old English translation is to some extent a simplification of Felix's elaborate style, and many of his difficult phrases and words are avoided by judicious omissions. But the main thread of the story is followed faithfully enough. Old English scholars have neglected this piece and have hardly done justice to the unusual skill of the translator, or the importance of the piece in the development of translation technique during the Anglo-Saxon period.

1 For a description of the manuscript and the latest edition of the text see Gonser, pp. 31 ff., 100 ff.

2 For a facsimile of this manuscript see M. Förster, *Il codice Vercellese* (Rome, 1913).

In the Exeter Book,[1] another early eleventh-century collection of Old English poetry now in the Chapter Library, Exeter, are two poems on the subject of Guthlac. The first consists of 818 lines, the second of 560 lines, but this is incomplete. They are generally known as Guthlac A and Guthlac B. The first part (Guthlac A) seems to have apparently little connexion with Felix but several of the main facts are there, such as his period of ungodliness during his youth, his conversion, his dwelling on a barrow, the attendance of an angel upon him, and particularly the story of his being carried to hell and his rescue by St Bartholomew. As Liebermann[2] has pointed out, there are even one or two verbal echoes. Thus when Felix calls the robbers of the tumulus 'avari lucri', the Anglo-Saxon poet remarks that Guthlac, when he established himself there, 'nales þy he giemde þurh gitsunga lænes lifwelan'; again, Felix's 'sine ulla molestia' becomes 'ne laþes wiht', and 'suavitate quietissimo' becomes 'smeþe and gesefte'. Much of the rest of the poem deals in a vague and verbose way with his temptation by devils and how he overcame them. But no real additional information is given beyond what could have been derived from the Life. It is therefore pretty clear that the poet had a vague knowledge of Felix's work and that for the rest he depended on his own invention. In the second part the influence of the Life is clearly seen, and there are a certain number of verbal likenesses. There can be no doubt that the poet who wrote Guthlac B (probably a different man) was familiar at any rate with the latter part of the Life, the part which would normally be used as lections during the octave of the saint.

Of the numerous references to the saint which occur in the medieval chronicles, there is very little which does not go back directly to Felix. The anonymous epitome of the Life forming part of a twelfth-century chronicle in B.M. Cott. Jul. D vii,

1 *The Exeter Book, Pt. I*, ed. I. Gollancz (E.E.T.S. 1893). *The Exeter Book, Pt. II*, ed. W. S. Mackie (E.E.T.S. 1934). R. W. Chambers, M. Förster and R. Flower, *The Exeter Book* (London, 1933).

2 Liebermann, *Neues Archiv*, XVIII, p. 247. For a summary of the conflicting opinions held by scholars as to the relationship between Guthlac A and the Life, see Forstmann, pp. 1–3. Forstmann himself maintains that there is no connexion between the two, *op. cit.* p. 17.

is based on Felix; the abbreviator seems anxious to avoid the more elaborate and ornate language of the original, even though his own language is not altogether free from the charge of over-elaboration. The story is interrupted from time to time to introduce the names of contemporary kings both of Mercia and the other kingdoms, and occasionally to refer to contemporary events. Sometimes too the writer adds comments of his own, as where he describes how Tatwine (c. xxv) was familiar with the marches between Peterborough and Ely,[1] or describes Æthelred as the founder of the abbey of Peterborough.[2] He tells the story of the saint's vision of hell and adds that Guthlac was in the habit of answering friends who blamed him for his ascetic life by declaring that he had seen much harder things—obviously a memory of Bede's account of Dryhthelm.[3] In another place the writer declares that 'immediately after Æthelbald came to the throne, he began to change the hermitage into an abbey' ('heremiticum locum in abbatiam'), evidently echoing the later Crowland tradition which Ordericus put into writing and which the Pseudo-Ingulf elaborated.[4]

There is also another epitome of the Life found both in Matthew Paris and in the *Flores Historiarum*.[5] One piece of information based on Ordericus is found in William of Malmesbury,[6] that the monastery at Crowland 'inter tot bel-

1 In point of fact, Tatwine met Guthlac at Cambridge, and took him to Crowland, so that the remark would suggest that the writer of the epitome was not very familiar with the geography of the Fen district.

2 Æthelred, according to the Peterborough version of the *A.S.C.*, was not the founder but the generous patron of the abbey. This agrees with what Hugo Candidus says in his Chronicle. The idea that he was the founder was perhaps due to the forged charter which appears in the same version of the *A.S.C.* under the year 675. Cf. also *The Chronicle of Hugo Candidus*, ed. W. T. Mellows (Oxford, 1949), pp. 7, 9, 13, 16 ff.   3 *H.ecc.* v, 12.

4 Part of the Guthlac epitome from this MS. has been printed by Thomas Gale in *Scriptores XV* (Oxford, 1691), pp. 527–9. The whole Chronicle of which the epitome forms a part is soon to be published for the Royal Historical Society by Dr R. Vaughan of Corpus Christi College, Cambridge, to whom I am indebted for a transcript of the Guthlac section. The epitome used to be attributed to John of Wallingford, but Dr Vaughan informs me that this attribution is untenable.

5 Matthew Paris, *Chronica Majora*, ed. H. R. Luard (R.S. 1872), I, pp. 326 ff.; *Flores Historiarum*, ed. H. R. Luard (R.S. 1890), I, pp. 362 ff.

6 William of Malmesbury, *Gesta Pontificum*, ed. N. E. S. A. Hamilton, p. 321.

lorum turbines, inter tot temporum volubilitates' was never destroyed. Higden in his *Polychronicon*[1] repeats this phrase and then adds the additional information, doubtless based on local tradition, that Guthlac had special power over devils and made them do building for him. He also describes how the saint shut up an evil spirit in a boiling pot. John of Trevisa in his translation of the *Polychronicon* duly translates this into English.

Among other abbreviations of the Life outside the chroniclers, is the summary made by Peter de Blois, archdeacon of Bath, in the twelfth century at the request of Henry Longchamp. This Life has come down to us only in a thirteenth-century book of saints' lives originally from Westminster Abbey, now T.C.D. B 2.7.[2] A copy of the Life, now lost, is mentioned in the 1395 catalogue of Durham books.[3] It was the existence of this Life to which that Pseudo-Peter, who continued the Ingulf forgeries under the name of Peter de Blois, referred in the forged introductory letter addressed to Henry Longchamp. The Pseudo-Peter refers to the Life which he had written in accordance with Henry's commands 'in a straightforward and pleasant style'.[4] It was also upon Peter de Blois's epitome that John of Tynemouth based his epitome which he included in the *Sanctilogium Angliae* (MS. Cott. Tib. E i). This collection has been generally associated with the name of John Capgrave under the title of *Nova Legenda Angliae*, a title given to it by Wynkyn de Worde when he rearranged and published it in 1516. The epitomes of both Peter and John have been printed by Horstmann in his edition of the *Nova Legenda Angliae*.[5]

Use was also made of Peter de Blois's epitome in a poem dealing with the life of the saint to which reference has already been made. It is contained in MS. Dd. xi. 78, a thirteenth-

1 *Polychronicon of Ranulf Higden, with Trevisa's Translation*, ed. J. R. Lumby (R.S. 1876), VI, pp. 166–9.

2 P. Grosjean, 'Cat. codd. hag. lat. bibl. dubliniensium', in *An. Boll.* XLVI (1928), pp. 86–8; and P. Meyer, 'La vie latine de S. Honorat', *Romania*, VIII (1879), pp. 484–6.

3 *Catt. vet.* (Surt. Soc. VII, 1838), p. 55.

4 *Petri Blesensis Continuatio*, in *Rerum Anglicarum scriptorum veterum* (Oxford, 1684), tom. I, p. 110.

5 *Nova Legenda Angliae*, ed. C. Horstmann (Oxford, 1901), pp. 1–10, 698–719.

century manuscript in the University Library, Cambridge. It is written in Latin hexameters and was certainly composed by Henry of Avranches though, owing to a confusion of John Leland, the poem has usually been associated with a certain William of Ramsey and an eighteenth-century hand has added at the top of fo. 62, 'Autore Gulielmo monacho Ramesiensi'. The manuscript is written in a series of hands of the thirteenth century, but the one that appears most frequently is that of Matthew Paris himself, though the part containing the Guthlac poem is written in another hand. On the verso of the fly-leaf is an inscription, the top line of which has been partly cut away by the binders; it reads: 'Hunc librum dedit [Frater Ma]theus Deo et ecclesiae S. Albani quem qui abstulerit anathema sit. Amen.' The book is therefore of considerable interest as a possession of Matthew Paris compiled and partly written by himself. In the *Chronica Maiora* (iii, p. 43) he speaks of the 'liber fratris M. Parisiensis quem habet de versibus Henrici de Abrincis', and without much doubt is referring to this volume. The poem on Guthlac extends from fos. 61*a*–92*a* and consists of 1655 lines, though the scribe, at the end of the poem, maintains that it consists of 1666 lines; probably the latter is merely a slip in counting, for no part of the poem appears to be lost. This long piece follows Peter de Blois's epitome fairly closely, often borrowing phrases and words, but he has access to Felix and to other sources too, perhaps to local tradition. He borrows Peter's chapter titles for the most part; he puts long speeches into the mouths of his characters, such as Guthlac and Bartholomew, mostly based on Peter, though he makes considerable additions even to Peter's adornments of Felix's original text. He has also long digressions on the nature of the conversion of the saint and the difference between an anchorite and a monk. He adds, moreover, a few additional stories on his own account: for instance, he tells a story about the loss of the saint's psalter of which neither Peter nor Felix knows anything; he describes how the devils stole it and dropped it into the marsh, whence it was recovered unharmed seven years afterwards, and was still preserved in Crowland covered with silver and precious stones. He further relates the story of how Bartholomew provided the saint with a whip to drive away the devils, a well-known Crowland tradition, already mentioned, but not found in Felix nor Ordericus. Further, he tells a story about Pega which is unknown in any other source. He describes that in the early stages of Guthlac's hermit life she was living on the island of Crowland with her brother. On one occasion the devil assumed her appearance in order to persuade Guthlac to take food before sunset, contrary to his vow. The saint speedily discovered the origin of the trick and to prevent further attacks of the enemy from this direction, he bade his sister leave the island, and never saw her again. The poem is written in reasonably good hexameters which often show much dexterity in borrowing Peter's words and putting them into hexameter form.[1]

There is also a Middle English version of the Life in MS. B.M. Cott. Jul. D ix, fos. 297*b*–301*b*, consisting of 292 lines and forming part of a collection known as the South English Legendary.[2] This manuscript is in a handwriting of the fifteenth century and contains 105 pieces, mostly lives of saints. Of the same poem, 174 lines occur in MS. Corpus Christi College, Cambridge, 145, itself a fourteenth-century manuscript, but the Guthlac poem, written from fos. 210*b*–213*a*, is added in a different and apparently later hand, probably early fifteenth-century. Some 104 lines of the poem appear in a fifteenth-century manuscript, Oxford, Bodl. 2567 (779), fos. 163*a*–164*a*. The poem in Jul. D ix begins:

Seint Gutlac was i-bore, here in Englonde,

1 J. C. Russell, 'Master Henry of Avranches', *Speculum*, III (1928), p. 59; J. C. Russell and J. P. Heironimus, *The Shorter Latin Poems of Henry of Avranches* (Cambridge, Mass., 1935), pp. 6 ff., 105 ff.; *A Catalogue of the MSS. in the Library of the University of Cambridge* by various authors (Cambridge, 1856–), I, p. 472; Liebermann, *Neues Archiv*, XVIII, p. 252; Birch, pp. xxiv–xxviii, where extracts are printed; R. Vaughan, 'The handwriting of Matthew Paris', *Transactions of Cambridge Bibliographical Society*, I (1953), p. 391. Beccelmus, the form of the name Beccel which is found in this poem, appears to have been the traditional form at Crowland. It occurs in D but in no other MS. Cf. pp. 13, 186.

2 *The Early South English Legendary*, ed. C. Horstmann, E.E.T.S. LXXXVII (1887); Carleton Brown, *A Register of Middle English Religious and Didactic Verse* (Oxford, 1916), I, pp. 29 ff.; Forstmann, pp. 22–33, where he prints the text of Cott. Jul. D, IX and Bodl. 2567 and part of C.C.C.C. 145; Birch, pp. xxviii–xxx. The two Bodley MSS. mentioned by Birch (779 and 2567) are in fact the same MS.

and in each of the manuscripts the same beginning is found with slight variations; the three versions are substantially alike except in length.

Other interesting material relating to Guthlac is the reference in the Old English Martyrology found in MS. B.M. Cott. Jul. A x, a late tenth-century manuscript, at fo. 78a, and the almost identical entry in MS. Corpus Christi Coll. Camb. 196, a late eleventh-century manuscript, at p. 10. It is a brief reference to the meaning of the name Guthlac, the story of the hand that appeared at his birth, and the story of the angel who visited him each morning and evening.[1] All this is taken from Felix. Another vernacular reference to Guthlac is in the 'Resting places of English Saints'.[2] It merely states that Guthlac rests in the place called Crowland in the midst of the 'Girwan' fens. Lastly, reference may be made to a hymn to St Guthlac in fifteen stanzas of rhyming verse. This is found in a fifteenth-century manuscript, B.M. Arundel 201, fos. 92b–93b. The hymn has little literary merit and adds nothing to Felix's account. It forms one of a series of thirteen hymns, each addressed to a different saint. The inclusion of St Edmund, St Bartholomew and St Guthlac suggests a connexion with East Anglia.[3]

1 G. Herzfeld, *An Old English Martyrology* (E.E.T.S. 116, 1900), p. 56. Printed by Birch, p. 65.
2 *Die Heiligen Englands*, pp. 11–12.
3 Printed by Birch, pp. 72–4.

MANUSCRIPTS

1. R. British Museum, Royal 4 A xiv.[1] 11 × 7 in. (277 × 180 mm.), the present size of the page, which has been cut down. 2 fos. 27–28 lines to the page. Double column. Late eighth or early ninth century. This fragment consists of a bifolium used as two fly-leaves at the end of the book. The fly-leaves are now numbered fos. 107–8. They are written in what Lowe describes as 'an expert, rather fluent' Anglo-Saxon minuscule. The folios contain the prologue and the chapter headings of the first thirty-five chapters and part of the thirty-sixth. The first page of the prologue is only partly decipherable. Some of the prickings survive in the inner margin. The leaves have been bound into the MS. upside down. The rest of the book consists of 108 fos. containing a commentary on the Psalms, usually, though without authority, assigned to St Jerome. The hand is Anglo-Saxon of the late tenth century. Lowe considers that the Guthlac portion was written in south England and presumably at Winchester, for there is some evidence that the rest of the book is palaeographically connected with Winchester. In the early seventeenth century the MS. was at Worcester. It came into the possession of John Theyer of Cooper's Hill, Brockworth, Gloucester, probably between 1644 and 1646.[2]

2. C$_1$. Corpus Christi College, Cambridge, 307.[3] 9¾ × 6½ in. (248 × 167 mm.). 52 fos. 24 lines to the page. Single column. Written in a good clear insular minuscule hand of the ninth century. It consists of two fly-leaves with six gatherings of

---

1 E. A. Lowe, *Codices Latini Antiquiores* (Oxford, 1935), II, p. 28 (216) with facsimile; G. F. Warner and J. P. Gilson, *Catalogue of Western MSS. in the Old Royal and King's Collections*, I (1921), pp. 81–2; Birch, p. xviii; Bernard 6399; K. Zangemeister, 'Bericht über die im Aufträge der Kirchenväter-Commission unternommene Durchforschung der Bibliotheken Englands', *Sitzungsber. Wien. Akad., Philos-hist*, Vienna, LXXXIV (1877), p. 28 (510).

2 Cf. *Patrick Young, Catalogus librorum manuscriptorum bibliothecae Wigornensis*, ed. I. Atkins and N. R. Ker (Cambridge, 1944), pp. 18, 32, 63. See *D.N.B.* *s.v.* John Theyer.

3 M. R. James, *A Descriptive Catalogue of the MSS. in the Library of Corpus Christi College, Cambridge* (Cambridge, 1912), II, pp. 105 ff.; Birch, pp. xix ff.

eight leaves, and a seventh gathering of four leaves. Gatherings one to six are numbered. The arrangement of the sheets of vellum is unusual in that the hair side seems to be on the outside of all the sheets. The MS. contains the Life as well as the Prologue and a list of chapters. Following immediately at the end and in a somewhat smaller script, but apparently by the same scribe[1] are some verses which form an acrostic. These are in two sections, the first part consisting of ten lines and the second of seventeen. The acrostic of the first part reads (initials) EDUUALDUS, (finals) ISTA PINXIT. The verses are in crude Latin and seem to explain that the MS. was finished on the twentieth day before the Kalends of December, which presumably, is intended to mean 12 November, but they are so confused as to be almost meaningless. The second series of six lines read (initials) CALDUG and (finals) MUDEAA. CALDUG is of course GUDLAC reversed while as James points out[2] MUDEAA is a confusion of the scribe and should read GUDLAC. The next twelve lines, which follow the above without a break, read initially BEATUS GUDLAC and the finals read BARTHOLOMEUS. These lines are equally obscure, but seem to have been intended for the saint's shrine, probably the one built for him by King Æthelbald after the elevation of his relics (c. LI).

Bound up with this volume is a fourteenth-century volume consisting of four works by John Wallensis or Waleys[3] and the *De ente et essentia* of Thomas Aquinas.

3. C₂. Corpus Christi College, Cambridge, 389.[4] 9 × 5½ in. (228 × 141 mm.). 66 fos. 19 lines to the page. Single column. Tenth century, probably second half. Insular minuscule. This beautifully written MS. belonged in the fourteenth century to St Augustine's, Canterbury.[5] On fo. 1a it has the inscription, 'Di. ixᵃ Gradu tercio V.' Below on the same page in a twelfth-century hand is 'Vita sancti Pauli primi heremite' and 'Vita sancti Guthlaci' and beneath that in a fourteenth-century hand is 'Liber sancti Augustini Cant'. Below in a seventeenth (?)-

---

1 James (*op. cit.* p. 105), thinks that the verses are by another scribe.
2 *Op. cit.* p. 106. See also Birch, p. xx.
3 Cf. *D.N.B. s.v.* John Wallensis. He flourished about 1280.
4 James, *op. cit.* II, pp. 239ff.
5 Ker, *Med. Lib.* p. 26.

century hand is written, 'Hic liber scriptus ante conquestum'. There are eight gatherings of which gatherings 6 and 8 consist of nine leaves and the rest of eight. As in the other Corpus MS. (C_1) the hair side of the skin is outside on each sheet.

On fo. 1 b is a full-page drawing of St Jerome, tonsured and sitting at a desk writing. He is outlined in brown, wears a green robe touched in with red and purple, and brown boots. He holds a pen in one hand and a knife in the other. A dove is hovering close to his ear. Around the picture is an architectural background consisting of shafts having acanthus capitals, roughly touched in with green and red. The drawing is considered by Professor Wormald to be later than the MS.[1] From fo. 2a to fo. 16b is Jerome's Life of St Paul (*B.h.L.* 6596). On fo. 17b is a faint sketch of a king seated in state on a throne with a sword across his knee while he raises his finger towards a beardless tonsured youth on his right. Little more than the head and the neck of the youth are visible. It may possibly represent Felix offering his book to King Ælfwald. There are some good initials in black and red outline on fos. 2a, 4a, 18a, and 22b. They consist of interlacing work with biting bird and animal heads. The Life runs from fo. 18a to 66a. Eight lections are marked in the margin, the first one beginning with 'Contigit ergo' (c. L) on fo. 57b, while the eighth lection begins on fo. 63b and runs to the end of c. LII. They represent, of course, the lessons for the octave of the saint. There are numerous underlinings in red chalk such as are usual in the Parker MSS. One of the Corpus MSS. of the Life is noted by John Joscelyn as belonging to Archbishop Parker, so presumably this is the one.[2] On fo. 67b is a pen-proof in green and beneath in a sixteenth-century hand is the name 'Edwarde Wyllyams'.

4. A and A_2. British Museum, Royal 13 A xv.[3] $9\frac{5}{8} \times 6\frac{5}{8}$ in.

---

1 Cf. Francis Wormald, *English Drawings of the Tenth and Eleventh Centuries* (London, 1952), p. 55 and pl. 36.

2 James, *op. cit.* I, p. xviii and C. E. Wright, 'Monastic libraries and the beginning of Anglo-Saxon studies', *Transactions of the Cambridge Bibliographical Society*, I (1951), pp. 228 ff.

3 G. F. Warner and J. P. Gilson, *Catalogue of Western MSS.* II, p. 84; Birch, pp. xviii f.; C. P. Cooper, *Report on Rymer's Foedera*, appendix A (London, 1869), pl. 26.

(243 × 168 mm.). 45 fos. 20 lines to the page. Single column. Late tenth century. This MS. contains only the Life. It contains neither the prologue nor the list of chapters. The nail rust marks of the clasp on the last three pages would suggest that this was always the only item, though possibly and less likely it may have been the last item in a larger volume. It consists of five gatherings of eight leaves and one gathering of five leaves. In the fifth gathering a stub shows between fos. 34 and 35 and another stub between fos. 37 and 38 which suggests that a new fo. 38 has been inserted to replace an older folio which has been cancelled. The MS. is palaeographically interesting. It is written in two different hands, both of the late tenth century, one of which is English minuscules and the other Caroline minuscules. The first gathering of eight leaves is written in the English hand. Then follow three gatherings in the Caroline hand. In the fifth gathering, fos. 36 to 38 are in the English hand and the rest in the Caroline hand. The make-up of this gathering would therefore suggest that the sheet numbered 36 and 37 was inserted together with sheet 38 of which the stub appears between fos. 34 and 35. These take the place of the older sheets of which the stub of the original fo. 38 still remains. The English hand is smaller and it is clear that the scribe has spaced out his words on 38 *b* so as to reach the point where the Caroline hand restarts. The Caroline hand continues to the end. It would seem probable that the English hand represents the later (though very little later) completion of a faulty copy of the Life. The present third gathering is marked on fo. 24 *b* with the figure iii which would suggest that like Nero C. vii (n), it never had a prologue or list of chapters or else that the original beginning was lost and the book made up again by the scribe who wrote the English hand and the first gathering. The source of the MS. is unknown though the name Lumley[1] (now erased

1 John, Lord Lumley, who died in 1609, possessed a large library, a catalogue of which, compiled within two years of Lumley's death, still survives in the library of Trinity College, Cambridge (O. 4. 38). It covers 420 pages. This library was bought by King James I for the use of his eldest son, Prince Henry, and was afterwards incorporated in the Royal Library and so in 1757 reached the British Museum. Some 308 of the MSS. mentioned in the Lumley Catalogue can be identified in the Royal Collection. Our MS. is perhaps the

but still visible) occurs on fo. 1. This MS. was taken by Birch as the basis of his text.

Throughout the book in a late eleventh-century hand are a series of emendations and interlineations and marks of omissions. The new text thus formed is the basic text of E_2 and G (see below, p. 49). This new text formed by the variations in A, I have followed Birch in calling A_2.

5. H. British Museum, Harleian MS. 3097.[1] $10\frac{7}{8} \times 6\frac{3}{4}$ in. (277 × 172 mm.). 128 fos. Mostly 32 lines to the page. Single column. Mid-eleventh century. There are sixteen gatherings of which all except the last two consist of eight leaves. The fifteenth and sixteenth gatherings both have nine leaves. The handwriting changes at fo. 34a and then continues to 48b when the first hand takes up again until fo. 116a where another change of hand occurs. This hand continues until the middle of fo. 123a after which the hand seems to change again while still another hand appears on fo. 125a. Half-way down fo. 126b, the first hand appears again and goes to the end of fo. 127b. The initials are in red, blue and green and the rubrics in red and green up to fo. 64, after which, to the end of the book, only red is used for initials and rubrics.

The book contains first of all an exposition on the prophet Daniel by St Jerome, followed by Othloh's Life of St Nicholas (*B.h.L.* 6126), Folcard's Life of St Botulph (*B.h.L.* 1428), Lives of St Tancred, Torhtred and Tova,[2] followed by an account of the 'translation of the saints who rest in Thorney monastery'. The Life comes next (fos. 67b–84b). It has the prologue but no list of chapters and ends in the middle of a page and the middle of a sentence ('Deinde...', c. LIII). Then follow four sermons of St Ambrose and after that the prologue to the Life of St Nicholas, followed by selections from the Life and miracles of the same saint (*B.h.L.* 6104, 6161, 6172, 6174 and 6133). The

'Vita Guthlaci confessoris manuscripti incerti' mentioned on fo. 253. On the other hand, in the list of MSS. of the Royal Library made in 1666 (Royal MSS., appendix 71, fo. 6b) the only 'Vita Guthlaci' mentioned there is described as a quarto volume.

1 *A Catalogue of the Harl. MSS. in the Brit. Mus.* (London, 1808), II, p. 735.
2 Cf. W. Levison, *Das Werden der Ursula-Legende* (Köln, 1928), pp. 55 and 56, nn. 1 and 2.

MS. is from Peterborough and is found in the late fourteenth-century catalogue of Peterborough books printed by Gunton noted with the letter 'I'.[1] It is no. 628 in Bernard[2] where it is described as belonging to Charles Howard's collection at Naworth Castle. The MS. contains chainmarks. There are throughout the book a number of comments in a sixteenth-century hand with a variety of note-marks.

6. N. British Museum, Cotton. Nero E i (part 1).[3] $15\frac{3}{8}$ × $10\frac{3}{8}$ in. (473 × 260 mm.). 208 fos. 42 lines to the page. Written in a neat, mid eleventh-century hand. This volume, together with Nero E i, pt. 2 (a modern division of what was originally one book) and Cambridge, Corpus Christi College 9 (C.C.C. 9), forms a mid eleventh-century passional deriving from Worcester. Nero E i, pt. 1 begins on fo. 3 a with the Life of St Oswald of Worcester and York (*B.h.L.* 6374) followed by the Life of St Egwin of Worcester (*B.h.L.* 2432). Then follow the translation and miracles of St Swithin (*B.h.L.* 7944-5). After this come the miracles of St Andrew (*B.h.L.* 430) and then on fo. 55 a the passional proper begins with a list of contents in the hand in which the rest of the book is written. This list does not altogether correspond with the present arrangement of the book. The *Vita Guthlaci* follows after the piece numbered XLII. It is not numbered and does not appear in the index and appears to have been added as an afterthought. The Life extends from fo. 185 a to fo. 196 a (new foliation). It is clear that the first 54 folios have been added to the original passional at a later date.[4] The rest of the passional consists of fifty items beginning with St Martin (1 January) and ending with the Apostle Philip

1 S. Gunton, *History of the Church of Peterborough* (London, 1686), p. 174; M. R. James, 'Lists of MSS. formerly in Peterborough Abbey Library', Supplement to the *Transactions of the Bibliographical Society*, V (1926), p. 31; Ker, *Med. Lib.* p. 84.

2 Bernard, II, p. 14.

3 *A Cat. of the MSS. in the Cott. Lib. in the Brit. Mus.* (London, 1802), pp. 239-41; W. Levison, *Script. rerum Merov.* VII, pp. 545 ff., 601 f.; N. R. Ker, 'Membra disiecta, second series', *Brit. Mus. Quart.* XIV (1939-40), pp. 82 f.; P. Young, *Catalogus librorum mss. bibliothecae Wigornensis* (ed. Atkins and Ker), pp. 10, n. 5, and 70.

4 There are ancient dedications to both St Swithin and St Andrew in Worcester. Cf. F. Arnold-Foster, *Studies in Church Dedications* (London, 1899), III, pp. 315 f.

(1 May) (*B.h.L.* 6814). The second part (fos. 1–151) extends from May to September, and now contains seventy-one items, but some leaves are missing between fos. 48 and 49. The items on fos. 151–66 do not belong to the original passional while fos. 166–80, together with fos. 187–8, form part of the original second volume, the rest of which is now C.C.C.C. 9. This latter MS. on pp. 61–458 contains the rest of the volume up to December. There is a very close connexion between these two volumes (Nero E i and C.C.C.C. 9) on the one hand, as both Levison and Ker have pointed out, and Bodleian MSS. Fell 1 and 4 on the other. These MSS. originally belonged to Salisbury.[1] In both cases practically the same saints have been chosen (though the *Vita Guthlaci* does not occur in them). There is a separate list of contents for the section running from October to December. It is highly probable that both sets derive from the same exemplar.

There is one illuminated initial in pt. 1 of Nero E i on fo. 55 *b*. It is decorated with heads of dragons and birds and with interlace and acanthus leaves.[2] The smaller initials and rubrics are red. The *Vita* is the only one in either part of the Nero volume to have any glosses. These are closely associated with the glosses in C_2, a Canterbury book. It is quite possible that C_2 may have been borrowed at some time by Worcester.

7. n. British Museum, Cotton, Nero C vii.[3] $13\frac{1}{2} \times 9\frac{1}{2}$ in. (335 × 242 mm.). 225 fos. A composite volume of various dates and various hands. Fos. 29–79 form part of the third volume of a set of passionals from Christ Church, Canterbury. This volume, which is written mainly in two hands of the first half of the twelfth century, has 39 lines to the page. Double columns. Further sections of this same passional are to be found in Harl. 315, fos. 1–39 and Harl. 624, fos. 84–143.[4] The Life occupies fos. 29 *b*–40 *b*. It has neither prologue nor list of

---

1 Ker, *loc. cit.*; also *Med. Lib.* p. 97.
2 F. Wormald, 'Decorated initials in English MSS. from A.D. 900 to 1100', *Archaeologia*, XCI (1945), p. 135.
3 *A Cat. of the MSS. in the Cott. Lib. in the Brit. Mus.* p. 235; *Script. rerum Merov.* VII, p. 601.
4 N. R. Ker, 'Membra disiecta, second series', *Brit. Mus. Quart.* XII (1937/8), pp. 131–2; XIV (1939/40), pp. 83 ff.; *idem, Med. Lib.* p. 105 n.

chapters. The first part of the book (fos. 1–28) is taken up with the Lives of St Alban and Amphibalus (*B.h.L.* 213) and the Life of St Augustine (*B.h.L.* 783). The passional proper begins on fo. 29*a* containing the end of the Life of Irenaeus of Sirmium (*B.h.L.* 4466). After St Guthlac there are six other April saints ending on fo. 59*b* with part of the Life of St Ursmar (*B.h.L.* 8416?), but the end of the life is missing. On fo. 60 begins another section of the passional in a second hand and extending to fo. 72 containing Willibald's Life of St Boniface (*B.h.L.* 1400) and a translation of St Alphege (*B.h.L.* 2519). A third section of the passional in the same second hand begins at fo. 73 and continues to fo. 79. This section contains the end of the Passion of St Symphorosa (*B.h.L.* 7971), and lections from Adelard's Life of St Dunstan (*B.h.L.* 2343); the metrical Life of St Anselm (*B.h.L.* 533) which concludes this section is in a different but contemporary hand. On fos. 80*a*–84*a* are four leaves of a Thorney Chronicle which originally belonged to a MS. now in St John's College, Oxford (number 17). On fos. 85*a*–215*b* is a 'reddituale' and description of the lands of Peterborough monastery situated in Northamptonshire in a fifteenth-century hand which is followed by a brief chronicle from A.D. 1–1141. It ends with an Elizabethan rental on the last two folios, dated 1578.

The passional has some elaborate initials in green, red, and blue with brown outline. The initials in the translation of St Alphege on fo. 46*a* and fo. 46*b* are particularly elaborate. The Life is written in the first of the two hands which are associated with the passional and begins at chapter 1 with a particularly elaborate initial. This capital F is in red, green, brown and white. It consists of running spirals of acanthus and one attractive little lizard-like creature, biting the side of the column up which it climbs. There are two human faces in the roundel ends of the horizontal strokes and several of the upper spirals end in biting animal heads. The initial is reminiscent of the less elaborate F at the beginning of the first chapter of the Life in C_2, which the illuminator may well have seen, for both are Canterbury books (see p. 27 above).

3   CSG

8. V. Arras MS. 812 (1029).[1] $7\frac{1}{4} \times 5$ in. (184 × 127 mm.). 154 fos. 18 lines to the page. In two or three hands of the late tenth and early eleventh century.[2] This MS. is one of the books presented to the monastery of St Vaast at Arras by Abbot Seiwold of Bath, when for political reasons he fled to Flanders some time after the Norman Conquest, taking some MSS. with him. He presented 33 volumes to Arras and the list is still preserved in an eleventh-century catalogue of the monastic library.[3] This volume is made up of twenty gatherings normally consisting of eight sheets and numbered from 1 to 20 on the first sheet of each gathering. The numbering is modern. The first piece in the book is the Anonymous Life of St Cuthbert in an English hand. In the first gathering which consists of only six leaves, there is about as much of the Anonymous Life of St Cuthbert missing (the first piece in the book) as would have covered a leaf. It would appear therefore that the first leaf of the gathering is missing. Between the second and third gatherings, as much is missing of the same piece as would have comfortably filled another gathering. In gathering four (present numbering) there are six leaves or rather four leaves and two stubs (fos. 4 and 6) which are not folioed. These four leaves are in the wrong order and should run: fos. 25, 26, 23, 24. Fo. 24 b is a blank. The *Vita Guthlaci* begins (in the middle of a sentence in c. x) at the fifth gathering (fo. 27 a) but in a continental hand, of the late tenth century, and naturally without a prologue or list of chapters. It is quite possible that there was once a gathering which contained them, for the missing parts would have about covered a gathering. It is significant that on fo. 24 b is a pen-

1 *Cat. gén.* 4to, IV (1872), p. 322; Stubbs, *Dunstan*, pp. xxxviii–xxxix; *Script. rerum Merov.* V, p. 575 and n. 2; VII, p. 555; *Neues Archiv*, II (1877), p. 318; P. Grierson, 'Les livres de l'Abbé Seiwold de Bath', *Revue bénédictine*, LII (1940), pp. 96 ff.

2 The later part of the MS. can hardly be earlier than the beginning of the eleventh century, for the Life of Dunstan is dedicated by its author 'B' to Ælfric whom he styles archbishop. Ælfric was archbishop of Canterbury from 995 to 1005. Furthermore, Stubbs maintains that this MS. is not the original. He puts the date of the composition of the Life as approximately the year 1000. Stubbs, *Dunstan*, pp. xi, xxvii.

3 G. Becker, *Catalogi bibliothecarum antiqui* (Bonn, 1885), p. 143; *Two Lives*, pp. 18 f.; P. Grierson, *loc. cit.* pp. 107 ff.

proof, 'In domino dominorum', the first three words of the
Guthlac prologue. Between the sixth and seventh gatherings
there is a break in the text equivalent to another gathering, and
the Life ends with the ninth gathering on fo. 65 b. On fo. 66 a
begins the Life of St Dunstan by 'B' (B.h.L. 2342) in a later
(early eleventh-century) English hand. After the tenth gathering
there is again a gap in the text and two gatherings are missing,[1]
the Life ending on fo. 106, an odd leaf attached to the fifteenth
gathering. The Life of Filibert, abbot of Jumièges (B.h.L. 6806)
begins at fo. 107 a and occupies the rest of the book as it stands
at present, ending abruptly before the end of the Life on fo. 154,
the end of the twentieth gathering. This Life is again written
in the English hand. In the seventeenth century the volume
also contained a Life of St Aichard (B.h.L. 181) for it is mentioned in the seventeenth-century list of contents in the first
folio. It was used by the Bollandists (AA.SS. Sept. v, pp. 85–99)
for the text of the Life of St Aichard in the Acta Sanctorum.
So it must be after the date of this volume (1755) that the MS.
was rebound; the missing gatherings were perhaps lost at this
time too and the gatherings renumbered. The MS. may well
have been written originally at Bath which would account for
the mixed English and continental hands. As Grierson points
out, it is quite possible that the Flemish monks of St Bertin
who left their abbey rather than submit to the reforms of
Gerard de Brogne and who were settled in Bath by King
Edmund in 944, imposed their style of handwriting on the
Abbey scriptorium.[2] The Life of Guthlac which is written in
a late tenth-century hand could well have been written in Bath
by a monk who came over with these Flemish brethren.

   9. B. Boulogne, Public Library 637 (106).[3] 10 × 7¼ in.
(254 × 184 mm.). 171 fos. 19 lines to the page in the Life,
but differs in other parts of the MS. Single column. About
A.D. 1000. The book is in a late seventeenth-century binding,
and on the front are the arms of Bethune des Planques, abbot

1 Stubbs, Dunstan, p. xxxviii.
2 P. Grierson, loc. cit. p. 104.
3 Cat. gén. (4to), IV, p. 637; Script. rerum Merov. VII, p. 561; Neues Archiv,
XVIII (1892), pp. 567 ff.

of the monastery of St Bertin at St Omer.[1] He held the abbacy
from 1677 to 1705. Inside the binding are some pieces of MS.
in a late eighth- or early ninth-century insular hand which
seem to be fragments of a Gospel commentary. The book
consists of 23 gatherings mostly of eight leaves, of which
gatherings 14, 15 and 16 have been inserted. At the left-hand
bottom corner of fo. 1a is a list of contents in a fifteenth-century
hand but the last item or items have been cut away by the
binder. The list includes the lives in the inserted gatherings.
At the top of the same page is the inscription in a fifteenth-
century hand 'De libraria sancti bertini', with the figure 312
in the right-hand corner. Below in a seventeenth-century hand
is 'Vitae gemeticenses'.

The first item in an early eleventh-century hand is a Life of
St Walaric (B.h.L. 8762), followed at fo. 41b by a Life of
St Filibert (B.h.L. 6806) in a different but contemporary hand.
On fo. 55a begins the Life of St Aichard (B.h.L. 181), followed
at fo. 83b by the Life of St Bavo (B.h.L. 1049, Prol. 2). The
Life begins at fo. 85a and continues up to the thirteenth
gathering which consists of only two leaves (fos. 91 and 92),
where it breaks off abruptly. The hand is continental of about
A.D. 1000. It is similar to the hand in which the *Vita Guthlaci*
is written in V: it is hardly the work of the same scribe but
it may well have been written in the same monastery. At this
point are inserted the three gatherings (fos. 93–119) which are
written in what Dom A. Wilmart describes as the Odbert
hand.[2] They contain the Lives of Fuscianus, Victoricus and
Gentianus (B.h.L. 3224), followed by Eufrosina (B.h.L. 2723),
Eufrasia (B.h.L. 2719) and the Passion of Spes, Fides and
Karitas (B.h.L. 2970). This is followed by the beginning of the
Life of Sabina (B.h.L. 7408), all in the same hand, and ends
abruptly at the end of the sixteenth gathering which consists of
ten folios. This part of the MS. was almost certainly written
at the Abbey of St Bertin and inserted into the MS. at least
before the end of the fifteenth century, as the list of contents

---

1 J. Guigard, *Nouvel Armorial du bibliophile* (Paris, 1890), I, p. 237.
2 Dom. A. Wilmart, 'Les livres de l'Abbé Odbert', *Bulletin historique de la
société des antiquaires de la Morinie*, XIV (1929), p. 180.

shows. At the beginning of the seventeenth gathering (fo. 119) the Life begins again in the same hand as before and concludes at the end of the nineteenth gathering. The rest of the book, in this same hand (fos. 142–71) contains a series of sermons attributed to Eusebius and Augustine and others, for Easter, Ascension and Pentecost, ending with one for St John the Baptist's Day.

Among the most striking features of this volume are two full-page miniatures on fo. 1 *a* and fo. 1 *b*. On fo. 1 *a* is a representation of eleventh-century date of Christ in Majesty. He is bearded and has a cruciferous nimbus coloured green. His left hand holds a book bound in green with red decoration, jewelled and clasped. His right hand is raised in blessing, the third and fourth fingers being bent. Across his shoulders and covering his left side is a blue mantle with a green lining beneath which can be seen a further light brown garment with jewelled borders and the portion of a third green garment. His feet are bare and are coloured with a faint green wash. On either side is written in a later (twelfth-century) hand: 'deus abraam *et* deus ysaac deus iacob.'

On fo. 1 *b* is a representation contemporary with that on fo. 1 *a*, but by a different artist. It is another representation of Christ in Majesty. He is seated and wears a cruciferous nimbus with a violet rim, yellow background and green cross-pieces. He has reddish-brown curls. He holds a small circular red object in his right hand and the inner part of the hand is coloured bluish-green. In his left hand He holds a clasped book with decorated cover in light green and in its top dexter corner is an Alpha, the Omega being hidden by the fingers. At his feet is a round object in which are depicted three rows of heads; those in the top row are nimbed with yellow, the background of the second row is brown, the third green. The divisions between the three rows consist of clouds of green, red and yellow. There are four nimbed heads in the top row, the two outer ones having the left and right hand respectively held outwards with the thumb raised; in the second row there are six heads, two of whom are bearded, while in the bottom row are five heads. It is possible that they may represent the souls

in Paradise, Purgatory and Hell. Christ is wearing an undergarment of violet which has a yellow edging at the neck, wrist
and foot, with an outer garment of bluish buff. At his side,
standing in an attitude of adoration is St Bertin with a yellow
nimbus, a green crook in his left hand and a book in his right.
He is bearded and wears a violet dalmatic with yellow undergarment, green hose and brown shoes. He stands on an animal's
head which is an offshoot from the decorative frame. Above his
head is written in a twelfth-century hand: 'bertinus abbas.'

On the dexter side above is an angel representing St Matthew
and on the opposite side an eagle representing St John. The
angel has a violet nimbus, green outer garment and yellow
undergarment and carries a very large book while his wings
are in yellow, purple, green and white. The eagle stands on
a decorated book of which only part appears; it has a violet
nimbus with green rim. Its feathers are yellow, green, purple
and white. The whole of the figures are crowded into a portico
which is not quite square with them. It consists of two pillars
springing from pedestals and an upper piece attached to the
pillars by roundels at each end. Both these are divided into
four and contain triquetrae in each quarter. The top piece of
the portico consists of one panel of interlacing plaitwork while
the dexter pillar has three panels of unequal length, the two
larger of which consist of plaitwork and the smaller at the
bottom is filled with an S-shaped running leaf-scroll. The
sinister pillar is filled with a design of S-shaped leaf-scrolls.
The whole outer frame is coloured yellow. The general effect
of the illuminated page is as if the artist had been copying a
Christ in Majesty in which the symbols of the four evangelists
originally appeared at each corner. But in order to find room
for St Bertin and also to fit the figures into the somewhat narrow
framework, he has been obliged to omit the symbols of St Mark
and St Luke.

On fo. 34 a, at the beginning of the *Vita Walarici* is an amusing
initial. There is an oblong arranged in double lines occupying
about half the page. Inside the oblong frame are the words,
'Incipit transitus sancti Gualarici abbatis kl. Aprilis'. There is
then a capital 'Q', the initial of the first word in the chapter.

It is formed of three fishes, two of which form the circle of the 'Q' while the third fish forms the tail.

The book clearly belonged to and was partly written at the monastery of St Bertin at St Omer. Whether the part containing the *Vita Guthlaci* was written at St Omer or Bath must remain a matter of conjecture. But the close similarity of the text and handwriting of V and B would suggest that the first and last sections of the book (fos. 1–92 and fos. 119–71) may well be the products of the Abbey of Bath: these sections were afterwards returned to St Bertin where the illustration on fo. 1 *b* was added and the other sections inserted.

10. D. Douai, Public Library 852.[1] 10⅜ × 6⅞ in. (265 × 175 mm.). 207 fos. A volume written in various hands and at various dates. The Life is written in a twelfth-century hand and contains 27 lines to the page. The book originally belonged to the monastery of Crowland and was doubtless written there. It was still there in the sixteenth century when John Leland visited Crowland about 1540 and made a transcript of part of it which is preserved in the British Museum (Add. MS. 38132, fos. 3 *a*–12 *a*). D begins with a brief account of the translation of St Neot in a thirteenth-century hand, followed by a list of contents in the same hand. These correspond to the present contents of the volume. There follows the Life in a twelfth-century hand beginning on fo. 3 *a*, concluding with a chapter from Ordericus Vitalis[2] on fo. 32 *a*. The first 'I' of the Prologue and the 'F' of the first word of the first chapter are very elaborate, especially the latter with fully coloured scroll work and extremely vigorous birds, and beasts and two human figures climbing about the scrolls and the upright of the 'F'. The initial reaches from the top to the bottom of the page. The Life is marked throughout for lections. There are first of all nine main divisions of the whole Life, ending with c. LII. In addition cc. XV–XXIV are divided up into eight lections. C. XXV (from 'Contigit enim divina') to the end of c. XXVII

---

1 *Cat. gén.* 4to, VI (1878), pp. 598–602; *Anal. Boll.* XX (1901), pp. 406f.; L. Toulmin Smith, *The Itinerary of John Leland* (London, 1908), II, pp. 122ff.; Liebermann, *Neues Archiv*, XVIII, pp. 249ff.

2 See Ordericus Vitalis, *Historiae ecclesiasticae libri tredecim*, ed. A. le Prévost (Paris, 1838–55), II, pp. 268ff. and Migne, 188, cols. 362ff.

is divided up into three lections, cc. XXIX and XXX are divided into a further three lections, while cc. XXXVII–XL are divided into eight lections. But the most important set, judging by the more prominent marginal figures, are the twelve lections into which cc. XLVI–LII are divided. These were presumably the lections used for the octave of the saint. Throughout the Life the more difficult words are glossed, accents are occasionally added to assist in pronunciation and extra chapter headings are added in the margin. In one place in c. XLIX where the sixth lection begins with a speech of the saint to Æthelbald, the words 'inquit sanctus Athelbaldo' are added above to make the reference clear. See p. 45 below.

On fos. 32b–38 is the 'Translatio sancti Guthlaci' written in another and later twelfth-century hand. This piece (B.h.L. 3731) was written some twenty years after the event, which took place under Abbot Waltheof of Crowland in 1136. The Bollandists, who print it in AA.SS. April, II, p. 54, describe it as being 'ex MSS. Anglicanis' but it is fairly clear that they derive it from this MS. Nor is it apparently found elsewhere. The 'Miracula S. Guthlaci' (B.h.L. 3732) are found in fos. 38a–46b and these too are not found elsewhere. They are printed from this same MS. by the Bollandists (loc. cit.) and apparently were written at about the same time as the 'Translatio'. A folio is missing and the end is lost. An epitome of these miracles including the lost ones, written by Peter of Blois, is found in MS. T.C.D., B. 2. 7. See p. 22.

The last of the Guthlac series is the Abbreviatio (B.h.L. 3725) which Ordericus made at the request of Prior Wulfwine, when he visited Crowland at the invitation of the Abbot Godfrey of Orleans sometime before 1124.[1] It was afterwards incorporated by Ordericus in the fourth book of the *Historia ecclesiastica*. This piece is in a thirteenth-century hand. After a brief history of the abbots of Crowland,[2] there follow a series

---

1 Le Prévost, II, pp. 268–79.

2 On fo. 52b where the 'Gesta abbatum Croylandiae' begins there is a list of the abbots beginning with 'Kenulfus' and ending with Philippus Everard (thirty-six in all). Everard was abbot about 1497–1504. The handwriting of the list as far as Henry Longchamp (1191–1236) is the same but the rest of the names have been added later.

of pieces of great importance to Crowland history and tradition relating to Earl Waltheof of Northumbria who was beheaded in 1076 by the order of William the Conqueror.[1] He was buried in Crowland with William's permission and in 1219 his body was transferred to a marble tomb by Abbot Henry Longchamps. These eight pieces fill fos. 57b–66b. They are in some confusion and consist of three parts (with some repetition) of an epitaph on Waltheof written by William of Ramsey in leonine verse together with a summary account of his life. There is also a 'Gesta antecessorum comitis Waldevi', giving an account of the deeds of Siward, Waltheof's father. This may also possibly be the work of William, as also may be the *De comitissa* which follows it. This gives an account of Waltheof's widow, Judith, her descendants and the earls of Huntingdon up to Earl David of Scotland who died in 1219. The most important piece is the Life of Waltheof (*B.h.L.* 8779) though in fact it is largely borrowed from William of Malmesbury, Ordericus and Florence of Worcester. The last piece of the series which appears to be in a somewhat earlier hand than the rest is the 'Miracula S. Waldevi gloriosi martyris'. These miracles are undated but the date of one must be before 1137 and after 1093. The conclusion is missing. It looks as if they belonged to about the middle of the twelfth century or a little earlier.

At fo. 71a occurs the Life of St Neot (*B.h.L.* 6054) written about the time when Abbot Henry translated the relics of the saint to Crowland in 1213. It was also the work of William of Ramsey. After this follow some pieces in a twelfth-century hand which have no special Crowland connexion, the 'Historia Lausiaca' of Palladius (*B.h.L.* 6532), the 'Planctus Angliae de morte Lanfranci', a treatise 'De singularitate clericorum' and Isidore 'De fide catholica'. At fo. 194, again in a thirteenth-century hand, are three pieces on the origin, life and translation

---

1 These Waltheof pieces are found only here and most of them have been printed by Francisque Michel, *Chroniques anglo-normandes* (Rouen, 1836), II, pp. 99–142. See also C. E. Wright, *The Cultivation of Saga in Anglo-Saxon England* (Edinburgh, 1939), pp. 127 n. 1 and 129 ff.; and Forrest S. Scott, 'Earl Waltheof of Northumbria', *Archaeologia Aeliana* (4th ser.), XXX (1952), p. 151 and notes.

of St Ivo (*B.h.L.* 4621–3). They end on fo. 206*b*. St Ivo's relics were brought to Ramsey from St Ives in 1001.

11. E₁. Trinity College, Dublin. B.4.3 (Abbott 174). 10¾ × 6¾ in. (274 × 171 mm.). 124 fos. 45–6 lines to the page. Single column. Written in various hands of the late eleventh century. The volume consists of two separate parts with separate lists of contents. The first part extends from fo. 1 to fo. 48, the second from fo. 50 to fo. 123. The contents of the second part have been added below the first list of contents on the old fly-leaf before fo. 1 in a later hand and again copied on to the otherwise blank folio, 49*b*, in a sixteenth-century hand. It is probable that these lists were inserted when the two parts were bound together, which, judging by the hand, would be some-time in the sixteenth century. The script throughout the two parts of the book is fairly uniform and generally rather untidy but there are probably two or three hands involved.

The contents of both parts consist of various hagiographical pieces, lives, passions and homilies, connected with apostles and saints. The first piece comprises the miracles of St Andrew (*B.h.L.* 430) and the last piece is the preface to the Life of St Paternus, bishop of Vannes, by Fortunatus (*B.h.L.* 6477). The second part begins at fo. 50 with the Life of St Giles by Fulbert (*B.h.L.* 93) and consists of the same mixture of lives and homilies, mostly hagiographical, as the other. On the verso of the last folio are fragments of litanies and a version of the familiar morning prayer of which only the beginning is written, 'Domine sancte pater omnipotens sempiterne Deus qui nos ad principium huius diei pervenire fecisti tua nos'. The MS. originally also contained some sets of verses which are now missing.

On the recto of the first old fly-leaf is in late eleventh-century script 'of searbyrig ic eom'. The book comes in fact originally from Salisbury, being one of the six MSS. which Archbishop Ussher borrowed from Salisbury in 1640. Two of these were not returned, having been seized in 1643 from Ussher's library at Chelsea. This particular volume was one of the two, but it must have been returned to him afterwards, as some of the other books were, which were taken at the same time. In due course it found its way with his other MSS. to Trinity College, Dublin.[1] It bears the Ussher pressmark, HHH13. The saints are not associated with any special part of the year and it looks as if the association may have been the relics of a religious house.

The Life occupies fos. 73*a*–85*b* and the text bears a strong likeness to the text found in the two passionals from Canterbury and Worcester (C_2 and N). See pp. 50–1 below.[1]

12. E_2. B.1.16 (Abbott 171). $15 \times 11\frac{1}{8}$ in. (380×282 mm.). 252 pages. 34 lines to the column. Double columns. Written in a good thirteenth-century hand. This is part of a legendary once belonging to and probably written at Jervaulx. On p. 2 is an index of the contents and in the same elaborate hand the inscription: 'Liber. Sce. Marie. de Jorevalle.' The hand is the same as that of the rest of the book. There are twenty-nine items in the book though thirty-two appear in the index. The missing ones are the 'Passio S. Torpetis', the 'Passio S. Maximini' and the 'Vita S. Germani'. The legendary as it stands reaches from 1 March (S. Albinus, *B.h.L.* 234) to 28 April (S. Vitalis, *B.h.L.* 3514). The three missing Lives would have been for 28 and 30 April and 28 May. A folio is missing between pp. 72 and 73 and between pp. 220 and 221, and the last Life is unfinished.

The *Vita* extends from p. 138 to p. 164. It has, as we should expect, no prologue nor list of chapters. The text shows a close connexion with the Life in Gotha, 1, 81 (G; see below, p. 49) and both are based ultimately on the readings and alterations made to MS. Brit. Mus. Royal 13 A xv (A and A_2; see pp. 28, 49).[2]

13. G. Gotha, Herzogliche Bibliothek 1. 81. $12\frac{1}{2} \times 9\frac{1}{4}$ in. (313×230 mm.). 230 fos. 48 lines to the page. Double columns. This very interesting codex in an early fourteenth-

1 T. K. Abbott, *Catalogue of the MSS. in the Library of Trinity College, Dublin* (Dublin and London, 1900), p. 23; P. Grosjean, 'Catalogus codicum bibliothecarum Dublinensium', *An. Boll.* XLVI (1928), p. 88; N. R. Ker, 'Salisbury Cathedral manuscripts and Patrick Young's Catalogue', *Wiltshire Archaeological and Natural History Magazine*, LIII (1949), pp. 172 and 179.

2 T. K. Abbott, *op. cit.* p. 22; P. Grosjean, *loc. cit.* pp. 84 ff.; W. Levison, *Script. rerum Merov.* VII, p. 582; M. Esposito, *Journal of Theological Studies*, XIV (1913), pp. 72 ff.; Ker, *Med. Lib.* pp. 57, 136.

century hand contains altogether sixty-four items. It consists entirely of lives of English, Welsh and Cornish saints, the first twenty pieces dealing with the lives, passions and miracles of martyrs, while numbers 21–49 are devoted to the lives and miracles of confessors; of these, numbers 41–49 are associated with saints from the west country. Lastly, pieces 50–64 are devoted to women saints. This MS. contains the lives of a number of saints which do not occur elsewhere and were otherwise known only by the epitomes of John of Tynemouth in his collection known as *Nova Legenda Angliae*. See p. 22.[1]

The text of the Life occurs on fos. 104*b*–113*a*. Like A and E₂ it has no prologue nor list of chapters. As has been noted above it is a version founded on the revisions based on the text of A₂; see above.

LOST MANUSCRIPTS

Glastonbury Abbey. The 1248 catalogue of the library mentions three MSS. of the Life:

Vita sancti Gutlaci et translacio capitis sancti Stephani.

Vita sancti Gutlaci et liber Pronosticorum, et de animabus defunctorum et de ultima resurrexione et ænigmata multorum.

Vita sanctorum Gutlaci, Georgii, Erasmi et Eustachii. (*Johannis monachi Glastoniensis chronica*, ed. T. Hearne, Oxford, 1726, II, pp. 436–7.)

Ramsey Abbey, in a thirteenth-century catalogue:

114. Vita sancti Gutlaci. (*Chronicle of the Ancient Abbey of Ramsey*, ed. W. D. Macray, R.S., 1886, p. lxxxix.)

1 F. C. W. Jacobs and F. A. Ukert, *Beiträge zur ältern Litteratur* (Leipzig, 1843), III, 2, pp. 271–2.
It was the brief record in this place which led to a fresh examination of the MS. by scholars in 1939. It was taken temporarily to Munich and examined by the late Professor M. Förster and later the MS. was lodged with the Bollandists. Here it was thoroughly examined and described in detail by Père P. Grosjean in an account published in *An. Boll.* LVIII (1940), pp. 90–204. When the war broke out it was returned to Gotha. Unfortunately it has now disappeared, having been removed, it is said, by the Russians in 1945. My collation is based upon a photostat of the Life, obtained when the MS. was in Munich, in 1938, through the kindness of Professor Förster. See also *Two Lives*, p. 37. The account there given requires correction in the light of Grosjean's description.

Rievaulx Abbey, in a thirteenth-century catalogue:

124. Vitae patrum. Vita S. Guthlaci, liber qui dicitur formula vite honeste in 1° volumine.[1] (M. R. James, *A Descriptive Catalogue of the MSS. in the Library of Jesus College, Cambridge*, p. 49.)

Titchfield Abbey, from a catalogue of about 1400:

E IIII. Vita sancti cuthlaci anacorite. (R. M. Wilson, 'The mediaeval library of Titchfield Abbey', *Proceedings of the Leeds Philosophical and Literary Society*; Literary and Historical Section, v, pt. iii, 1940, p. 165.)

B. M. Lansdowne 436. This fourteenth-century MS. from Ramsey Abbey once contained a Life of St Guthlac, as is apparent from the late fourteenth-century index on fo. 1 *b*. The last four Lives are missing, namely those of Aldhelm, Patrick, Guthlac, and Æthelbert. They are all marked 'desunt' in an eighteenth-century hand. (See P. Grosjean, *An. Boll.* LVI, 1935, p. 339.)

Lyre. The text of the *Vita* in Mabillon's edition is based, according to the editor, on a MS. from Lyre. No such MS. can now be found, but the text follows D so closely that it would seem likely that the Lyre MS. is a transcript of D, possibly made for Mabillon in the seventeenth century. Where the text differs from D, the difference can nearly always be explained as a correction or alteration of an unusual form by the editor, or even a misreading as for example, c. XLI, *lunali* for *limali*, or *clementia* for *dementia* in the same chapter. There is one place where in c. XLIX, the words *inquit sanctus Aethelbaldo* are added in the margin in D, at the beginning of a new *lectio*, to make the reference clear. This marginal note is inserted in Mabillon's text. He also adds the extract from Ordericus with which the D text alone ends. So in the circumstances it does not seem wise to postulate a lost MS. from Lyre. The Lyre MS. is referred to in the notes occasionally as *Uticensis*, that is from Saint-Évroul.

---

[1] The last treatise is presumably the work of Martin of Braga. Cf. M. Manitius, *Geschichte der lateinischen Litteratur des Mittelalters* (Munich, 1911), I, p. 110.

Arras. The editor also refers in his introduction to a MS. from Arras. This is almost certainly V, but the first part of the Life in this MS. is now missing (see p. 34 above). Mabillon refers to a reading from the prologue in this MS., and in fact he inserts it in his text. In the prologue Felix refers to himself as 'catholicae congregationis vernaculus', and over the latter word a glossator in B has written 's. Beda' (i.e. 'scilicet Beda'). Now the connexion between B and V is very close. Either the above phrase was misread and copied by the scribe of V from the common exemplar and inserted in the text as 'sancti Beda vernaculus', or, more probably, the gloss in V and B was identical and Mabillon's informant misread it thus. Anyhow Mabillon introduces the above reading into the text with an apology in the notes for the form 'Beda'. Needless to say the reading caused much confusion amongst later writers who imagined from this that Felix must have been a monk at Jarrow.

THE RELATIONSHIP OF THE MANUSCRIPTS

The twelve MSS. of the Life (not counting R which is only a fragment) divide themselves, as a study of the variants will show, into four groups, namely:

I. V and B.
II. H and D.
III. A (with A_2, E_2 and G).
IV. C_2, N, E_1 and n.

C_1 is less easy to assign, though it has close connexions with groups I and III.

Group I. V and B are so closely connected that it is clear that either one was a copy of the other, or, what is more likely, that both are from the same exemplar. Both are written in continental hands which closely resemble one another; one (V) is definitely connected with Bath (see p. 34) while the other (B) through St Omer has close connexions with Bath; V appears to be slightly the older though they were probably written within twenty years of one another. The readings are extremely close throughout and their differences may generally be explained as a slip or an idiosyncrasy on the part of one or other of the scribes (e.g. *reminiscens* B: *reminisscens* V, c. XVI; *meditatione* B: *meditatio* V and *persequutorum* B: *persecutorum* V, c. XVIII). In a few cases obvious mistakes are common to both as c. XIX, *avino* changed to *avito* in B while *avito* is the original reading in V. In c. XLI B reads *devomerat* for *demoverat* while B begins by writing *demoverat* and then changes it to *devomerat*. The glosses are almost confined to c. XLI in both and are identical with one exception, though in one place B glosses *valitudinem* as *infirmitatem* while V more correctly glosses it as *firmitatem*. Even the sporadic numbering of some chapters only, between XXX and LII, is identical, though cc. XXXIII–XXXVIII are now missing in V. In c. XXXI where B, like C₁ and A, omits a passage of ten words ('sed caelo...tegebant'), it is added in the margin in B in a different (?) though probably contemporary hand. In V the passage is incorporated in the text. This may perhaps be explained by the fact that, in the exemplar, the missing passage was added in the margin. V inserted it, while in B it was added by the corrector.

Both scribes are familiar with the insular script, in which their exemplar was certainly written. Both scribes, when writing out proper names, are inclined to use insular forms of *g, r* and *s*, and the runic *thorn* and the ligature *æ* while B occasionally uses the runic *wynn*. B also once uses the insular sign *par excellence*, the tailed *h* for *autem* (cf. W. M. Lindsay, *Notae Latinae*, Cambridge, 1915, p. 13). In this case V writes out *autem* in full; B uses ÷ twice for *est* and V uses it once. Probably the easiest solution of all these peculiarities is that both V and B copied an English original at Bath, as has already been suggested (see pp. 35, 39 above).

Group II. The two MSS., H and D, the former from Peterborough, the latter from Crowland, are so closely related that there seems to be a strong case for supposing that D is a copy of H. The two MSS. agree together in readings, against all the other MSS., very frequently. These two alone omit words and phrases in several places as, for example, *prodigium* c. X or *ac venerabile* c. XLVIII, or *de illo* c. XLIX. On the other hand, a few phrases are inserted by these two alone, such as

Mediterraneorum Anglorum in c. XXIV, or *quae lingua Anglorum* in c. XXV. The same attempts are made to clarify a difficult reading in c. XXX where the original reading was *fascibus*. The exemplar which H used probably read *farcibus*, the reading which is common to groups I and IV, a very easy mistake in insular script. H tries to make sense by reading *faucibus* and D follows him. Again the rare word *sincelli*, c. XLV, was a difficulty to all the scribes. H and D again combine in inventing the phrase *sine celle*, which H glosses ·i· *extra domo*, and D adds the same gloss but changes *domo* to *domum*. Again both of them get nearer than any of the other MSS. to what was probably the original reading when they give *ergo lucri* (c. XXVIII) and gloss *ergo* with *causa*. All the other MSS. flounder over this phrase mostly inserting the gloss into the text. Mistakes are common to both and to these two alone as in *quidem* for *quodam* in the prologue, *globis* for *globosis* in c. XXXI, and *cursu* for *curru* in c. XXXIII.

But even if D is copying H, he does not always slavishly follow. Occasionally he corrects H where the latter is obviously wrong. Thus in c. XXIX, H has *ablueri* which D corrects to *ablui*. In c. XXX the word which was almost certainly *insolentiam* originally, caused all the scribes a good deal of difficulty, perhaps owing to a mistake in the archetype. All group IV together with C_I and A read *olentiam*; H like B and V reads *inolentiam*, but D, possibly as the result of a happy guess, wrote *insolentiam*, a solution also adopted, probably independently, by A_2 and followed by E_2 and G. In the same way D also writes his own version of proper names such as *Beccelmus* for H's *Beccel* or *Conredi* for H's *Coinredi*. It is very probable that D consulted another exemplar besides H, for H has no list of chapters and never had one. D's chapter headings, in any case, conform only partly to the normal pattern and have many variations not found elsewhere. For instance c. XXXI and c. XXXII are divided into three separate chapters in D alone, and each has a separate chapter heading.

In a number of places, as the variant readings show, groups I and II are found agreeing together against the rest. Thus the problem of *insolentiam* or the phrase *lucri ergo* is solved basically in the same way. All add the phrase *quod Anglorum vocabulo nuncupatur* in c. XX. It would therefore seem likely that these two groups go back to a not very remote common ancestor.

C_I shows certain similarities to group I. Thus in c. X *percepit* is omitted in all three MSS. In c. XXI the phrase *in eo* is also omitted in each and *in illo* substituted earlier in the sentence, while the chapter heading to c. XXX has *pseudalitate* for *pseudo-sodalitate*. In c. XLV all agree in *detrisset* against *detruditur* and in *finem* against *terminum* in c. L. Other examples will also be found in the variants.

C_I also sometimes joins with A and its group against the rest of the MSS. The most striking likenesses are the two passages where both omit several words. One is in c. XVIII where C_I and A omit a passage of thirteen words after *peregissent* up to *quieverunt*, and the passage in c. XXXI mentioned above, where it is also omitted in B and added in the margin. In c. XXXIII, where B and V have *analeta* for *athleta*, A has *anthleta* with the *n* expunctuated, while C_I has *athleta* but an *n* has clearly been erased. One may therefore suggest that C_I and A derive from an exemplar which was itself the exemplar or, more probably, a copy of it, from which both groups I and II ultimately derive.

Group III. As we have already seen, the text of A was used by a glossator to establish a new text used by E_2 and G. As the variants show, in most cases E_2 and G follow the emendations closely, but there are a number of instances where E_2 and G either together or separately differ from A_2 (i.e. the emended text of A). Thus in c. XXX instead of *quo facto*, A_2 has *quo dicto*; G follows, but E_2 reads *quo audito*. In c. XL, for *pulsato signo* A_2 has no alternative reading, but E_2 and G both have *appulsi*. The sentence in A *et manicam sibi ostendit* in c. XL reads *quam cum eis ostendisset* in both, again without any alteration being noted in A_2. Further E_2 and G differ frequently enough to suggest that one is not a copy of another. For example, G is alone in substituting *coram* for *ante* before *aeterno Deo* in c. XXXVI and so altering the sense of the passage; or changing *conprobat* to *significat* (last word in c. XLIX). E_2 on the other hand is alone in substituting *iustus* for *in cuius* in c. XXVII and in omitting the phrase *plurima his* in c. XXXI. It would also seem by the look of the MSS. that it was in A that the alterations which formed the new text were originally made; indeed, one or two mistakes which occur in A are carried on into E₂ and G. Thus in c. XXIX, A has *depependit fixa* for *defixa pependit*, and both E₂ and G have the same. In c. XXX A has *neca* for *necari* and so have E₂ and G. Most convincing of all is the fact that the sentence mentioned above which was omitted from A in c. XXXI is also missing in E₂ and G. It is therefore likely that E₂ and G were copies, not from A₂, but from an intermediate MS., a copy of A₂.

Group IV. The last group consists of the MSS. C₂, N, E₁ and n. The origin of each of them is known, C₂ and n coming from Canterbury, N from Worcester, and E₁ from Salisbury. C₂ is tenth, N mid eleventh, E₁ late eleventh, and n late twelfth century. There is no prologue or list of chapters in n. C₂, N and E₁ begin the *Vita* proper with the same elaborate introduction: *In nomine trino et divino. Incipit liber de vita sancti Guthlaci strenuissimi ac perfectissimi anachoritae.* The first phrase is omitted by n who begins at *Incipit*. Throughout the *Vita*, as the variant readings show, the group keeps closely together and very frequently differs from the rest, as when all four omit *lassi quieverunt* in c. XVIII or *inrumpentesque* c. XXXI, or *et sponsarum* in c. XLVIII. All of them agree in their rendering of the difficult passage in c. XXVIII as *erga causam lucri*, and all of them agree on certain peculiar readings such as *strinebant* for *stridebant* in c. XXXVI, though n, feeling something was wrong, put a *d* above the *n*. Three of them have *strimulantes* for *strimulentas* in c. XXXIV, but E₁ here attempts to correct by reading *stimulantes*, though his correction does not make sense. It is clear then that these four go back to the same exemplar, though probably not immediately. There is no evidence that any one of them is a copy of the other. They all have individual readings. Thus E₁ omits *funesti* in c. XLI but N does not. C₂ has *saeculari* in c. XIX where n agrees with the rest in reading *saecularibus* and again n agrees with the others in c. III in reading *adoptata sibi coaetanea virgine*, while C₂ alone reads *adoptatam sibi coaetaneam virginem*. It is pretty certain, however, that N had access to C₂ for a large number of glosses coincide, including a note on *rivigarum* in c. XXIV, a grammatical note on *cerneres* in c. XXXI and a note on the three rivers of Hades in the same chapter. N also has a certain number of glosses of his own, including a note on *cratium* in c. XXXI and a long note on *fulcris* in c. XLIII. Of course one cannot entirely rule out the possibility of an intermediate MS. glossed in the same way as C_2 but with additions, though there is no evidence of it. There are, however, a few places where C_2 and n agree against N and E_1. For instance in c. XLIII, C_2 and n have the reading of most of the MSS., *praesentibus absentia*, while N and E_1 both read, like C_1, *praesentibus praesentia, absentia absentibus*. Near the end of c. XLIV, E_1 and N read *agreste* while C_2 and n read correctly *agrestis* or again C_2 and n, like group I, read *locuta* in c. XLVI while E_1 and N have *locutas*. A few more instances, all minor differences, mark these as standing in two groups, so that it is quite possible that C_2 and n, both coming from Canterbury, had the use of one exemplar, while the Worcester and Salisbury books had another.

The group as a whole occasionally agrees with group I and occasionally with group II, but there is no close connexion between it and any other group.

The following is an attempt to show the possible relationship between the MSS.:

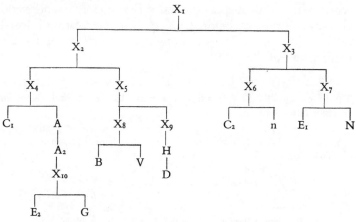

X_1, X_2, ..., X_{10} represent hypothetical exemplars.

It will be clear from a study of the variants that none of the

MSS. available is outstanding either on account of its age or obvious accuracy of tradition. I have therefore attempted, when deciding upon a reading, to choose the variant which seemed to be most in keeping with Felix's general style. So the text may be described as 'reconstructive', that is to say, an attempt has been made to get as close as possible to what Felix wrote, by taking into consideration the various features of his style, his fondness for the unusual word or form, his use of Aldhelmian phraseology and rhythm on the one hand, and his dependence upon Bede on the other.

So far as orthography is concerned, I have tried to get as near as possible to early eighth-century orthography as revealed in the earliest MSS. of Bede, though this is not always easy, in the case of place and personal names. I have kept throughout certain unassimilated forms such as *adl-*, *ads-*, *inm-*, etc., rather than the corresponding assimilated forms such as *all-*, *ass-*, *imm-*. Forms such as *sullimis* for instance would hardly be possible in the eighth century. But assimilated forms such as *acc-*, *arr-*, *comm-*, *corr-*, *coll-*, *succ-*, which are regularly found in the earliest Bede MSS. have been kept in the text. I have used *cumque* and *namque* instead of *cunque* and *nanque* and also *caelum* rather than *coelum*. I have also written out the *ae* in full, whether the MS. used *ae*, the tailed *e* or merely *e* alone; and also *-ti-* and not *-ci-* before a vowel. The punctuation is based on the demands of sense, though it follows generally the punctuation of the MSS.

OLD ENGLISH GLOSSES

The following Old English glosses occur in MSS. A, N and C₂, all in eleventh-century hands:

A

c. XXIX:
  fo. 9*b*   *versat: þoh*
          for *þohte* (A. S. Napier,
          Old English Glosses, Ox-
          ford, 1900, p. 202)
          versuta: fæ
          for *fæcne* (Napier)
  fo. 10*a*   *ðonan*
  (in margin) Probably a sign to the
          scribe or reader, or a
          mere pen-proof

c. XXX:
  fo. 12*a*   *strofosus: fa*
          for *facenful* (Napier)
          videretur: þu
          for *þuhte* (Napier)
          adsumpta: fa
          for *fangen* (Napier)

c. XXXI:

fo. 12 b intermissis: asend
Cf. Gloss on Aldhelm,
De laud. Virg. MS.
Digby, 146
intromittitur: asend
(Napier, p. 130, 5118)
catervis: pi
for *wigheapum?*
(Napier)

fo. 13 a comis: loc
for *loccum*
vagitibus: pa
for *wanunge* (?)
crepidinem: pes
for *westnesse?*

fo. 14 a discurrentes: yr
for *yrnende* (Napier)

c. XXXII:

fo. 15 a furvae: deor
for *deorc* (Napier)

c. XXXIII:

fo. 15 a nimia: spiþ
for *swiþe*

c. XXXIV:

fo. 16 b spiculis: or
for *ordum* See H. D.
Meritt, *Old English
Glosses* (Oxford, 1945),
p. 23
levare: he
for *hebban* (Napier)
millenas: þus
for *þusend* (Meritt)

c. XXXV:

fo. 17 a dementia: witleas
for *witleasnes*

fo. 17 b flagitiosas: fac
for *facenfulle* (Napier)

c. XXXVI:

fo. 18 a mugitans: hlopende
fo. 18 b balatum: hlo
for *hlowunge* (Meritt)

c. XXXVII:

fo. 19 b stagnosa: fennegan
ligistra: hopu See
Napier, *loc. cit.* n. 14

fo. 20 a tangere: æthrinan

c. XLI:

fo. 24 a orientalium: est

c. XLIII:

fo. 27 a remeabili: hwyrf
for *hwyrfende* (Meritt)

fo. 27 b alium: oþer

c. XLV:

fo. 29 b exegisset: ðy
for *ðyldigode* (?)

fo. 30 a dampnum: hy
for *hynðu* (Napier)

c. XLVI:

fo. 30 b presagae: gewittigre
providentiae: forescea
for *foresceawunge*
(Meritt)

fo. 31 a pollicebatur: behet

c. XLVII:

fo. 32 a stupescere: fo
for *forhtian* (?)

c. XLIX:

fo. 33 b velut: 7 swa
fo. 34 b contigerunt: curon

c. L:

fo. 35 a stimulatio: sticel

c. LI:

fo. 41 a efficax: glau

c. LII:

fo. 41 b longinquis: fyr
for *fyrlenum*
Cf. Bosworth-Toller,
s.v. fyrlen

fo. 42 b annalem: gear
for *gearlic* (?) (Meritt)
dicebat: cwæþ

c. LII: (cont.)
fo. 43 a   *effecta: gepor* (?)
       for *geworden* (?)

N

c. XXX:
fo. 188 b   *framea: arpan*

c. XXXV:
fo. 189 b   *versutias:* ·i· *calliditates
        locu*
       for *lotu* (Napier)

c. XXXIX:
fo. 191 a   *garrulantes: pri*
       for *writiende* (see Napier,
         op. cit. p. 203, n. 3)

c. XLI:
fo. 191 b   *vastaretur: æsceue*
       No explanation of this
       Old English word
       seems to be forth-
       coming. For one sug-
       gestion, see Bosworth-
       Toller, Supplement,
       s.v. æscene (a misprint
       for *æsceue*)
       distabuerunt: weor
       for *weornodon* (Napier)
       The gloss is written
       over the preceding
       word *vires*

c. XLV:
fo. 192 b   *infigens: hwol*
       No explanation forth-
       coming
fo. 193 a   *qui: þe*
       þe is the relative par-
       ticle

c. LI:
fo. 195 a   *artuum flexibus:
        liþepacum*

c. LIII:
fo. 195 b   *trophea: sigeas*

C₂

c. XXX:
fo. 34 b   *strofosus: fræte*

c. XXXI:
fo. 35 b   *raucisonis: hasgrumelum*
       For a note on the mean-
       ing of *hasgrumelum*, see
       Meritt, *op. cit.* p. 22, n.
       horrescere: hlypan
       for *hlydan* (Meritt)

c. XXXVI:
fo. 41 a   *strinebant: scriccettan*
       See note in Meritt,
        op. cit. p. 22

c. XXXVII:
fo. 41 b   *forcipe:* ·i· *bile*

PREVIOUS EDITIONS

1. The edition of L. d'Achéry and J. Mabillon. *Acta sanctorum ordinis sancti Benedicti* (Paris, 1672, Saec. III, Pt. 1, pp. 263–84; Venice, 1734, Saec. III, Pt. 1, pp. 257–75). See above, p. 45.

2. The Bollandist edition. *Acta Sanctorum* (Aprilis, II, 1675), pp. 38–50. The editor mentions in his introduction a MS. from St Omer (presumably B, see above, p. 36) and also a MS. from Douai which is certainly D. He refers to the Arras MS. also in his notes. He speaks strangely enough of the *Vita* as having been 'hactenus inedita praelo' (p. 37, E), but nevertheless at the beginning of the text he declares that the Life is 'ex pervetusto MS. Bertiniano [i.e. B] collato cum editione Acheriana'. But he follows the text of Mabillon very closely, even to the extent of copying the mistaken dedication of the prologue to Æthelbald. He does not, however, insert the words *sancti Beda*, as Mabillon does,[1] in the prologue and he omits the puzzling reference to the feast of St Bartholomew in April or May (see p. 181). Where he differs from the text of Mabillon, it is mostly to correct the latter's misprints or to give a reading which appears in none of the MSS. now available and would appear to be his own attempts at emendation. He also follows Mabillon in adding the extract from Ordericus as the final chapter of the Life. In addition he adds further extracts from Ordericus and the Pseudo-Ingulf, finishing with the translation of 1136 'ex MSS. Anglicanis', by which he obviously means D, for it breaks off suddenly where D also ends, and in fact no account of this translation is known to exist in any other MS., except for the epitome mentioned above, p. 22.

3. Gough's edition. R. Gough, 'The History and Antiquities of Croyland Abbey in the County of Lincoln', *Bibliotheca Topographica Britannica*, XI (London, 1783), pp. 131–53. Printed from H. Gough also knew N and A. The list of chapters and the last two sentences (omitted in H) are derived from N.

1 See p. 46 above.

4. Birch's edition. *Memorials of St Guthlac of Crowland*, ed. W. de Gray Birch (Wisbech, 1881), pp. 1–64. Birch printed the prologue and list of chapters from R and collated with N and H. For the rest of the Life he used A, printing the text verbatim from the MS., and noting variant readings from A_2, N, n, H, and also the Bollandist text which he calls B. It is a very careful and accurate piece of work. It is a pity, however, that he made no use of the Cambridge MSS., though he knew of them. He also knew of the continental MSS. but does not appear to have seen any of them.

5. Gonser's edition. P. Gonser, *Das angelsächsische Prosa-Leben des hl. Guthlac* (Heidelberg, 1909), pp. 100–73, printed from the Bollandist edition. It is set out beneath the Anglo-Saxon version (see p. 19), and is intended merely to illustrate the latter. Sentences which do not occur in the Anglo-Saxon translation are omitted.

TRANSLATION

C. W. Jones, *Saints' Lives and Chronicles in Early England* (Cornell, 1947), pp. 125–60. Based on the Bollandist text with occasional use of Birch's text. To be used with discretion.[1]

1 For comments on the translation see *American Historical Review*, LIII (1948), pp. 528 ff.

SCRIPTURAL QUOTATIONS

There are thirty-five direct quotations from Scripture which have been noted in the margin, but there may well be other Scriptural echoes which have been missed. It is clear that Felix knew the Scriptures well, and it is likely that for the most part he used the Vulgate version, for twenty-five of the quotations noted agree exactly with the Vulgate. But it must be remembered that the quotations are often very brief and it would therefore not be safe to come to any very definite conclusion as to the type of text Felix was using for either the Old or the New Testament.

In one or two places, however, it is clear that he is using a non-Vulgate version as for instance in Ps. 117. 7 (c. xxix) where the Old-Latin version[1] printed by Sabatier (*Bibliorum Sacrorum Latinae Versiones Antiquae*, ed. Pierre Sabatier, 3 vols. Paris, 1743) reads *et ego videbo inimicos meos* identically with Felix and against the Vulgate reading of *despiciam*. In Ps. 55. 10 (c. xxx) other ancient versions read *convertantur* with Felix, while the Vulgate and the Old-Latin version read *convertentur*. In c. XLIX where Felix is quoting, or rather adapting a quotation, from Ps. 20. 12, the *quod* of Felix is supported by the Old-Latin version. In quoting Isa. 1. 19 (c. xxxviii) Felix uses *oboedieritis* (a reading supported by all the MSS. of the *Vita*) where the Vulgate reads *volueritis*. Sabatier (*op. cit.*) quotes from Fulgentius the reading *obaudieritis*, but no example of *oboedieritis* is mentioned. It is quite possible therefore that Felix may have misread *obaudieritis* in the version he was using.

In the New Testament, Matt. 24. 20 is quoted in c. XVIII. Here the *ne* of Felix is found as *ut non* in the Vulgate. This reading is also found in the Rushworth Gospels (cf. *Novum Testamentum secundum editionem S. Hieronymi*, ed. J. Wordsworth etc. Oxford, 1889, etc., *loc. cit.*). Of Felix's other three

---

1 For a concise account of Old-Latin versions before Jerome see H. F. D. Sparks, 'The Latin Bible' in *The Bible in its Ancient and English Versions*, ed. H. Wheeler Robinson, Oxford, 1940.

variations from the Vulgate in the New Testament two are in
Rom. 11. 25 and 11. 33 (Prologue and c. xxvii). In the former
Felix's reading of *subintraret* for Vulgate *intraret* is also found in
Origen while Felix's reading of *inscrutabilia* for *incomprehensibilia*
in Rom. 11. 33 is found in the Book of Armagh and other
ancient MSS. His only other quotation from Rom. (8. 30;
c. xxvii) corresponds with the Vulgate.

The third variation is from Matt. 17. 19 (c. xxxviii) where he
is clearly quoting, but his variations are not noted as occurring
in any other early text in Wordsworth, *op. cit.*

VITA SANCTI GUTHLACI AUCTORE FELICE

THE LIFE OF SAINT GUTHLAC
BY FELIX

VITA SANCTI GUTHLACI AUCTORE FELICE

[1] Incipit prologus de vita sancti Guthlaci.[2]

Bede,
Vit. Cuth.
metr.,
Praef.

Aldhelm,
De metris,
Praef.

Sulpicius
Severus,
Vita S.
Martini,
Praef.

Gregorii I,
Expos.
in Job,
epist. ad
Leandrum

[3] *In Domino dominorum domino* meo, *mihi*[4] *prae ceteris regalium* primatuum[5] *gradibus* dilectissimo[6] Ælfwaldo[7] regi[8], Orientalium Anglorum [9]rite *regimina regenti*[10], Felix[11] *catholicae* congregationis *vernaculus*[12], perpetuae prosper*itatis* in Christo *salutem*[13]. Iussionibus tuis obtemperans, *libellum quem de vita* patris beatae memoriae Guthlaci[14] conponi praecepisti, simplici[15] verborum vimine textum non absque procacitatis[16] inpudentia[17] institui. *Ea tamen fiducia* coram obtuli[18] obsecrans, ut *si* ullatenus, ut *fore arbitror*, illic *vitiosus sermo* aures eruditi *lector*is *perculerit*[19], litteram in fronte[20] paginae veniam poscentem[21] intendat[22]. Reminiscatur[23] quoque, efflagito[24], *quia regnum Dei non in* verborum facundia, *sed in fidei* const*a*ntia persistit. *Salutem*[25] quidem *saeculo non ab oratoribus, sed a piscatoribus praedicatam*[26] fuisse sciat; sancti quoque Gregorii[27] dicta meminerit, qui rem ridiculam esse arbitratus est, *ut sub regulis Donati* grammatici[28] *verba caelestis oraculi restring*eret[29]. Sed si forsitan alius[30] animosi-

1–2 Incip(it prolo)gus de vita sancti ...ae in Christo R. Incipit prologus sancti Guðlaci C₁. Incipit prologus in vita sancti Guthlaci C₂. Incipit prologus sancti Guthlaci anachoritae B. Incipit prologus sancti Guðlaci anachoritae H. Incipit prologus de vita sancti Guthlaci N. Incipit prologus de vita sancti Guthlaci presbiteri E₁. Incipit prefatio in vita sancti Guthlaci anachorite D. *No prologue* VAnE₂G. 3 *capital missing* E₁. 4 michi D. 5 primatum D. 6 dilecto E₁. 7 Ælfpoldo C₁. Ælfpaldo BE₁. Elfwaldo H. 8 regni HD. *ins.* regimina regenti HD. 9–10 *om.* HD. 11 *s. ego C₂N. 12 s. Beda B. †i.e. servus N. 13 s. mitto C₂. s. mitto vel opto N. 14 Gudlaci RH. Gutlaci E₁. *The normal forms of this name are:* Guthlac C₁C₂n, Guðlac VA, Guthlac Gutlac E₁, Gudlac Guðlac HD, Gudlac RE₂G, Guderlac E₂ (*perhaps a misreading of* Guðlac), Guthlac

★ *All glosses are above the line unless otherwise stated. Occasionally 'ab.' is prefixed to show that the word is a gloss and not a variant.*

† [·i·] *I have written this sign out as 'i.e.' throughout.*

THE LIFE OF SAINT GUTHLAC BY FELIX

🎔

Here begins the prologue of the Life of Saint Guthlac.

In the name of the Lord of Lords, to my lord King Ælfwald, beloved by me beyond any other of royal rank, who rules by right over the realm of the East Angles, Felix, a servant of the Catholic community, sends greeting and wishes him everlasting happiness in Christ.

In obedience to your commands, though not without a bold forwardness, I have drawn up the book which you bade me compose concerning the life of our father Guthlac of blessed memory, weaving the text in a simple pattern. In this confidence I have publicly presented it to you, praying that if, as will happen, my faulty language shall here and there have offended the ears of a learned reader in any respect, he may note at the beginning of the volume these words in which I ask his pardon. And let him also remember, I earnestly pray, that the Kingdom of God does not consist in the eloquence of our language but in the constancy of our faith. And let him know that salvation was preached to the world not by orators but by fishermen; let him remember the saying of St Gregory, who considered it to be a ridiculous thing to confine the words of the heavenly oracle within the rules of the grammarian Donatus. But if perhaps someone else may impute our seizing upon this work to our pride and impetuosity seeing that there are many other

Guþlac Guðlac BD. *The nominative case is usually uninflected, but sometimes* -us *is added esp. in* DNA$_2$E$_2$ *and* G. *The oblique cases are then normally inflected like Latin masculine nouns of the second declension.*   15 semplici R.   16 *ab.* se N.
17 inprudentia C$_1$B.   i.e. verecundia N.   18 obtulli R.   opt... D.
19 perculserit RC$_1$C$_2$BHNE$_1$.   20 i.e. in principio C$_2$N.   21 *om.* H.
22 i.e. inspiciat N.   23 reminiscetur RC$_1$BH.   24 efflato N.
25 *ins.* dominum C$_2$.   i.e. dominum N.   26 ...atum C$_1$C$_2$V.   vel u N.
27 Hieronimi RC$_1$C$_2$BHNE$_1$.   28 grama... C$_1$.   *ab.* quia catholicus sermo regulis gramaticorum non seritur N.   29 redigeret RHNE$_1$D.   *ab.* redigeret vel revocaret C$_2$.   *ab.* restringeret vel revocaret N.   30 i.e. quilibet N.

tatis¹ nostrae fastibus² hoc opus nos³ arripere inputat,
dum alii plurimi Anglorum librarii coram⁴ ingeniositatis
fluenta⁵ inter flores rethoricae⁶ per virecta litteraturae
pure⁷, liquide lucideque rivantur⁸, qui melius lucu-
lentiusve conponere valuerunt, sciat nos hoc opusculum
non tam volentiae⁹ quam oboedientiae gratia incepisse¹⁰.
Propterea¹¹ laboris mei votis, o lector, quisquis es, faveas¹²;
¹²ᵃsin autem¹³, ut adsolet¹⁴, more obtrectatoris successeris¹⁵,
cave, ut ubi¹⁶ lucem putaveris¹⁷, ne a tenebris obcaeceris¹⁸,
¹⁸ᵃid est¹⁹, ne cum rata²⁰ reprehenderis, ignorantiae tenebris fusceris²¹. Moris²² enim caecorum est, cum in luce
perambulant, tunc in²³ tenebris errare²⁴ putant. Lucem
enim nesciunt²⁵, sed in²⁶ tenebris semper oberrant.
Caecitas enim²⁷ in scripturis ignorantia est, ut ait²⁸

Rom.
II. 25

apostolus²⁹: *Caecitas ex parte contigit in Israhel, donec pleni-
tudo gentium subintraret.* Origo quidem totius mali ab
ignorantia venit. Quapropter ³⁰te admoneo³¹, lector, ut
aliena non reprehendas³², ne ab aliis quasi alienus re-
prehendaris. Sed³³ ne sensus³⁴ legentium³⁵ prolixae³⁶
sententiae³⁷ molesta defensio obnubilet³⁸, pestiferis ob-

Ps. 57. 5

trectantium³⁹ *incant*ationibus *aures obturantes*⁴⁰, velut⁴¹
transvadato vasti gurgitis aequore, ad vitam sancti Guthlaci
stilum flectendo⁴² quasi ad portum vitae pergemus⁴³.

Vit. Ant.
Prol.

*Quoniam igitur exegisti*⁴⁴ *a me, ut de*⁴⁵ sancti Guthlaci⁴⁶ *conversatione* tibi *scriberem, quemadmodum coeperit, quidve ante*⁴⁷
*propositum sanctum*⁴⁸ *fuerit,* vel *qualem vitae terminum
habuerit*⁴⁹, prout a dictantibus idoneis testibus, quos scitis,
audivi, addendi minuendique modum vitans eadem⁵⁰

---

1 i.e. superbiae nostrae N.   2 i.e. extollentia N.   3 *om.*
RC₁BHE₁D.   4 i.e. manifeste N.   5 i.e. flamma N.   6 re-
thoriae B.   7 i.e. sincere N.   8 rimantur RB. i.e. perqui-
runt N.   9 i.e. voluntatis N.   10 incedisse RC₁C₂BHD.
11 promptam E₁.   12 foveas R.   12a–13 Si etiam C₁B. sin
etiam RC₂HNE₁D.   14 s. fieri N.   *ins.* fieri C₂.   15 susc…
C₁.   16 *om.* C₁.   17 *ab.* prius N.   18 obcecaveris B.
18a–19 idem N.   20 i.e. dicta C₂. i.e. dictata N.   21 fuscaris
BNE₁. *ab.* vel e N.   22 mos C₁B.   23 *om.* RC₁.   24 s. se
D.   25 ness… B.   26 *om.* RHD.   27 autem RNE₁D.
ins. ex parte C₁C₂B.   28 *om.* C₂NE₁.   29 *ins.* dixit C₂NE₁.
30–31 adm. te C₁C₂B.   32 reprehendes RB. prehendes C₁.

English scholars in our midst who make the waters of genius flow in pure and lucid streams among the flowers of rhetoric and amid the green meadows of literature, men who could compose in a better and more splendid style than I, let him know that we entered upon this little work not so much for reasons of inclination as of obedience. Therefore, O reader, whoever you are, look favourably upon the purpose of my labours. But if, on the other hand, as sometimes happens you should approach as a disparager, beware lest, when you think you have the light, you be blinded by darkness—that is to say, lest when you would refute certainties, you be darkened by the blackness of ignorance. For it is the custom of the blind, when they walk in the light, to think that they are wandering in darkness. For they do not know the light, but always wander about in gloom. For blindness in the Scriptures typifies ignorance, as the Apostle says: 'Blindness in part has happened to Israel, until the fullness of the Gentiles be come in.' Indeed, the origin of all evil springs from ignorance. So I warn you, reader, not to blame a stranger's work lest you be blamed by others as yourself being strange. But for fear that my laboured defence and long drawn out periods may cast a veil over the minds of my readers, let us stop our ears against the pestiferous incantations of our detractors as though we were traversing the waters of a vast whirlpool and let us steer our pen towards the life of St Guthlac as though we were making for the haven of life.

Since therefore you have required of me that I should write for you about the career of St Guthlac, I have described how it began, what his manner of living was before his holy vow, and how his life ended, just as I learned it from the words of competent witnesses whom you know: and I have avoided, by the same right craftsmanship, any tendency to add to or subtract

33 set B.   34 i.e. intellectus per N.   35 i.e. discentium N.
36 i.e. longi N.   37 i.e. sermonis N.   38 obnubet C₁C₂BHNE₁D.
alt. to obnubilet D.   39 obtract... C₁B.   40 obd... R.
opt...NE₁.   41 velud C₁B.   42 flectando C₁B.   43 ab.
prius N.   44 exig... C₁C₂NE₁.   45 ins. vita C₁C₂B.   46 ins.
vel C₁C₂B.   47 ins. sanctum C₂.   48 om. C₁C₂B.   49 habuit R.
50 eodem C₂NE₁.

Bede,
V.pr.,
Prol.

Vit. Ant.
Prol.

ortodemia[1] depinxi, ad huius utilitatis commodum hunc codicellum fieri ratus[2], ut illis *qui* sciunt *ad*[3] *memoriam* tanti viri, nota *revoca*ndi fiat, his vero, *qui ignorant*, velut late pansae[4] viae indicium *note*scat. Non enim *sine certissima inquisitione rerum gestarum aliquid de tanto viro scriberem*[5], *nec tandem ea, quae scripsi, sine subtilissima indubiorum testium* sanctione libratim *scribenda*[6] *quibusdam dare praesumpsi*[7], *quin*[8] *potius diligent*issime[9] inquirens, quantacumque scripsi, *investig*avi a *reverentissimo* quodam[10] abbate Wilfrido et a *presbitero*[11] purae conscientiae, ut arbitror, Cissan[12], vel etiam ab *aliis*[13], *qui diutius cum viro Dei conversati vitam illius*[14] ex parte *noverant. Ergo quanta-cumque* de vitae ipsius ortonomia[15] stilo perstrinxero[16], *minima de magnis*, pauca de plurimis *audisse*[17] *aestimate*[18]. *Non* enim *ambigo illos* dictatores non *omnia* facta illius[19] *potuisse cognoscere*, nec ab illis tota dictata me descripsisse[20] glorifico. *Sed*[21] ut *tanti viri tanti*[22] *nominis relatio conpleatur*, prout ubique miracula illius[23] fulserunt *percunctamini*[24], ut, *singulis quae* novere *referentibus*[25], sequentis libelli materia adgregetur[26]. Igitur eximiae dilectionis tuae imperiis obtemperans, textum[27] praesentis cartulae[28], prout potui, digessi, maioris scientiae auctoribus maiorem partem linquens; principium in principio, finem in fine conpono[29].

[30]Explicit prologus[31]. Incipiunt capitula libri sancti Guthlaci[32] anachoritae.

I. [33]De temporibus parentum illius et vocabulis eorum.

II. De origine et mansione patris ipsius.

III. De legali adiunctione[34] parentum illius.

1 ortothemio C_2NE_1. i.e. positione C_2N.   2 *ins.* sum C_1C_2B. 3 *om.* C_1B.   4 passae C_2NE_1. i.e. ample N.   5 scribebam C_2NE_1.   6 scribendo C_2NE_1.   7 praesumsi R.   8 cum C_1.   9 ...issimi C_1.   10 quidam R.   quidem HD. 11 presp... R.   12 Cyssa D.   13 alis R.   14 ipsius $RHNE_1D$.   15 i.e. directa lege H. i.e. regula N. ortho... D. 16 perstrincx... RC_1.   17 audiisse R.   18 estimato H. 19 ipsius HD.   20 scrips... H.   21 set B.   22 *add.* -que C_1C_2B. s. et N.   23 ipsius C_1C_2BH.   24 *ins.* referentibus C_1BHD.   percont... C_2.   25 percunctantibus RC_1C_2BHD. *ab.* referentibus R.   26 gregetur $RHNE_1D$.   27 texum C_1.

from their account. I considered that this little book should be composed for this useful purpose that, for those who know, it may serve as a sign to call them back to the remembrance of so great a man, and for those who do not know may be an indication to direct them on a wide open way. For I would not write anything about so great a man without an exact inquiry into the facts; nor have I at length presumed to hand my notes to anyone to be written in the form of a book without taking scrupulous care to have them confirmed by credible witnesses: nay, rather, it was with most diligent inquiries that I sought information about whatever I wrote from a certain most reverend Abbot Wilfrid and from a priest Cissa, a man, I believe, of pure conscience, as well as from others who for any length of time had dealings with the man of God and knew his life in part. So however much my pen has touched upon concerning his rule of life, you should realize that you have heard only brief accounts of great matters and very few out of many things. For I do not doubt that those informants of mine could not have known all the facts about him, nor do I boast that I have written down all the information they gave me. But in order that the story of so great a man may be completed, you should, inasmuch as his miracles shone forth everywhere, make further inquiries so that when each one has related what he knows, the material for an additional book may be gathered together. Therefore, obeying the commands of your exceeding love, I have, so far as I could, set in order the text of the present document, leaving the greater part of the story to authors with greater knowledge; and I put first things first and last things last.

Here ends the prologue. Here begins the list of chapters of the book of St Guthlac the hermit.

I. Concerning the times of his parents and their names.

II. Concerning the origin and the dwelling-place of his father.

III. Concerning the lawful marriage of his parents.

28 carthulae R.   29 *ins.* finis R.   30–31 *om.* D.   32 *ins.* confessoris atque B.   33 *No list of chapters in* VAHnE₂G.   34 coniunct... B.

IV. De conceptione et epidendarum[1] dierum cursu.

V. De prodigio in tempore nativitatis ipsius manifestato[2].

VI. De turbis videntibus et admirantibus signum.

VII. De manu ab aere[3] missa ostium[4] domus[5] in qua natus [6]est signante[7].

VIII. De varia sententia stupentis turbae.

IX. De rumigerulo[8] illius prodigii[9] famine.

X. De baptismate illius et vocabulo sibi ex appellatione[10] patriae indicto[11].

XI. De nutrimento [12]et edoctione illius[13] in aula paterna.

XII. De modestia infantiae illius et puerili simplicitate.

XIII. De docibilitate et sagacis[14] mentis ipsius ingenio[15] discendarum[16] artium.

XIV. De illius oboedientia senioribus et dilectione erga illum coaetaneorum.

XV. De omnibus de illo testimonium perhibentibus[17] et gratia divina[18] in vultu ipsius radiante[19].

XVI. De repentina commutatione[20] ipsius[21].

XVII. Quomodo tertiam partem predatae gazae possidentibus remittebat[22].

XVIII. Quomodo spiritalibus[23] stimulis instigatus se Dei famulum fieri devoverit[24].

XIX. Quomodo relictis comitibus suis solus viam pergens Hrypadun[25] pervenit[26].

XX. Quomodo tonsuram apostolicam accipiens ab omni[27] sicerato liquore[28] abstinuerit[29].

XXI. Quomodo ob id omnibus cohabitantibus[30] aspero odio[31] habebatur, et postea eius mansuetudinem dinoscentes in affectum sui[32] animos omnium convertit.

---

1 epidarum RC₁.   2 mani N.   3 aethere E₁.   4 hostium
C₁B.   5 om. B.   6–7 om. N.   titles of chs. vi and vii interchanged D.   8 ab. foremere R.   9 prodii C₁.   10 apell....
C₁BD.   11 indigito E₁.   indito D.   12–13 ill. et edoc.
C₁C₂BE₁.   14 saga gie R.   alt. to sagacitate C₁, sagacitate B,
sagaciae C₂NE₁.   15 genimo R.   genimio C₁.   gremio NE₁.
16 discentium C₁C₂B.   17 referentibus C₁C₂BNE₁.   18 divino
RC₁.   19 radi N.   20 commot... RB.   21 ins. ad his

IV. Concerning his conception and the course of the days of pregnancy.

V. Concerning the prodigy manifested at the time of his birth.

VI. Concerning the crowds who saw and marvelled at the sign.

VII. Concerning the hand sent from the sky which marked the door of the house in which he was born.

VIII. Concerning the various opinions of the amazed crowds.

IX. Concerning the widespread report of that prodigy.

X. Concerning his baptism and his name derived from the name of his country.

XI. Concerning his upbringing and education in his father's hall.

XII. Concerning the sobriety of his infancy and his childish simplicity.

XIII. Concerning his docility and wise disposition of mind in learning the arts.

XIV. Concerning his obedience to his seniors and the love of his fellows for him.

XV. Concerning the witness all bore to him and the divine grace shining in his face.

XVI. Concerning his sudden change of disposition.

XVII. How he used to restore a third part of the pillaged treasure to the owners.

XVIII. How, urged by spiritual impulses, he vowed that he would become a servant of God.

XIX. How, having left his comrades, he made his way alone to Repton.

XX. How, after receiving the apostolic tonsure, he abstained from all intoxicating liquor.

XXI. How he was intensely hated by all his fellows on account of this and afterwards, when they recognized his gentleness, how he turned the hearts of them all to an affection for him.

peragium RC₁B. *ins.* in priscorum more D.   22 remitterit C₁E₁.
...erat B.   ...eret D.   *om.* C₂.   23 spiritual... D.   24 devovet R.
...erat B.   25 Hrypandum NE₁. Ripadum D.   26 pervenerit
C₁C₂NE₁D. ...erat B.   27 omini E₁.   28 *ins.* se C₁C₂NE₁D.   29 abstinuit R.   ...erat B.   30 coevit... RB.   31 hodio R.   32 *om.* E₁.

XXII. Quomodo psalmis[1] et[2] monasticis disciplinis gratia inlustrante inbuebatur[3].

XXIII. Quomodo universorum proprias virtutes imitari[4] studebat.

XXIV. Quomodo post biennium clericatus sui heremum petivit[5].

XXV. Quomodo a proximis habitatoribus heremi in missa sancti Bartholomei usque in Crugland[6] deductus[7] est[8].

XXVI. Quomodo fratres resalutare[9] dehinc Hrypadun[10] remeavit.

XXVII. Quomodo rursus die viii Kalendarum Septembrium qua sancti Bartholomei missa[11] celebrari solet Crugland reversus est.

XXVIII. [12]Quomodo ortonomiam[13] vitae ducebat[14].

XXIX. Quomodo primam temptationem[15] disperationis[16] a Satana[17] pertulit[18].

XXX. Quomodo illum[19] zabulus[20] pseudosodalitate[21] ieiunare docuit[22].

XXXI. Quomodo corporaliter maligni spiritus ad portas inferni illum asportaverunt[23].

XXXII. Quomodo[24] Bartholomeus illic sibi apparuit et reportari illum iussit.

XXXIII. Quomodo[25] inmensa quietudine ad sedes suas ab inmundis spiritibus [26]reportatus est[27].

XXXIV. [28]Quomodo fantasticas turbas satellitum cantato primo versu lxvii psalmi[29] fugavit[30].

XXXV. [31]Quomodo prophetico[32] spiritu funestas cogitationes alicuius venientis clerici [33]interimere se volentis cognoscebat[34].

---

1 spalmis R.   2 om. C₁C₂BNE₁D.   3 imbueretur D.   ab. vel imbuebatur D.   4 imitare RC₁C₂BNE₁.   ins. et exercere D. 5 petierit. Et de heremo palustri D.   6 Cruglond C₁C₂BNE₁. *The normal spelling of this place-name in the MSS. is:* Crugland Cruglond RC₁CV₂BNE₁, Cruwlond A, Crouland H, Cruland nDA₂E₂G; *only variations will be noted.*   7 ductus C₁.   8 om. B.   9 resalutaret et D. 10 Hreopandun B.   Hrypandun N.   Hrypandun E₁.   11 misa R. 12–14 Qualiter in scisso latere tumuli superimposito tugurio habitaret, vel orthonomiam heremitalis vitae quomodo habuerit D.   13 orto-

XXII. How he was instructed in the psalms and in the monastic discipline while grace illuminated him.

XXIII. How he strove to imitate the individual virtues of all.

XXIV. How after two years of life as a cleric he sought the desert.

XXV. How he was guided to Crowland by those who lived closest to the desert, on the feast of St Bartholomew.

XXVI. How he returned to Repton to salute his brethren again.

XXVII. How he returned again to Crowland on 25 August, the day on which it is customary for the feast of St Bartholomew to be celebrated.

XXVIII. How he carried out his rule of life.

XXIX. How he endured the first temptation of despair, sent by Satan.

XXX. How the devil, in false friendship, instructed him how to fast.

XXXI. How the evil spirits carried him bodily to the gates of hell.

XXXII. How Bartholomew appeared to him there and ordered him to be carried back.

XXXIII. How he was carried back by the foul spirits with the utmost quiet to his dwelling.

XXXIV. How, by singing the first verse of the 67th psalm, he put to flight the phantasmal bands of the devil's train.

XXXV. How by the spirit of prophecy he perceived the deadly intentions of a certain cleric, who had come wishing to slay him.

nomia B.   14 *ab. in later hand* require in libro C_1.   15 temt... C_1.
16 desp... C_2E_1D.   17 Sathana D.   18 pertullit R.   pertulerit
$C_1C_2NE_1$. ...erat B.   19 *om.* B.   20 Satanas $C_1C_2BNE_1$.   21 speudo...
RC_1.   pseudosolidate E_1.   pseuda D.   i.e. falsa D.   21–22 ieiunium
docere temptaverit D.   23 ans... RB.   ass... C_2.   24 *ins.*
sanctus D.   25 *ins.* cum RD.   26–27 reportabatur D.   28–30 Quomodo fantasticas demonum turmas qui se Brittanicum exercitum simulavere
orationibus fugavit D.   29 spalmi R.   31–34 Quomodo prophetico
spiritu demones per fantasmata decipere se volentes cognovit D.   *ab. i.e.*
cogitationes malignas clerici cuiusdam intellexit D.   32 profet... RB.
33 R *ends here at* in-.

XXXVI. Quomodo nocte quadam maligni spiritus in diversarum bestiarum formis illum terrebant.

XXXVII. Quomodo corvus cartulam in medio stagni dimisit[1] nec illam[2] aquae laedere valuerunt[3].

XXXVIII. Quomodo[4] ad vocem illius alites heremi et pisces paludis[5] veniebant.

XXXIX. [6]De hirundinibus in scapulis ipsius se inponentibus[7].

XL. Quomodo domi sedens duas manicas a corvis [8]sublatas cognoscebat et iterum restitutas predixit[9].

XLI. Quomodo quendam per quadriennium[10] a maligno spiritu vexatum[11] saluti restituit[12].

XLII. Quomodo comitem Ecgan[13] subzonam[14] suam sibi donando ab inmundi spiritus infestatione[15] sanavit[16].

XLIII. Quomodo[17] cuiusdam abbatis ministrorum longe repositorum[18] culpam[19] manifestando prodidit[20].

XLIV. Quomodo[21] duobus clericis ad se venientibus [22]flasculas[23] binas quas in via abscondebant, monstravit[24].

XLV. [25]Quomodo[26] comitem postquam melote[27] suo induit, vulnere spinulae sanavit[28].

XLVI. [29]Quomodo Wigfritho[30] verba quae illo absente[31] dicebat, providentiae spiritu renarravit[32].

XLVII. Quomodo ab episcopo Headdan[33] officium sacerdotale[34] accepit.

XLVIII. Quomodo Ecgburge[35] interroganti illum quis heres loci eius[36] post se foret, respondisse fertur [37]in gente pagana fuisse[38], nec adhuc baptizatum.

XLIX. Quomodo exulem Æthilbaldum[39] ad se

---

1 dimiserit D.   2 ins. oranti sancto Guthlaco D.   3 reval... B.
4 ab. in later hand requir. C₁. ins. nequitiam corvorum pertulit et D.
5 paludes B. plaudis N.   6–7 Quomodo hyrundines in scapulis ipsius modulis vocibus cantantes, atque modulantes insidebant D. 8–9 predatas intellexit, et iterum restitutas fore in eadem et eodem momento quo vir Dei predixit D.   10 quadrienium C₁.   11 ins. pristinae D.   12 i.e. reddidit D.   13 Egcgan C₁C₂NE₁D. 14 zonam D.   15 ins. dicto citius D.   16 sanaverit D. ab. -vit D.   17 qualiter D.   18 a se positorum D. ab. manentium D. ins. occultum D.   19 crimen D.   20 prodebat D. ab. manifestabat D.   21 qualiter D.   22–24 bina flascula quae in via absconderunt, ludibri verborum famine prophetiae monstravit D.

XXXVI. How one night the evil spirits terrified him in the form of various beasts.

XXXVII. How a jackdaw dropped a document into the middle of a pool and how the waters could not harm it.

XXXVIII. How the birds of the desert and the fish of the marsh came to his call.

XXXIX. Of the swallows that perched on his shoulders.

XL. How, seated in his house, he perceived two gloves being carried off by jackdaws and how he predicted that they would be restored again.

XLI. How he restored to health a certain man who had been vexed for four years by an evil spirit.

XLII. How he healed the *gesith* Ecga from the troubling of an unclean spirit, by giving him his girdle.

XLIII. How he disclosed and made known the fault of the servants of a certain abbot though they were far away.

XLIV. How he made known to two clerics who came to him, about the two flasks which they had each hidden by the wayside.

XLV. How, after having wrapped a *gesith* in his sheepskin, he healed him of the wound caused by a thorn.

XLVI. How, by the spirit of foresight, he repeated to Wigfrith words which he had spoken when absent.

XLVII. How he received the office of priest from Bishop Headda.

XLVIII. How when Ecgburh questioned him as to who would inherit his dwelling after him, he is said to have answered that it would be a man of heathen race who was not yet baptized.

XLIX. How he consoled the exile Æthelbald when he came

23 *om.* C_2NE_1. fascinas C_1B.   25–28 Quomodo rumor virtutum ipsius fines Brittanniae pervagavit, vel quomodo comes quidam postquam melote sua se induit vulnere spinulae sanatus sit D.   26 *ab. in later hand* require C_1.   27 melo C_2NE_1. melotine C_1B.   29–32 Quomodo Wigfrido verba quae locutus est, illo absente renarraverit et quomodo ab episcopo Headda officium sacerdotale acceperit D.   30 Wifritho C_1. Wilfritho N. Þilfrido E_1.   31 adsente E_1. *ab.* vel b E_1.   33 Eaddan E_1. 34 sacerdotali B.   35 Egcburge D.   36 ipsius D.   37–38 iam adhuc paganum D.   39 Aedilbaldum D.

venientem consolatus est, et regnum sibi [1]futurum promisit, et inimicos suos subtus calcaneum suum redactos prophetavit[2].

L. Qualiter[3] egrotus temptamenta pertulerit, [4]vel quomodo[5] de sua sepultura commendaverit, quae novissima mandata sorori commendavit aut inter verba orationis spiritum quomodo emisit[6].

LI. Qualiter[7] corpus ipsius sine corruptione post duodecim menses repertum est.

LII. Quomodo post obitum suum Æthilbaldo[8] tunc exuli visione nocturna se ostendit, et regnum sibi a domino per [9]intercessionem ipsius donatum monstravit[10], et ad haec [11]confirmanda signum dedit[12].

LIII. [13]Quomodo caecus qui tot dierum voluminibus lucem a tenebris discernere nequiebat[14], tactu salis ab eo sacrati inluminatus est[15].

[16]FINIUNT CAPITULA[17].

[18]INCIPIT VITA[19]

I.[20] Fuit itaque in diebus Æthelredi[21] inlustris Anglorum regis quidam vir de egregia [22]stirpe Merciorum[23] cognomine Penwalh[24], cuius mansio in Mediterraneorum[25] Anglorum partibus diversarum rerum fluxu praedita constabat.

1–2 mox futurum fore predixit D.   2 prof... B.   3 quomodo B.   4–6 aut quid de sua commendaret sepultura quae novissima mandata sorori commendaverit, aut quomodo emiserit spiritum inter verba orationis. Qualiter turris illa ignea a ministro illius visa sit, et de angelico cantu et quomodo sepultus sit D.   5 quo B.   7 quomodo B.   8 Ethilbaldo E₁. Aedilbaldo D.   9–11 (-cessionem...to con-) om. E₁.   10 monstraverit D.   12 dederit D.   13–15 Qualiter caecus quidam post obitum ipsius per sacratum ante ab eo salem illuminatus est D.   14 nequibat C₂N.   16–17 om. C₂D. Expliciunt capitula libri sancti Guthlaci B. Explicunt capitula NE₁.   18–19 In nomine trino et divino. Incipit liber de vita sancti Guthlaci strenuissimi ac perfectissimi anachoritae C₂NE₁. Incipit liber de vita sancti Guthlaci strenuissimi ac perfectissimi anachoritae n. Incipiunt militia ipsius to him, promising that the kingdom would be his and prophesying that his enemies would be brought beneath his heel.

L. How he endured temptations in his sickness and about his commands concerning his burial, of the last injunctions entrusted to his sister and how while praying he yielded up his spirit.

LI. How twelve months afterwards, his body was found without corruption.

LII. How, after his death, he showed himself in a vision of the night to Æthelbald who was then an exile and revealed that by his intercession the kingdom had been granted to Æthelbald by the Lord; and how he gave him a sign to confirm these things.

LIII. How a blind man who in the course of many days had not been able to discern light from darkness, was given sight by the touch of salt consecrated by him.

Here the Chapter list ends

Here the Life begins

I. Now there was in the days of Æthelred the illustrious king of the English a certain man of distinguished Mercian stock named Penwalh, whose dwelling, furnished with an abundance of goods of various kinds, was in the district of the Middle Angles.

---

contra malignorum spirituum incursus B.   Vita sancti Guthlaci confessoris A. Vita sancti Guhtlaci confessoris A_2.*   Hic imitatoris Pauli simul Antoniique orditur sancti Guthlaci vita legenda H.   Incipit vita sancti Guthlaci strenuissimi ac piissimi anachoritae D.   Incipit vita sancti Gudlaci confessoris iii id. Aprilis E_2.   Incipit vita sancti Gudlaci confessoris G.   20 *Chapters* I–XXVII *are not numbered in* C_2AHnDE_2G. *Chapters* III–VII *are numbered* II–VI *and then numbers end in* B.   21 Edelredi H.   Ethelredi DG.   Edrelredi E_2. 22–23 Merc. st. AHE$_2$G.   Mertiorum styrpe D.   24 Penwald H.   Penwaldus D.   Penwallus E_2.   Penulballus G   25 Mediteran´... C_1BE_2G.

---

* Throughout A words and phrases are underlined for omission and sometimes alternative words and phrases are substituted above or in the margin, all in a later (eleventh-century) hand. These later readings I have followed Birch in calling A_2. They form a fresh version of the Life which in E_2 and G is seen as the basic text. See pp. 28 ff. above.

II. Huius etiam viri progenies per nobilissima inlustrium regum nomina[1] antiqua[2] ab[3] origine Icles[4] digesto ordine[5] cucurrit.

III. Itaque cum iuvenilis aevi viridante vigore florebat[6], adoptata[7] sibi coaetanea[8] virgine[9] inter nobilium puellarum agmina, condecentibus[10] nuptiarum legibus uxorem duxit, vocabulo Tette[11], quae a primaevis rudimenti[12] sui diebus in puellari verecundia vivere studebat.

IV. Evolutis ergo aliquorum temporum curriculis, quibus se coniugalis iuris[13] conditionibus indidissent[14], contigit, humana cogente natura, ut concipiens pregnasset[15]. Peractis vero mensium epidendarum[16] cursibus, cum parturiendi tempus inmineret et viscera[17] nixandi [18]inscia ignota[19] violentia vexarentur, extimplo[20] [20a]prodigium divinum[21] caelestis oraculi portentum circumadstantibus[22] et undique concurrentibus[23] turbis videbatur[24]. Nam pius[25] omnitenens[26], futurorum praescius, cui omnia praesentia persistunt, sigillum manifestandi militis sui internae[27] memorationis indicium praemisit.

V. Igitur cum nascendi tempus advenisset, mirabile dictu! ecce humana manus croceo rubri nitoris splendore fulgescens[28] ab aethereis Olimpi[29] nubibus ad patibulum cuiusdam crucis ante ostium[30] domus, qua[31] sancta[32] puerpera futurae[33] indolis infantulum[34] enixa est[35], porrecta videbatur.

VI. Cumque insolito stupore omnes ad prospiciendum miraculum concurrere certabant[36],

VII. en[37] subito, signato praedictae domus ostio[38],

1 *ins.* ab G.   2 *om.* C₂NE₁n.   3 *om.* G.   4 Ycles D.
5 *ab.* composito vel disposito D.   6 floreret ADE₂G.   7 adob...
C₁. adoptatam C₂.   8 coetaneam C₂.   9 virginem C₂.
10 condecetis C₁C₂BAHNE₁. *alt. to* condecentis C₁E₂. *ab.* vel
condecentibus C₂. condecretis D. *ab.* i.e. oportunis vel aptis D.
11 Tetthe D.   Tettam E₂G.   12 *ab.* i.e. iuventutis suae D.
13 fidei E₂G.   14 incidissent B.   15 impregnaretur A₂E₂G.
16 *add.* -que BA.   decem novemque A₂G.   novem E₂.   id est
decem H.   17 *ins.* eius A₂E₂G.   18–19 incognita A₂E₂G.

II. Moreover the descent of this man was traced in set order through the most noble names of famous kings, back to Icel in whom it began in days of old.

III. And so when he was flourishing in all the bloom and vigour of youth, he took to himself as wife, in accordance with the seemly laws of marriage, a damsel of like age from among the ranks of noble maidens: her name was Tette, and from her earliest days she had been zealous to live in maidenly modesty.

IV. So, some time having passed after their entrance into the estate of matrimony, it happened in the natural course of things that she conceived and became pregnant. When the months of her pregnancy had passed and the time of the birth of her child drew near and her inward parts were suffering from the violent pains of labour hitherto unknown to her, suddenly a heavenly prodigy, the portent of a divine announcement, was seen by those who stood near and by the crowds who ran up from every direction. For the Holy One Who rules all things and knows the future, to Whom all things are perpetually present, sent a sign to make His soldier known and as a token that He remembered him in His heart.

V. For when the time of his birth had arrived, marvellous to relate, a human hand was seen shining with gold-red splendour, and reaching from the clouds of the heavenly Olympus as far as the arms of a certain cross, which stood in front of the door of the house in which the holy woman, now in labour, was bearing an infant son destined to greatness.

VI. And when, with no ordinary amazement, they ran together eagerly to see this miracle,

VII. lo! suddenly, after it had marked the door of this

18 *ins.* quadam A_2E_2G.   20 *alt. to* extempio n.   20a–21 div.
prod. $AHDE_2G$.   22 circumastant... nDE_2.   circumstant... G.
23 i.e. demonstratis N.   24 apparuit A_2E_2G.   25 *om.* AE_2G.
26 omnipotens C_1.   27 *alt. in later hand to* in eterne A.   in aeternae H.
28 fulgens AE_2G.   29 Olimphi E_1.   30 host... C_1BAHG.
31 quam H.   32 sanctam H.   33 futuri C_1.   34 infantem
AE_2G.   35 *om.* H.   36 certarent E_2G.   37 *om.* A_2E_2G.
38 host... C_1BAHG.

aethereas in auras manus reducta recessit[1]. Hoc novo
stupefacti prodigio omnes, qui intererant, in loco sanctae
apparitionis[2] prostrati, supplices pronis vultibus Dominum[3] gloriae magnificabant[4].

VIII.[5] Transactis vero orationum deprecationibus,
convertentes[6] ad invicem versari[7] coeperunt, quidnam
esset hoc novum[8], quod[9] scrupulum multis[10] excitavit.
Illis ergo[11] cum inmenso stupore variis sermocinationibus
multa inter[12] sese[13] conferentibus[14], ecce ex aula propiante[15], qua supradictus infans nascebatur, mulier inmensa velocitate currens[16] clamabat: 'Stabilitote[17], quia
futurae gloriae huic mundo natus est homo.' Alii vero
hoc audientes ex divino praesagio ad manifestandam
[18]nascentis[19] gloriam[20] illud prodigium[21] fuisse per-
hibebant. Alii vero[22] sagacioris sententiae coniecturis[23]
promere [24]coeperunt hunc[25] ex divina dispensatione in
perpetuae beatitudinis praemia praedestinatum[26] fore.

IX.[27] Erat ergo[28] magna [29]admirantium turba[30], in
tantum ut illius miraculi vagabundus[31] rumor, priusquam
luciflua solis astra occiduis finibus vergerentur, Mediterraneorum Anglorum totos pene terminos inpleret.

X.[32] Igitur[33] decursis bis quaternis[34] dierum[35] voluminibus, cum ad salutaris lavacri [36]sacratas undulas[37]
propinquasset[38], ex appellatione[39] illius tribus, quam[40]
dicunt Guthlacingas[41], proprietatis vocabulum velut[42] ex
caelesti consilio Guthlac percepit[43], quia[44] ex qualitatis[45]
conpositione adsequentibus meritis conveniebat. Nam

1 conc... C₁.   abs... C₂HNE₁nD.   abc... A₂.   2 i.e.
ostensionis D.   3 Deum C₁VB.   4 magnificant HD.
5 *ch. numbered* VII NE₁.   *ch. title* De varia sententia stupentis turbae
quae inter se serebant D.   6 i.e. simul vertentes C₂N.   *ins.*
se E₂G.   7 scrutari A₂E₂G. i.e. investigare D.   8 s. prodigium C₂N.   9 *ins.* plurimis H.   10 plurimis AE₂G.
om. H.   11 vero NE₁.   12 in E₂G.   *alt. to* inter A.
13 se HE₂G.   14 convertentibus C₁.   i.e. colloquentibus D.
15 *ab.* vel propinqua N.   16 cucurrens C₁B.   concurrens AE₂G.
17 scitote A₂E₂G.   stabili estote E₁.   18-20 glor. nasc. E₂.
19 i.e. nati N.   21 *om.* HD.   22 autem AHDE₂G.   23 *in*

same house, the hand was withdrawn and disappeared into the clouds of heaven. All those who were present, amazed by this new miracle, fell prostrate on their faces at the scene of this holy vision, and humbly magnified the Lord of glory.

VIII. When, however, they had finished praying, those who had come together began to consider among themselves what new thing this was which aroused questionings among many. So while they had much debate among themselves in vast amazement and with manifold discussions, a woman came rushing at great speed out of the house near by in which the said child was being born, and cried out: 'Stand still, for a man child who is destined to future glory has been born into this world.' Now some, when they heard this, asserted that the marvel was a divine presage to manifest the infant's glory. Others, interpreting the sign more wisely, began to declare their opinion that this child was, by divine dispensation, predestined to enjoy the reward of everlasting bliss.

IX. There was indeed such a crowd of people marvelling at it, that the rumour of the miracle spread afar, and before the sun's radiant glory had sunk in the western horizon, it had reached almost to the furthest boundaries of the Middle Angles.

X. And so after eight days had run their course, and he was brought to the sacred waters of the life-giving font, he received the personal name of Guthlac from the name of the tribe known as the Guthlacingas; it being as though by divine plan, because by virtue of its formation, it fitted and matched his qualities. For, as those who are familiar with that race relate,

marg. i.e. estimationibus vel suspitionibus D.   24–25 hunc cep. G.
26 om. C₁.   27 ch. title De rumigerulo illius famine D.   28 enim
C₁BAE₂G.   29–30 turb. adm. C₁B.   31 vagib... C₁B.   32 ch.
title De baptismate illius et vocabulo sibi ex appellatione patriae indito D.
33 capital missing H.   34 i.e. octo D.   35 V begins here.
36–37 undas A₂E₂G.   38 propinquaret C₁.   39 apell... C₁VAE₂.
40 quem C₁VBNE₁.   41 Guthlacyngas C₁.   Guðlacringas V.
Guðlacingas AD. Guderlacingas E₂.   42 velud C₁VB.   43 om. C₁VB.
44 quod C₂ANE₁nD.   45 qualitates V.

ut illius gentis gnari[1] perhibent, Anglorum lingua hoc nomen ex duobus integris constare videtur, hoc est 'Guth' et 'lac', quod Romani sermonis nitore personat 'belli munus', quia[2] ille[3] cum vitiis bellando munera[4] aeternae beatitudinis[5] cum triumphali[6] infula[7] perennis[8] vitae percepisset[9], secundum apostolum dicentem: *Beatus vir qui suffert temptationem*[10], *quoniam cum probatus fuerit, accipiet coronam vitae, quam repromisit Deus diligentibus se.*

James I. 12

XI.[11] Postquam ergo sacrati[12] fontis limphis spiritalibus[13], divino gubernante numine, abluit parentum delicta[14], infans mirae indolentiae[15] nobilibus antiquorum[16] disciplinis [17]aulis[18] in[19] paternis[20] inbuebatur.

XII.[21] Igitur transcensis infantiae suae temporibus, cum fari pueriliter temtabat[22], nullius molestiae[23] parentibus nutricibusve seu coaetaneis parvulorum coetibus fuit. [24]Non puerorum lascivias, non garrula matronarum[25] deliramenta[26], non vanas vulgi fabulas, non ruricolarum[27] bardigiosos[28] vagitus[29], non falsidicas[30] parasitorum[31] fribulas[32], non variorum volucrum diversos[33] crocitus, ut adsolet illa aetas, imitabatur[34],

XIII. sed eximia sagacitate[35] pollens[36], hilari[37] facie, sincera mente, mansueto animo, simplici vultu,

XIV. in pietate[38] parentibus, in oboedientia senioribus, in dilectione conlactaneis[39], neminem seducens, neminem increpans, neminem scandalizans, *nulli*[40] *malum pro malo reddens,* [41]aequanimis utebatur[42].

Rom.
12. 17

1 i.e. sapientes D.   2 *ins.* nimirum A₂E₂G.   3 ipse AE₂G.
4 *om.* D.   5 *ins.* munera D.   6 *ab.* superabili vel invincibili C₂N.   7 i.e. dignitate C₂N.   *in marg.* victoria triumpho C₂. insula VB.   i.e. dignitate vel facultate D.   8 perhen... HDE₂G.
9 percepit A.   percepturus erat A₂E₂G.   10 temt... C₁.
11 *ch. title in marg.* De enutrimento et edoctione illius in aula paterna D.
12 sacri G.   13 spiritualibus nD.   14 originale peccatum A₂E₂G.
15 indolis A₂E₂G.   i.e. agilitatis vel certe spei D.   16 *om.* VB.
17–19 laribus A₂E₂G.   18 auleis A.   i.e. auli -as D.   20 i.e. moribus D.   21 *ch. title in marg.* De modestia infantiae illius et puerili simplicitate D.   22 temptabant VB.   posset A₂E₂G.   23 i.e. meroris vel tristiciae D.   24–34 *om.* A₂E₂G.   25 matronum

the name in the tongue of the English is shown to consist of two individual words, namely 'Guth' and 'lac', which in the elegant Latin tongue is 'belli munus' (the reward of war), because by warring against vices he was to receive the reward of eternal bliss, together with the victor's diadem of everlasting life, as the apostle says: 'Blessed is the man that endureth temptation: for when he is tried, he shall receive the crown of life which the Lord hath promised to them that love Him.'

XI. So after he had cleansed himself, under the governance of the divine will, from the sins of his parents in the mystical waters of the sacred font, this infant of marvellous nature was instructed in the noble learning of the ancients in his father's halls.

XII. And as the time of his infancy passed and he tried to speak in his childish way, he was never troublesome to his parents or nurses or to the bands of children of his own age. He did not imitate the impudence of the children nor the nonsensical chatter of the matrons, nor the empty tales of the common people, nor the foolish shouts of the rustics, nor the lying triflings of flatterers, nor the different cries of the various kinds of birds as children of that age are wont to do;

XIII. but possessing remarkable wisdom, he showed a cheerful face, a pure mind, a gentle spirit, a frank countenance;

XIV. he was dutiful to his parents, obedient to his elders, affectionate to his fosterbrothers and sisters, leading none astray, chiding none, causing none to stumble, recompensing no man evil for evil, always even-tempered.

$C_1C_2VBANE_1n$.   26 delera...$VBANE_1$.   27 ridiculorum C_1. ruricolorum VBA.   28 bardigiosas $C_1C_2ANE_1$. i.e. stultas C_2N. bardiosos VB. i.e. ineptos H. i.e. ineptos vel irrationabiles D.   29 i.e. cachinationes N. i.e. flebiles voces D.   30 falsidica D.   31 parasitum C_1VBA. i.e. memorum vel buccellariorum D.   32 frifulas C_1. fribolas C_2. frivolas AHN. frivola D.   33 diversas ANn.   35 i.e. capacitate C_2. i.e. alacritate vel ingenio D.   36 i.e. lucens C_2.   37 i.e. alacri C_2. 38 s. pollens C_2. s. inpietate N.   39 coaetaneis H. *ab.* collectaneis H. collectaneis *alt. to* collact... D.   40 s. et N.   41–42 omnibus se commendabat E_2G.   42 *ch. title to XV* De docibilitate et sagacis mentis ipsius ingenio discendarum artium D.

XV. Erat enim[1] in ipso[2] nitor spiritalis[3] luminis[4] radescens[5], ut per omnia omnibus, quid[6] venturus[7] esset, monstraretur.

XVI. Igitur cum adolescentiae[8] vires increvissent, et iuvenili in pectore egregius [9]dominandi amor[10] fervesceret, tunc valida pristinorum[11] heroum[12] facta reminiscens[13], veluti ex sopore evigilatus[14], mutata mente, adgregatis satellitum[15] turmis[16], sese in arma convertit.

XVII. Et cum adversantium sibi urbes et villas, vicos et castella igne[17] ferroque vastaret, conrasis[18] undique diversarum gentium sociis, inmensas praedas gregasset[19], tunc velut[20] ex divino consilio edoctus tertiam partem adgregatae gazae[21] possidentibus remittebat.

XVIII. Igitur transcursis novem [22]circiter annorum[23] orbibus[24], quibus persecutorum[25] suorum[26] adversantiumque sibi[27] hostium famosum excidium[28] crebris vastationum[29] fragoribus[30] peregisset, [31]tandem defessis viribus post tot praedas, caedes rapinasque quas[32] arma triverunt[33], lassi quieverunt.[34] [34a]Itaque[35] cum supradictus vir beatae memoriae Guthlac[36] inter dubios [37]volventis[38] temporis eventus[39] et atras[40] caliginosae vitae nebulas, fluctuantes[41] inter saeculi gurgites iactaretur[42], quadam nocte, dum[43] fessa membra solitae quieti dimitteret[44] et[45] adsueto more [46]vagabunda mente[47] sollicitus curas[48] mortales[49] intenta meditatione[50] cogitaret, mirum dictu[51]! extimplo velut[52] perculsus[53] pectore, spiritalis[54] flamma omnia praecordia supra memorati viri incendere coepit.

1 om. AE₂G.   2 ins. radescens H.   3 spiritualis H.   4 ins. paulatim A₂E₂G.   5 exardescens A₂E₂G. om. H. radiascens D.   6 quis D.   7 futurus A₂E₂G.   8 ins. suae C₁VB. 9–10 am. dom. A₂E₂G.   11 priscorum D. i.e. antiquorum D. 12 i.e. fortium D.   13 reminisscens V.   14 evigilans C₁VB. 15 i.e. sociorum N.   16 i.e. exercitibus D.   17 igni C₁AE₂. 18 i.e.—C₂. conrosis HN. contrasis E₁. corrasisque D. et deletis A₂E₂G.   19 gregaret HD. con... C₁G. s. et cum N.   20 veluti AE₂G.   21 pecuniae A₂E₂G. ins. ante E₂G.   22 octo E₂G. 22–23 ann. circ. G.   24 ordibus VB.   25 persequut... BH. 26 om. C₂NE₁n.   27 om. D.   28 i.e. transversionem N. 29 vastationibus C₁.   30 ins. in later hand -que C₁. i.e. strepi-

XV. For the brightness of spiritual light shone in him so brilliantly that in all things it was clear to all what manner of man he was to be.

XVI. Now when his youthful strength had increased, and a noble desire for command burned in his young breast, he remembered the valiant deeds of heroes of old, and as though awaking from sleep, he changed his disposition and gathering bands of followers took up arms;

XVII. but when he had devastated the towns and residences of his foes, their villages and fortresses with fire and sword, and, gathering together companions from various races and from all directions, had amassed immense booty, then as if instructed by divine counsel, he would return to the owners a third part of the treasure collected.

XVIII. So when about nine years had passed away during which he had achieved the glorious overthrow of his persecutors, foes and adversaries by frequent blows and devastations, at last their strength was exhausted after all the pillage, slaughter, and rapine which their arms had wrought, and being worn out, they kept the peace. And so when this same man of blessed memory, Guthlac, was being storm-tossed amid the uncertain events of passing years, amid the gloomy clouds of life's darkness, and amid the whirling waves of the world, he abandoned his weary limbs one night to their accustomed rest; his wandering thoughts were as usual anxiously contemplating mortal affairs in earnest meditation, when suddenly, marvellous to tell, a spiritual flame, as though it had pierced his breast, began to burn in this man's heart. For when, with wakeful mind, he

dis C_1. i.e. strepitus N. 31 peregissent VBHD. peregesset A. peregit A_2E_2G. 31–34 om. C_1AE_2G. 32 quae C_2BHNE$_1$D. om.Vn. 33 triverat C_2NE$_1$n. 33–34 om. C_2VBNE$_1$n. 34a–36 om. A_2E_2G. 35 ecce C_1VB. 37–39 ev. volv. temp. AE$_2$G. 38 i.e. transeuntis N. 40 om. A_2E_2G. 41 fluctuantis $C_2AE_1nE_2$G. ab. s. et N. 42 lact... VB. 43 cum NE$_1$. 44 i.e. deorsum inclinaret N. 45 s. dum N. 46–47 om. A_2E_2G. 47–49 cur. sol. mort. E$_2$. 48 om. HD. 49 mortalia HD. 50 meditatio V. 51 dictum N. 52 s. esset C_2N. velud A. 53 percussus nG. 54 spiritualis D.

Nam cum antiquorum regum stirpis suae per transacta retro saecula miserabiles exitus[1] flagitioso[2] vitae termino[3] contemplaretur, necnon[4] et caducas[5] mundi divitias contemtibilemque temporalis vitae gloriam pervigili mente consideraret, tunc sibi proprii obitus sui imaginata[6] forma [7]ostentatur[8], et[9] finem inevitabilem brevis vitae curiosa mente horrescens, cursum cotidie [10]ad finem[11] cogitabat, [12]immo etiam[13] audisse se[14] recordabatur, *ne*[15] *in hieme*[16] *vel*[17] *sabbato* [18]*fuga vestra*[19] *fiat*[20]. Haec et alia his similia eo cogitante ecce subito instigante divino numine se ipsum[21] famulum Christi[22] venturum[23] fore, si in crastinum vitam servasset, devovit[24].

Matt.
24. 20

XIX. [25]Ergo exutis[26] umbrosae noctis caliginibus, cum sol *mortalibus* [27]*egris* igneum demoverat ortum et[28] matutini volucres avino[29] forcipe pipant[30], tunc indutos[31] artus agresti de spatulo[32] surgens arrexit, et signato cordis gremio salutari sigillo, se[33] comitantibus[34] praecepit, ut ducem alium itineris sui elegissent, nam[35] se divinae servituti destinasse[36] perhibebat[37]. Hoc audito, comites ipsius, inmenso perculsi stupore, supplicibus obsecrationibus, ne hoc[38], quod dicebat, incepisset[39], exorabant[40]; qui contemtis eorum precibus, in eo, quod inceperat, inmotus[41] perstabat[42]. Ita[43] enim[44] in illo divinae gratiae inflammatio[45] flagrabat[46], ut non solum regalis indolentiae[47] reverentiam despiceret, sed[48] et[49] parentes et patriam comitesque adolescentiae suae contempsit. Nam cum aetatis suae xxiiii[50] annum peregisset, [51]abrenuntiatis[52] saecularibus[53] pompis[54], spem indubitatae[55] fidei fixam in Christo tenebat.

Virg. *Aen.*
II, 268, etc.

---

1 *ins.* et VB.   2 flagitiosae C₁. flagitiosum VBHD. flagitiosa E₁. i.e. otioso N.   3 terminum VBHD. i.e. fine N.   4 *om.* A₂E₂G.   5 s. cum N.   6 imaginatam D. ymag... E₂. 7 formam D.   7–9 *om.* A₂E₂G.   8 ostentat C₁C₂ANE₁n. ostendit VBHD. i.e. ostendit N.   10 quot... C₂H. 10–11 finemque A₂E₂G.   12–13 maxime qua A₂E₂G.   14 *om.* C₁.   15 *ins.* fiat fuga vestra C₁VB.   16 hyeme E₂. 17 *ins.* in VBAE₂G.   18–20 *om.* C₁VB.   19 nostra E₂. 21 *om.* A₂E₂G.   22 Dei C₂NE₁. *ab.* Christi C₂.   23 *om.* A₂E₂G.   24 devovet C₂NE₁.   25–26 ex. erg. A₂E₂G.

contemplated the wretched deaths and the shameful ends of the ancient kings of his race in the course of the past ages, and also the fleeting riches of this world and the contemptible glory of this temporal life, then in imagination the form of his own death revealed itself to him; and, trembling with anxiety at the inevitable finish of this brief life, he perceived that its course daily moved to that end. He further remembered that he had heard the words: 'Let not your flight be in the winter neither on the sabbath day.' As he thought over these and similar things, suddenly by the prompting of the divine majesty, he vowed that, if he lived until the next day, he himself would become a servant of Christ.

XIX. So when the mists of the dark night had been dispersed and the sun had risen in fire over helpless mortals, while the winged tribe chirped their morning songs from the beaks that birds possess, then he dressed and raised his limbs from his rustic bed and, signing himself with the sign of salvation on his breast, bade his companions choose another leader for their expedition; for he declared that he had devoted himself to the service of God. His comrades when they heard this were struck with overwhelming amazement, and besought him with prayers and supplications not to undertake what he proposed; but he despised their prayers and persisted, unmoved, in his undertaking. Indeed, the flame of divine grace burned so fiercely in him that he not only disregarded the reverence due to his royal blood, but he also spurned his parents, his fatherland, and the comrades of his youth. For when he had completed the twenty-fourth year of his age, he renounced the pomps of this world, and kept his unwavering faith and trust fixed in Christ.

27–33 illucesceret A₂E₂G. 28 in quo HD. s. cum N. 29 avito V. alt. to avito B. 30 pippant C₁. ripant VB. 31 indutus A. 32 spatula E₁. 34 ins. se A₂. 35 mam E₁. 36 i.e. devovisse vel commodare D. 37 i.e. narrabat N. 38 oc B. 39 incip... C₁A. inciperet A₂NE₂G. 40 orabant A₂E₂G. 41 i.e. stabilis D. 42 i.e. permanebat D. ch. title in marg. Quomodo relictis comitibus suis solus viam pergens Ripadum pervenit D. 43 itaque AE₂G. 44 ita AG. om. E₂. 45 inflamatio A. 46 i.e. ardebat N. 47 nobilitatis A₂E₂G. 48 set B. 49 om. C₁VBD. 50 vicesimum tercium E₂G. 51–54 om. A₂E₂G. 52 abrenuntians C₂n. 53 saeculari C₂. saeculi VB. 55 indubite H.

XX. Exin coepto[1] itinere, relictis omnibus suis, monasterium[2] Hrypadun[3] usque pervenit, in quo misticam[4] sancti Petri apostolorum proceris[5] tonsuram accepit [6]sub abbatissa[7] nomine[8] Ælfthryth[9], ac deinde, accepto clericali habitu, praeterita piacula[10] expiare certabat[11]. Ab illo enim tempore, quo apostolicae tonsurae indicium suscepit[12], [12a]non ullius inebriantis[13] liquoris aut alicuius delicati[14] libaminis[15] haustum, excepto communicationis tempore, gustavit.

XXI. Hac igitur ex causa omnibus fratribus illic[16] cohabitantibus aspero[17] odio[18] habebatur. Probantes[19] vero[20] vitae illius sinceritatem et serenae mentis modestiam, cunctorum[21] animos in *affectum*[22] suae caritatis[23] convertit. *Erat enim forma praecipuus*[24], *corpore castus*, facie decorus, *mente devotus*, aspectu dilectus, sapientia inbutus, vultu floridus[25], *prudentia praeditus*, colloquio blandus, *temperantia clarus*[26], *interna fortitudine robustus*, *censura iustitiae stabilis*, *longanimitate largus*[27], *patientia firmus*, *humilitate mansuetus*[28], *caritate*[29] sollicitus. *Ita enim*[30] *omnium virtutum decorem sapientia* [31]*in eo*[32] *adornabat*[33], *ut secundum apostolum sermo illius semper sale* [34]*divinae gratiae*[35] *conditus fulgebat*[36].

XXII. Cum[37] enim[38] litteris[39] edoctus[40] psalmorum canticum[41] discere maluisset[42], tunc frugifera supra memorati viri praecordia roscidis roris caelestis imbribus divina gratia ubertim inrigabat. *Summis* autem *providentibus* magistris[43], auxiliante *gratia divina*[44], *sacris litteris*[45] *et monasticis disciplinis erudiebatur*.

Vita Fursei, c. 1

Vita Fursei, c. 1

1 accepto HD.   2 *ins.* quod Anglorum vocabulo nuncupatur VBHD.   3 Hrypandun C₂VB. Rypadun AE₂G. Hripadun H. Hrypandum NE₁. Ripadum D.   4 mysticam AN.   5 principis AE₂G. i.e. principis D.   6–9 *om.* A₂E₂G.   7 abatissa D. 8 *om.* C₁.   9 Ælfðryð C₂A. Ælftryð VB. Aelfdrid H. Ælfþryð N. Ælfthryð E₁. Ælfþrið n. Elfrida D.   10 *ab.* sua A.   11 *ch. title in marg.* Quomodo tonsuram apostolicam accipiens ab omni sicerato liquore se abstinuerit D.   12 accepit A₂E₂G.   12a–15 nullius A₂E₂G.   13 inebriati C₁C₂NE₁n. inebriati A.   14 delicatae C₁NE₁.   15 liquaminis C₂NE₁n. 16 illum C₁C₂NE₁n. illi A₂. illi, *alt. in later hand to* illico G. 17 *om.* A₂E₂G. i.e. contrario vel duru D.   18 hodio C₁VB.

XX. Then he began his journey and, leaving everything he possessed, he came to the monastery of Repton, in which he received the mystic tonsure of St Peter the chief of the apostles, under an abbess whose name was Ælfthryth; and, assuming the dress of a cleric, he strove to make expiation for his past sins. And from the time when he received the mark of the apostolic tonsure, he never again took any draught of intoxicating drink or any sort of choice liquor except at the time of holy communion.

XXI. For this cause he was intensely hated by all the brethren who lived with him there. But when they had proved the sincerity of his life and the modesty and serenity of his mind, the hearts of them all were turned to an affectionate love of him. He was distinguished in appearance, chaste of body, handsome of face, devout in mind, and attractive to look at. He was endowed with wisdom and prudence, bright of countenance, pleasant in converse, outstandingly temperate, strong with inward strength, steadfast in his judgement of what was right, abundant in forbearance, firm in patience, submissive in humility and solicitous in love. For his wisdom enhanced in him so greatly the splendour of all his virtues that, in the words of the apostle, 'his speech always shone, seasoned with the salt of divine grace'.

XXII. When indeed, after having been taught his letters, he set his mind to learn the chanting of the psalms, then the divine grace sprinkled this same man's fertile heart copiously with the moist showers of heavenly dew. Cared for moreover by the best teachers and aided by the heavenly grace, he was instructed in the Holy Scriptures and in the monastic discipline.

19 licet mox ob A_2E_2G.   20 *ins*. ab C_1.   *om*. A.   autem C_2NE_1n.
21 aliquorum A_2E_2G.   22 i.e. in amorem D.   23 kar... H.   i.e.
pacis N.   24 *ab*. mycel D.   25 i.e. decorus N.   26 modestus
HD.   27 *ab*. tolerabilis C_1.   longanimis VB.   patiens HD.   28 subiectus HD.   29 kar... H.   30 *ins*. in illo C_1VB.   31 sapientiae
VB.   31–32 *om*. C_1VB.   33 ornabat G.   34–35 *om*. VB.
35 *ins*. esset A_2E_2G.   36 *ins*. gratiae VB.   *om*. A_2E_2G.   37 dum HD.
38 vero E_2G.   39 *alt. to* literas C_1.   40 edoctis C_1.   41 *om*. C_1.
cantica AE_2G.   42 maluiset D.   43 *ins*. et VBHD.   44 supernae
pietatis HD.   45 liter... C_1.

XXIII.[1] Igitur [2]canticis, psalmis[3], hymnis[4], orationibus moribusque ecclesiasticis[5] per biennium inbutus[6] *proprias singulorum* secum cohabitantium virtutes imitari[7] studebat. *Illius* enim oboed*ientiam, istius* humil*itatem*; ipsius *patientiam, alterius* longanimitatem; illorum abstinentiam, utriusque sinceritatem; omnium temperantiam, cunctorum suavitatem; et ut brevius dicam, *omnium in omnibus* imitabatur virtutes.

XXIV.[8] Decursis itaque [9]bis denis bis binisque alternantium[10] mensium[11] circulis, quibus sub clericali habitu vitam inmensae moderantiae[12] peregit[13] heremum cum[14] curioso[15] eximiae sollicitudinis animo petere meditabatur. Cum[16] enim priscorum monachorum solitariam vitam legebat[17], tum inluminato cordis gremio[18] avida cupidine heremum quaerere fervebat[19]. Nec plura[20], intervenientibus aliquorum dierum cursibus, cum seniorum [21]licita volentia, incoepto[22] aeternae prosperitatis itinere, solitudinem[23] invenire perrexit[24]. Est in meditullaneis[25] Brittanniae[26] partibus inmensae magnitudinis aterrima[27] palus, quae, a Grontae fluminis ripis[28] incipiens, haud[29] procul a castello quem[30] dicunt[31] nomine[32] Gronte[33], nunc[34] stagnis, nunc flactris[35], interdum nigris[36] fusi[37] vaporis laticibus, necnon et[38] crebris insularum nemorumque[39] intervenientibus[40] flexuosis[41] rivigarum[42] anfractibus, ab austro in aquilonem mare tenus longissimo tractu protenditur. Igitur cum supradictus vir beatae memoriae Guthlac illius vastissimi[43] heremi inculta loca conperisset[44], caelestibus auxiliis adiutus[45], rectissimo[46] callis tramite [47]tenus[48] usque[49] perrexit.

1 *ch. title in marg.* Quomodo psalmis monasticisque disciplinis gratia illustrante imbuebatur D.   2–3 ps. cant. C_2HNE_1nD.   4 ymn... VBANE_1nE_2G.   himn... HD.   5 ecl... C_1VD.   aeccl... B.
6 intuitus A_2.   intentus E_2G.   7 imitare C_1VBA.   8 *ch. title in marg.* Quomodo post biennium clericatus sui heremum petierit D.
9–11 xxiiii annorum A_2E_2G.   10 alternantibus C_1.   *om.* HD.
12 modestiae AE_2G.   13 degebat C_1VB.   egit AE_2G.   14 *om.* A_2E_2G.   15 curiosa C_1.   curiose V.   16 dum HD.   17 legeret A_2E_2G.   18 intuitu A_2E_2G.   19 satagebat A_2E_2G.   20 s. dico C_2N.   s. sunt dicenda D.   21–24 licentia inceptum opus aggreditur A_1E_2G.   22 incepta C_1.   i.e arepto D.   23 *om.* C_1A.   24 per-

XXIII. So for two years he was initiated in canticles, psalms, hymns, prayers, and church routine, and at the same time he sought to imitate the individual virtues of each one of those who dwelt with him: the obedience of one, the humility of another, the patience of this one, the longsuffering of that one; the abstinence of some, the sincerity of others, and the temperance and agreeableness of all and sundry; to put it briefly, he imitated the virtues of all of them in all things.

XXIV. And so when four and twenty months had run their course during which he lived a life of the greatest self-restraint in the habit of a cleric, he planned to seek the desert with the greatest diligence and the utmost earnestness of mind. For when he read about the solitary life of monks of former days, then his heart was enlightened and burned with an eager desire to make his way to the desert. Briefly, after some days had passed, with the willing consent of the elders, he started out on the path to eternal bliss and proceeded to look for a solitary place. There is in the midland district of Britain a most dismal fen of immense size, which begins at the banks of the river Granta not far from the camp which is called Cambridge, and stretches from the south as far north as the sea. It is a very long tract, now consisting of marshes, now of bogs, sometimes of black waters overhung by fog, sometimes studded with wooded islands and traversed by the windings of tortuous streams. So when this same man of blessed memory, Guthlac, had learned about the wild places of this vast desert, he made his way thither with divine assistance by the most direct route.

reit A. *ch. title* De heremo palustri C₂NE₁D. 25 meditula... C₁A. mediterra... VB. Mediterraneorum Anglorum HD. in mediterraneis A₂E₂G. 26 Bryttann... B. Brittan... A. Britann... H. Britan... E₁. 27 acerrima C₁VBAHDE₂G. i.e. assperrima D. 28 rivis A₂E₂G. 29 haut C₂BANnG. 30 quod ADE₂G. 31 dicitur E₂. 32 *om.* AE₂G. 33 Gronta bricc A₂. Granto-brige E₂. 34 *ins.* in NE₁. 35 *ab.* flatibus A₂E₂G. i.e. incisuris D. 36 nigri C₂VBANE₁nE₂G. 37 *alt. to* flui C₂. fusis HD. *om.* A₂E₂G. 38 *om.* HD. 39 nemoribus C₁VBHD. 40 interventibus E₁. i.e. inruptionibus D. *ins.* et HD. 41 *add.* -que VB. flexosis C₁C₂VBANE₁n. 42 i.e. rivulosarum HD. *note in marg.* riviga dicitur ubi congregatur aqua C₂N. rivorum A₂E₂G. 43 vastissimae HD. 44 repper... H. 45 i.e. confortatus N. 46 rectissimae C₁. rectissima C₂VBNE₁n. 47–49 *om.* HD. 48 i.e. illuc C₂N. illuc A₂E₂G.

XXV. Contigit ergo, cum a[1] proximantibus[2] accolis illius[3] solitudinis experientiam sciscitaretur[4], illisque plurima ipsius spatiosi heremi inculta[5] narrantibus, ecce quidam de illic adstantibus [6]nomine Tatwine[7] se scisse aliam insulam in abditis[8] remotioris[9] heremi partibus confitebatur[10], quam multi inhabitare temtantes[11] propter incognita heremi monstra et diversarum formarum terrores reprobaverant[12]. Quo audito, vir beatae recordationis Guthlac[13] illum locum monstrari sibi a narrante[14] efflagitabat[15]. Ipse enim[16] imperiis[17] viri[18] annuens[19],

Virg. *Aen.*
IV, 151

arrepta piscatoria scafula[20], per *invia lustra* [21]inter atrae[22] paludis margines Christo viatore ad [23]praedictum locum [24]usque pervenit[25]; Crugland dicitur[26], [26a]insula media in palude posita[27] quae ante paucis[28] propter[29] remotioris[30] heremi solitudinem inculta [31]vix nota[32] habebatur[33].

Bede,
V.pr.
c. 17

Nullus[34] *hanc ante famulum* Christi Guthlacum[35] *solus habitare colonus valebat,* [36]*propter videlicet*[37] illic *demorantium* [38]*fantasias demonum*[39], in qua vir Dei Guthlac[40], contempto hoste, caelesti[41] auxilio adiutus, inter umbrosa solitudinis nemora solus habitare coepit[42]. Contigit enim, [43]divina dispensante gratia[44], ut aestivis temporibus, die quo[45] missa[46] sancti Bartholomei[47] venerari debet, insulam Crugland[48] [48a]beatus Guthlac[49] devenisset, qui in[50] sancti Bartholomei[51] auxiliis[52], cum omni fiducia heremum habitare coeperat. Igitur, adamato[53] illius loci[54] abdito [55]situ velut[56] a Deo sibi donato[57], omnes dies vitae suae illic degere[58] directa[59] mente devoverat[60].

---

1 *om.* G.   2 approx... C₂G.   3 *ins.* vastissimi AE₂G.
4 sciscitabatur VB.   5 s. loca C₂N.   6 astant... nDE₂G.
6–7 *om.* A₂E₂G.   7 Tatpine V.   Tatuuine B.   Tatuinus D.
8 auditis C₁.   9 i.e. longioris N.   10 adserebat H.   asserebat D.
i.e. affirmabat D.   fatebatur A₂E₂G.   11 i.e. probantes N.
12 reprobaverunt C₂VBANE₁nE₂G.   amiserant HD.   13 Guðlac
C₂.   14 i.e. demonstrante C₁C₂.   i.e. monstrante N.   narante E₁.
15 efflagitat C₁C₂NE₁n.   i.e. postulat C₂N.   16 autem AHDE₂G.
17 i.e. precibus N.   18 *ins.* Dei C₂VBHDE₁n.   19 i.e. consentiens C₂N.   20 scaphula C₁C₂ANnE₂.   scapula VBE₁.   i.e.
cistiba vel navicula D.   *in marg. partly legible:* (nav)iculas dicimus,
(vi)mine factas et corio N.   21–22 *alt. to* in tetrae D.   23–24 predictam insulam HD.   24–25 quae lingua Anglorum HD.
26 vocatur HD.   *ins.* pervenit HD.   26a–27 *om.* HD.   28 pacis E₁.
om. HD.   paucum A₂E₂G.   29 praeter C₁.   vel propter C₁.   30 re-

XXV. It happened accordingly that when he was questioning those who lived near as to their knowledge of this solitude and they were telling him of many wild places in this far-stretching desert, a certain man among those standing by, whose name was Tatwine, declared that he knew a certain island in the more remote and hidden parts of that desert; many had attempted to dwell there, but had rejected it on account of the unknown portents of the desert and its terrors of various shapes. Guthlac, the man of blessed memory, on hearing this, earnestly besought his informant to show him the place. Tatwine accordingly assented to the commands of the man and, taking a fisherman's skiff, made his way, travelling with Christ, through trackless bogs within the confines of the dismal marsh till he came to the said spot; it is called Crowland, an island in the middle of the marsh which on account of the wildness of this very remote desert had hitherto remained untilled and known to a very few. No settler had been able to dwell alone in this place before Guthlac the servant of Christ, on account of the phantoms of demons which haunted it. Here Guthlac, the man of God, despising the enemy, began by divine aid to dwell alone among the shady groves of this solitude. For it happened through the dispensation of divine grace that the blessed Guthlac reached the island of Crowland in the summer time, on the day on which the feast of St Bartholomew is due to be celebrated. So he began to inhabit the desert with complete confidence in the help of St Bartholomew. He loved the remoteness of the spot seeing that God had given it him, and vowed with righteous purpose to spend all the days of his life there.

motionis B. i.e. longioris D. 31 s. loca C_2. 31–32 ignota VB. et ignota HD. i.e. incognita D. 33 manebat HD. 34 ins. vero A_2. 35 Guðlacum n. 36–37 vid. prop. A_2E_2G. 38–39 dem. fant. HD. 40 Guðlacus n. 41 caeleste NE_1. 42 chap. title in marg. Quomodo a proximis habitatoribus heremi in missa sancti Bartholomei usque in Cruland deductus est D. 43 autem A_2E_2G. 43–44 divinae dispensanti providentia gratiae AE_2G. 44 providentia HD. 45 om. E_2. 46 om. $AHDE_2G$. 47 ins. missa AH. ins. solemnitas A_2E_2G. ins. festivitas D. 48 Cruplond A. 48a–49 om. C_1. 49 Guðlac C_2. 50 ins. ipsius A_2E_2G. 51 ins. apostoli VB. 52 ins. specialiter fisus A_2E_2. ins. specialiter confisus G. 53 i.e. adoptato D. 54 om. E_2. 55–56 om. C_1. 57 donatum AG. 58 ins. devovit AE_2G. i.e. conversari D. 59 promptissima A_2E_2G. i.e. intenta N. 60 devovit C_1. devovet C_2VBNE_1n. om. AE_2G. i.e. promiserat D.

XXVI. Aliquot itaque diebus illic[1] permanens, omnia[2] quaeque[3] illius[4] loci diligenti investigatione considerans, versari[5] coepit, ut ad sodalium[6] suorum colloquium[7] veniret[8], quos[9] sibi[10] eximiae fraternitatis caritas[11] [11a]in gremio[12] catholicae congregationis iungebat[13], nam quos[14] ante [15]insalutatos dimittebat[16], iterum [17]salutaribus praeceptis[18] commendare disposuit[19]. Interea *mortalibus aegris* lux crastina demoverat[20] ortum, cum ille unde[21] egressus est[22], remeare coeperat[23]. Itaque intervenientibus[24] ter tricenorum[25] dierum curriculis quibus[26] sodales suos fraternis commendabat[27] salutationibus[28], ad supradictum locum, quasi ad paternae hereditatis habitaculum, binis illum comitantibus pueris, unde pervenit[29], regressus est.

Virg. Aen.
ii, 268

XXVII.[30] Deinde[31] peracto itinere, die [32]octava[33] kalendarum Septembrium[34], quo sancti Bartholomaei sollemnitas[35] celebrari solet, [36]in cuius[37] suffragio [38]omnia incoepta[39] heremi[40] habitandi[41] ex[42] divina providentia inchoaverat, Crugland pervenit. Erat ergo[43] annorum circiter viginti sex, cum[44] se[45] inter nubilosos[46] remotioris heremi lucos cum caelesti adiutorio veri Dei militem[47] esse proposuit[48]. Deinde praecinctus spiritalibus armis *adversus* teterrimi hostis *insidias scutum fidei, loricam spei, galeam* castitatis, arcum patientiae, sagittas psalmodiae[49], sese in aciem[50] firmans[51], *arripuit*[52]. Tantae enim fiduciae erat, ut inter torridas[53] tartari turmas sese contemto hoste iniecerit[54]. O quam admiranda est divinae miserationis

Eph.
6. 11–17
(cf. Hier.
Vita Pauli,
c. 8)

1 *ins.* fuit C₁.   istic AHDG.   2 *om.* D.   3 quaecumque NE₁n. quae A₂E₂G.   4 istius G.   5 versare AE₂G.   *ins.* mente A₂E₂G. i.e. regitare, cogitare D.   6 sodaliorum C₁.   i.e. sotiorum D. 7 colloquia VBD.   conloquia H.   8 perveniret VBHD.   9 quo A₂E₂G.   10 *ins.* eos A₂E₂G.   11 kar... H.   11a–12 *om.* C₁. 13 aggregaret A₂E₂G.   i.e. coadunabat D.   14 *om.* C₁A.   eos VBHD.   15–18 *om.* A₂E₂G.   16 dimiserat D.   17 *ins.* resalutatis VBHD.   17–18 *om.* HD.   18 *ins.* se HD. 19 studivit A.   20 i.e. exagitabat D.   21 inde C₁C₂NE₁n.   22 *om.* C₂AHDNE₁n.   23 coepit D.   24–25 aliquot A₂E₂G.   25 trienarum C₁. trigenarum C₂VBAHNE₁n. tricenum *ab.* tricenorum D.   26 ut HD. s. diebus N.   27 commendarat HD.   erudiebat A₂E₂G.   28 eruditionibus A₂.   exhortationibus E₂G.   29 venit D.   30 *ch. title* Quomodo rursus die viii Kalendarum Septembrium qua sancti

XXVI. And so, when he had remained there for some days and had investigated every part of that place with diligent search, he began to consider that he ought to go and have converse with his companions to whom he had been united by no common brotherly love in the bosom of a Catholic community, for he had previously forsaken them without any farewells; and so he determined to greet them again with wholesome words of exhortation. Meanwhile the light of the next day had risen over hapless mortals when he set out on his return journey. And so after he had spent a period of ninety days in greeting his companions with brotherly salutations, he returned to the above-mentioned place whence he had come, as though to a home inherited from his father, and was accompanied by two boys.

XXVII. He finished his journey and reached Crowland on 25 August, the day on which it is usual to celebrate the feast of St Bartholomew with whose help, under divine providence, he had made a beginning of his dwelling in the desert. He was then about twenty-six years of age, when he determined with heavenly aid to be a soldier of the true God amid the gloomy thickets of that remote desert. Then, girding himself with spiritual arms against the wiles of the foul foe, he took the shield of faith, the breastplate of hope, the helmet of chastity, the bow of patience, the arrows of psalmody, making himself strong for the fight. So great in fact was his confidence that, despising the foe, he hurled himself against the torrid troops of Tartarus. O how marvellous is the kindness of the divine

Bartholomei missa celebrari solet Crugland reversus est NE_1D (Cruland D).
31 dein n.   32-34 om. A_2E_2G.   33 octavo n.   ix ab. D.
34 septembris n. septemrium D. ab. vel septembrium'D.   35 solemni...
HD. sollenni...nE_2G.   36 adsolet VB. assolet HD.   36-37 iustus E_2.
37 s. Bartholomei D.   38-39 om. A_2E_2G.   39 i.e. inchoata B.
40 heremum A_2E_2G.   41 habitare A_2E_2G.   42 om. A_2E_2G.   43 autem
tunc A_2E_2G.   44 ins. dedisset C_1VB.   45 om. C_2NE_1n.   46 nubilos
C_1. nebulosos C_2NE_1n.   om. A_2E_2G. i.e. obscuros D.   47 miles
$C_1C_2ANE_1nE_2G$.   48 i.e. destinavit D.   49 ins. arripiens A_2E_2G.
50 arma AE_2G. i.e. in pugnam N.   51 om. C_1. convertit AE_2G.
52 et decenter in acie se firmavit A_2E_2G.   53 i.e. ardentes N.
54 interieceret C_1VB. iniecerat HD. iniceret C_2NE_1n. i.e. inmitteret N.

indulgentia, et quantum glorificanda sit[1] paternae[2]
dilectionis providentia, [3]en[4] in[5] quantum laudanda sit[6]
aeternae Deitatis praedestinatio, quam inscrutabilia sunt

Rom.   perpetui iudicis arbitria[7], ut apostolus confirmat[8], *quam[9]*
II. 33   *inscrutabilia[10] sunt iudicia eius et investigabiles viae* ipsius[11].
Cf. Acts   Nam, sicut egregium doctorem gentium Damascum per-
c. 9   gentem, quem ante saecula evangelium Filii sui nuntiare
praedestinavit, de tenebrosa[12] Iudaeorum erroris caligine
caelesti voce deduxit[13], sic et sanctae memoriae virum
Guthlac de tumido aestuantis saeculi gurgite, de obliquis[14]
mortalis aevi anfractibus, de atris [15]vergentis mundi[16]
faucibus [17]ad perpetuae[18] beatitudinis militiam[19], ad
directi[20] itineris callem, ad veri luminis prospectum[21]
perduxit; [22]et non solum praesentis saeculi famosa venerantia[23] beavit[24], sed[25] in gaudio[26] perennis[27] gloriae[28]
aeterna[29] beatitudine[30] constituit, sicut apostolica[31]

Rom. 8. 30   veritas[32] depromsit[33]: *Quos praedestinavit[34], hos et vocavit;*
et[35] quos[36] vocavit, illos[37] glorificavit[38].

XXVIII.   [39]*Qualiter in scisso[40] latere tumuli superinposito*
tugurio habitabat, vel quomodo ortonomiam [41]vitae
habuit heremitalis[42]

Igitur ut de sancti Guthlaci solitaria vita, sicut proposui,
scribere exordiar[43], quae[44] a [45]frequentatoribus eius
Wilfrido et Cissan[46] audivi[47], eodem ordine, quo conperi,
easdem res narrare curabo. Erat itaque in praedicta[48]
insula tumulus agrestibus glaebis coacervatus[49], quem olim

1 *om.* A₂E₂G.   2 *ins.* illius A₂E₂G.   3–5 o A₂E₂G.   4 et HD.
6 est A₂E₂G.   7 consilia A₂E₂G. i.e. indicia D.   8 i.e. ap-
probat D.   9 quia AE₂G.   10 incomprehensibilia E₂G.
11 eius AE₂G.   *ins.* et reliqua C₂HNE₁.   12 tenebrosi
C₁VBAHDE₂G.   13 eduxit E₂G.   14 i.e. tortuosis D.
15–16 mund. verg. G.   17–19 *om.* VB.   18 perpetuam HD.
20 recti C₂VHNE₁nD.   21 affectum G.   22–38 *om.* A₂E₂G.
23 i.e. honorificencia D.   24 s. illum C₂N.   25 set B.
26 gaudium HD.   27 perhennis HD.   28 vitae A.   29 s. et
in N.   eterne HD.   30 beatitudini VBHD.   31 apostoli A.
32 *om.* A.   33 i.e. manifestavit D.   *ins.* veritas A.

mercy and how glorious the providence of the Father's love,
how praiseworthy the predestination of the eternal Deity, how
inscrutable the judgements of the everlasting Judge, as the
apostle declares: 'How unsearchable are His judgements and
His ways past finding out!' For just as with a heavenly voice
He brought forth, out of the gloomy mist of the error of the
Jews, the supreme teacher of the Gentiles when on his way to
Damascus—him whom He had predestined before all worlds
to preach the Gospel of His Son; so also He led Guthlac a man
of saintly memory from the eddying whirlpool of these turbid
times, from the tortuous paths of this mortal age, from the
black jaws of this declining world to the struggle for eternal
bliss, to the straight path and to the vision of the true light.
And not only did He reward him with fame and veneration
in this present world, but He also established him in the joy
and eternal blessedness of perennial glory, as apostolic truth
foretold: 'Whom He did predestinate, them he also called:
and whom he also called, them he glorified.'

XXVIII. *How he dwelt in the side of a barrow which had
been dug open, building a hut over it; and how he carried
out his rule of life as a hermit*

So to begin the account of St Guthlac's solitary life as I have
proposed to do, I will seek to narrate the story as I heard it from
Wilfrid and Cissa who were his frequent visitors, and in the
order in which I learnt it. Now there was in the said island
a mound built of clods of earth which greedy comers to the

34 predist... C₁.   35 *om.* HD.   36 *ins.* autem HD.   37 *ins.*
et C₁A.   38 *ins.* et reliqua C₂HNE₁nD.   39 *At this point where
the second part of the life begins, chapter headings are found regularly in*
C₁C₂VBHNE₁D. *The chapter headings in D differ somewhat from those set out
in the list of chapters, where the differences have been noted (see pp. 66–72).
Any further differences are recorded in the footnotes.*   40 i.e. diviso N.
41 *in marg.* rectam legem V.   *ab.* rectam legem B.   i.e. consuetudinem vel
constitutionem N.   41–42 habuerit heremitalis vitae D.   43 exordior
C₂NE₁n.   i.e. incipiam D.   44 quas C₂NE₁n.   45 *handwriting
changes in A after* fre-.   46 Cissano AE₂G.   *alt. to* Cissa D.   47 *ins.*
et E₁.   48 praefata C₂HNE₁nD.   49 i.e. congregatus N.

avari solitudinis frequentatores [1]lucri ergo[2] [2a]illic[3] adquirendi [4]defodientes[5] scindebant[6], in cuius latere velut cisterna inesse videbatur; in qua[7] vir beatae memoriae Guthlac desuper inposito tugurio[8] habitare coepit. Vitae scilicet[9] illius haec inmota[10] ortonomia[11] fuit, ita[12] ut ab illo tempore, quo heremum habitare coeperat, non laneo, nec lineo vestimine[13], nec alterius cuiuscumque delicatae vestis [14]tegminibus usus est[15], sed[16] in pelliciis[17] vestibus omnes[18] dies[19] solitariae conversationis suae exigebat[20]. Cotidianae ergo[21] vitae ipsius tanta temperantia fuit, ut [22]ab illo tempore, quo heremum[23] habitare coeperat[24], excepta[25] ordeacei[26] *pan*is particula *et lutulentae*[27] *aquae*[28] poculamento[29] post solis occasum[30], nullius alicuius alimenti usibus vesceretur. Nam cum sol occiduis finibus vergeretur[31], tunc [32]annonam parvam[33] mortalis vitae[34] cum gratiarum actione gustabat[35].

Hier. *Vita Pauli*, c. 6

I Pet. 5. 8

XXIX. [36]*Quomodo primam* [37]*temtationem*[38] *disperationis*[39] *a Satana*[40] *pertulerit*[40a]

Sub eodem denique tempore, quo praefatus vir beatae memoriae heremitare[41] initiavit[42], cum quodam[43] die adsueta[44] consuetudine psalmis canticisque incumberet, tunc[45] antiquus hostis prolis[46] humanae, ceu[47] *leo rugiens*, per vasti aetheris spatia tetra[48] numina commutans[49] novas artes novo[50] pectore versat[51]. Cum[52] enim[53] omnes nequitiae suae vires versuta[54] mente temptaret, tum[55] veluti ab extenso arcu venenifluam desperationis sagittam

---

1–2 erga gratiam lucri C₁. erga causam lucri C₂NE₁n. erga lucri gratiam A. ergo lucri VBHD. *ab.* i.e. causa HD. lucri gratia A₂E₂G. 2*a*–4 adq. illic G.   3–5 def. adq. C₁C₂VBNE₁n.   4–6 scind. def. AE₂G.   6 scindebat H.   i.e. dividebat N.   i.e. rumpebant D. 7 i.e. cisterna D.   8 tegurio B.   *ab.* vel tu B.   9 vero A₂E₂G. 10 innota E₁.   immoto E₂.   11 *ab.* consuetudo AE₂.   i.e. consuetudo N.   i.e. legalitas D.   12 *om.* A₂E₂G.   13 vestimento A₂E₂G.   14–15 tegmini uteretur A₂E₂G.   16 set B.   17 pelliceis C₂NE₁n.   18 omnibus A.   19 diebus A.   20 faciebat A₂E₂G.   21 *om.* A₂E₂.   que G.   22–24 *om.* A₂E₂G. 23 eremum C₁.   25 excepto VBH.   accepta G.   26 ordeaci C₁. ordeacii C₂VBHNE₁.   ordeicei n.   ordeicii D.   27 luc... VH.

waste had dug open, in the hope of finding treasure there; in the side of this there seemed to be a sort of cistern, and in this Guthlac the man of blessed memory began to dwell, after building a hut over it. From the time when he first inhabited this hermitage this was his unalterable rule of life: namely to wear neither wool nor linen garments nor any other sort of soft material, but he spent the whole of his solitary life wearing garments made of skins. So great indeed was the abstinence of his daily life that from the time when he began to inhabit the desert he ate no food of any kind except that after sunset he took a scrap of barley bread and a small cup of muddy water. For when the sun reached its western limits, then he thankfully tasted some little provision for the needs of this mortal life.

XXIX. How he endured the first temptation, namely that of despair, sent by Satan

And so about the time when the said man of blessed memory, Guthlac, had begun his hermit life, he was engaged one day upon his usual task of singing psalms and hymns, while the ancient foe of the human race, like a lion roaring through the spaces of the limitless sky, was ever varying his foul demonic might and pondering anew fresh designs. So, testing all his wicked powers, with crafty mind he shot, as from a bow fully drawn, a poisoned arrow of despair with all his might, so that

ab. vel lutosae A. i.e. turbatae N. *in marg. in sixteenth-cent. hand:* lutulentus a luto dicitur et idcirco dicitur quod lutosus vel turbidus D. 28 quae H. 29 poculamenta CVBAH. poculo A_2E_2G. 30 ocas... A. 31 veg... N. 32–33 parv. ann. $AHDE_2G$. 34 *ins.* sustinendae A_2E_2G. 35 *ins.* salubriter H. 36–40*a* Qualiter illum zabulus instigationibus desperationis temptavit C_2NE_1. 37–39 desper. tempt. D. 38 tempt... H. 39 desp... VB. 40 Sata VB. 41 heremitari C_2NE_1n. i.e. in heremi conversari N. i.e. heremum habitare D. 42 i.e. inchoavit D. 43 quadam C_2NE_1n. 44 i.e. morali N. 45 *om.* A_2E_2G. 46 i.e. generis N. 47 i.e. sicut D. seu G. 48 i.e. nigra D. 49 commot... $C_1C_2VBNE_1$n. comitans D. 50 nova E_1. 51 *ab.* þoh A. i.e. insidiatur N. gustavit C_2NE_1. 52 dum HD. 53 ergo A_2E_2G. 54 *ab.* fæ A. i.e. callida D. 55 tunc $AHNE_1nDE_2G$.

totis viribus iaculavit[1], quousque in Christi militis mentis[2] umbone[3] [3a]defixa pependit[4]. Interea cum telum toxicum[5] atri veneni[6] sucum[7] infunderet, tum miles Christi totis sensibus turbatus[8] de eo, quod[9] incoeperat, desperare coepit et huc illucque turbulentum animum convertens, quo solo sederet, nesciebat. [10]Nam cum sua ante commissa crimina inmensi ponderis[11] fuisse[12] meditabatur, tunc sibi de se [13]ablui ea[14] non posse videbatur[15]. In tantum enim[16] desperare coepit, ut[17] infinitum[18] et inportabile opus[19] se incoepisse putasset. Deinde[20] *Christi famulus trium dierum vicissitudinibus, quo se verteret, nesciebat.* Die autem[21] tertio[22] sequenti nocte, cum validissimus [23]miles Christi[24] robusta mente pestiferis meditationibus resisteret, velut prophetico spiritu psallere coepit: *In tribulatione[25] invocavi Dominum, [26]et reliqua[27].* [27a]Ecce beatus Bartholomaeus, fidus auxiliator, in[28] matutinis vigiliis sese[29] coram[30] obtutibus[31] obtulit[32] illius[33]; nec sopor illud erat, sed[34] palam splendentis caelicolae cognovit[35] vultum. Igitur vir praefatus, veluti miles inter densas acies dimicans, cum caeleste adiutorium[36] angelicae lucis adventasse persensisset, extimplo[37] discussis nefandarum[38] cogitationum nebulis, inluminato turbulenti pectoris gremio[39], velut triumphali voce psallebat aiens[40]: *Dominus mihi[41] adiutor est, et ego videbo[42] inimicos meos[43].* Exin[44] sanctus Bartholomaeus, coram eo persistens, illum praeceptis spiritalibus confortare coepit, pollicens[45] ei in omnibus tribulationibus adiutorem sui venturum se[46] fore. Sanctus autem Guthlac[47], his auditis et creditis[48] fidelissimi amici sui dictis, spiritali[49] gaudio repletus, indissolutam eximiae valitudinis fidem[50] in Domino Iesu defixit. Nam

Hier. *Vita Pauli*, c. 3

Ps. 17. 7

Ps. 117. 7

---

1 i.e. emisit D. 2 *om.* C₂NE₁n. 3 *ab.* s. mentis C₂N.
3a–4 depependit fixa AE₂G. 5 i.e. veneficium D. 6 venesi VB.
7 succum E₂. 8 *om.* E₂G. 9 quae C₁VB. 10 *in marg.*
ðonan A. 10–15 *om.* A₂E₂G. 11 i.e. gravi D.
12 s. ea C₂N. 13–14 abluere C₁C₂VBAHNE₁n. ablueri H.
16 ergo AE₂G. 17 uti C₁VB. 18 *ins.* opus VB. 19 *om.* VB.
onus G. 20 dein AHNnDE₂G. 21 *om.* C₁VBAE₂G.
22 tertia C₁VBAE₂G. 23–24 Chr. mil. HDG. 25 *ins.*
mea HD. 26–27 *om.* nD. et exaudivit me in latitudine Dominus

it stuck fast in the very centre of the mind of the soldier of Christ. Now when meanwhile the poisoned weapon had poured in its potion of black venom, then every feeling of the soldier of Christ was disturbed by it, and he began to despair about what he had undertaken, and turning things over in his troubled mind he knew not in what place to rest. For when he remembered that the sins he had committed in the past were of immense weight, it seemed to him that he could not be cleansed from them. He began indeed to despair so utterly that he thought he had undertaken an infinite and insupportable labour. Then the servant of the Lord for the space of three days did not know whither to turn. But on the third day at nightfall, while the most valiant soldier of Christ, still stout of heart, was resisting these baleful thoughts, he began to sing as though through the spirit of prophecy: 'In my distress I called upon the Lord', etc. And lo! the blessed Bartholomew his trusty helper presented himself before his gaze in the morning watches. Nor was it just a dream; but he openly recognized the countenance of the resplendent citizen of heaven. So when this same man, like a soldier fighting in the serried ranks, had realized that the heavenly aid and angelic light had reached him, immediately the clouds of impious thought were dissipated, his troubled heart was enlightened and he sang triumphantly: 'The Lord is my helper and I shall see my enemies', etc. Thereupon St Bartholomew remained in his presence and began to comfort him with spiritual precepts, promising that he would come to his aid in all tribulations. St Guthlac moreover heard him and, trusting the word of his most faithful friend, and full of spiritual joy, he placed his faith with constancy and uncommon strength in the Lord Jesus. For from the triumphant success of his first

E_2G. 27a *ins*. et A_2E_2G. 28 *om*. A_2E_2G. 29 esse N. 30 *om*. A_2E_2G. 31 *ins*. illius HD. opt... NE_2. 32 opt... HDE_2G. 33 *om*. HD. 34 set HB. 35 agn... HC_2NE_1nD. 36 i.e. auxiliatorem D. 37 extemplo n. 38 i.e. iniquarum D. 39 obtutu A_2G. op... E_7. 40 *ab*. i.e. dicens BD. dicens E_2. 41 michi nD. 42 despiciam A_2E_2G. ridebo D. i.e. despiciam D. 43 *ins*. et reliqua HD. 44 exinde C_1VB. 45 i.e. promittens D. *om*. E_2G. 46 *om*. C_1VBH. *ab*. s. se D. 47 Guþlacus n. 48 credens E_2G. 49 spirituali G. 50 spem C_2NE_1n.

ex primi certaminis triumphali successu[1] spem futurae
[2]gloriae et[3] victoriae[4] robusto pectore firmabat. Ex illo
enim tempore numquam zabulus[5] adversus illum desperationis[6] arma arripuit[7], quia [8]ab illo[9] semel infracta
contra illum ultra praevalere nequiverunt.

XXX.   *Quomodo illum zabulus pseudosodalitate*[10]
ieiunium docere temtavit[11]

Quadam quoque die, dum de conversationis suae coti-
diano[12] moderamine meditaretur, subito coram illo, velut[13]
ex aere lapsi, efferis[14] vultibus duo zabuli humano habitu
se obtulerunt[15], ac veluti cum familiari fiducia loqui cum
illo exorsi sunt[16], dicentes: 'Nos experti sumus te, [17]et
fidei tuae valitudinem conperimus[18], perseverantiamque
patientiae tuae invincibilem probantes, variarum artium
adversus te arma suscepimus. Propterea insultare tibi
ultra[19] desistere conamur, et non solum propositi tui
ortonomias[20] disrumpere[21] nolumus, sed te antiquorum
heremitarum conversationes[22] erudiemus[23]. Moyses[24]
etenim et Elias[25] et ipse[26] humanae prosapiae[27] Salvator
primo omnium ad ieiunii fastigia[28] conscenderunt; sed
et famosi illi monachi[29] habitantes Aegyptum[30] humanae
infirmitatis vitia[31] abstinentiae framea[32] interimebant. Et
idcirco, si tu vis ante commissa crimina abluere[33], inmi-
nentia necare[34], carnem tuam abstinentiae flagellis adflige,
et animi tui insolentiam[35] ieiunii[36] frange[37] fascibus[38].
Quanto enim in hoc saeculo frangeris, tanto in perpetuum
solidaris: et quanto in praesenti[39] adfligeris, tanto in futuro
gaudebis. Nam cum in[40] ieiunio prostratus iacueris, tunc

1 i.e. fortuna D.   2–3 *om.* HD.   3 *om.* NE₁E₂G.   4 *om.*
NE₁E₂G.   5 diabolus A₂E₂G.   6 disp... C₁.   7 aripuit D.
8–9 *om.* E₂G.   10 pseudalitate C₁VB. pseudasodal.... D.
11 tempt... VBHD.   12 quot... H.   13 velud A.   14 efferis
C₁C₂NE₁n. efferens VB. i.e. inconvenientibus, i.e. indomitis vel
ferocibus N.   15 opt... E₂.   16 i.e. coeperunt N. i.e.
incipiebant D.   17–18 *ins. ab.* N.   19 ultro AE₂G.
20 consuetudinem A₂E₂G. i.e. legalia iura D.   21 dirump...

battle, the hope of future glory and victory grew strong in his robust heart. From that time never indeed did the devil seize the weapon of despair to use against him, because once Guthlac had broken it, it could never more prevail against him.

XXX. *How the devil, in false friendship, tried to teach him how to fast*

Now on a certain day while he was meditating upon the day to day ordering of his life, two devils, in human form and with wild countenances, presented themselves before him suddenly as though they had fallen from the sky, and began to speak to him in friendly confidence: 'We have tried you', they said, 'and have tested the power of your faith: we have tried your unconquerable perseverance and patience: we have taken up against you weapons and wiles of various kinds. Therefore we intend to desist from assaulting you further; and not only are we unwilling to destroy the rules of your undertaking, but we will instruct you in the lives of the ancient hermits. For Moses and Elijah and the Saviour of the human race Himself first of all scaled the heights of fasting: moreover those famous monks who inhabited Egypt destroyed the vices of human weakness with the sword of abstinence. And therefore if you wish to wash away your sins committed in the past and to destroy those that threaten, afflict your flesh with the whips of abstinence and crush the arrogance of your mind with the rods of fasting. For in so far as you are broken down in this world, you shall be made whole and firm in eternity; and to the degree that you are afflicted in this present life, so much shall you rejoice in the future. For when you shall lie prostrated with fasting,

nDE₂G.   22 conversatione AE₂G.   23 erudimus C₁VBAE₂.
24 Mois... G.   25 Helias C₂AHNE₁nE₂.   26 ipsae C₁C₂VB.
27 prosapiei C₂n.   28 fastigiam C₁.   i.e. summitates D.   29 mo-
nahi C₁.   30 Aegipt... VBA.   Egipt... G.   31 *ins.* in
C₁C₂VBHNE₁n.   32 *ab.* arpan N.   33 *ins.* et C₂NE₁n.   34 neca
AE₂.   35 olentiam C₁C₂ANE₁n.   inolentiam VBH.   36 ieiunis HD.
37 *om.* HD.   38 farcibus C₂VBNE₁n.   faucibus frange HD.   i.e.
impletianibus N.   39 s. te C₂N.   40 *om.* HDA₂E₂G.

excelsius coram Deo elevaris. Ieiunium ergo non bidui[1]
aut tridui[2] aut[3] cotidianae[4] abstinentiae[5] gastrimargia[6]
sit[7], sed septenarum[8] dierum valida castigatio [9]ieiunium
est[10]. Sicut[11] enim sex diebus Deus mundi plasma[12] for-
mavit et septimo die[13] requievit, ita etiam hominem decet[14]
sex diebus per ieiunii plasma[15] spiritu[16] reformari[17] et
septimo die comedendo[18] carni requiem dare.' His[19]

Ps. 55. 10

auditis beatus Guthlac exsurgens[20] psallebat: *Convertantur*[21]
inimici mei retrorsum, [22]et reliqua[23]. Quo facto[24] hostis

Virg. Aen.
XII, 592

strofosus[25] velut[26] *fumus a facie*[27] eius *vacuas* in *auras*
evanuit; ille vero zabulicum[28] magisterium despiciens[29],

Ps. 67. 2

ne ullus locus consentiendi[30] illis[31] in eo videretur[32],
tunc[33] adsumpta[34] ordeacei[35] panis particula victum suum
cotidianum[36] vesci[37] coepit. Maligni vero spiritus, con-
temptos se[38] esse intelligentes[39], lacrimoso clamore, flebili

Virg. Geo.
IV, 515

ululatu diversisque[40] singultibus plangentes, late[41] loca[42]
maestis *questibus* inpleverunt. Exin[43] vir Dei inmundorum spirituum fantasmata[44], percepto ubique certandi[45]
bravio[46], contempsit.

XXXI. *Quomodo corporaliter maligni spiritus ad portas inferni illum asportaverunt*[47]

Per idem[48] fere[49] tempus, paucis intervenientibus dierum
cursibus, cum vir beatae memoriae Guthlac adsueto
more vigil[50] inintermissis[51] orationibus[52] cuiusdam noctis
intempesto[53] tempore perstaret, en[54] subito teterrimis[55]

---

1 biduum C_1A_2. biduo E_2G. *ins.* tantum A_2E_2G.   2 triduum
C_1A_2. triduo E_2G. *ins.* servandum est A_2E_2G.   3 vel C_1VBA.
contra E_2G.   4 quot... H.   5 *om.* E_2G.   6 castimonia
$C_1C_2VBNE_1n$. gastrimonia A. castrimargie DE_2G.   7 s. tibi
C_2N. fit A. vitium E_2G.   8 *ab.* vel septimanarum C_2. sep-
tenariarum C_2NE_1n. septenarium VB. septimanam A_2. septimana
E_2G.   9–10 est ieiunium A. est vitiorum E_2G.   11 sic E_2.
12 plasmam $C_1C_2VBNE_1n$.   13 *om.* C_1.   14 i.e. oportet D.
15 plasmam $C_1C_2VBNE_1n$.   16 spiritum AE_2G.   17 re-
formare AE_2G.   18 comedendi $C_1C_2VBANE_1n$. i.e. mandu-
candi D.   19 hiis G.   20 exurgens C_2nDE_2G.   21 convertentur C_1.   22–23 *om.* nD. ^i_q.q.a.v.a.e. A_2. qui quaerunt
animam meam ut auferant eam E_2G.   24 dicto A_2G. audito E_2.
25 strophosus n. i.e. fraudulentus D. *ab.* frǣte C_2. *ab.* fa. A.

then you shall be raised higher in the presence of God. So let not your fast be a matter of two days or three days nor even of a daily abstinence from gluttony; but a fast of seven days is an effective chastisement. For as in six days the Lord moulded the world and rested on the seventh day, even so man ought to be remoulded in spirit by fasting for six days and on the seventh day give rest to the flesh in taking nourishment.' When the blessed Guthlac heard this he rose up and sang: 'Let mine enemies be turned back', etc. When the impostor his foe heard this, he vanished like smoke from his presence into thin air. But the saint, despising this devilish instruction, and lest there should appear any sign of his consenting to them, began even then to eat his daily food, taking a scrap of barley bread. The evil spirits, however, realizing that they had been despised, lamented with tearful clamour and mournful cries and with many a sob, filling the land far and wide with their sad complaints. Thereafter the man of God despised the phantoms and foul spirits, having obtained everywhere the prize in the fight.

XXXI. *How the evil spirits carried him bodily to the gates of hell*

About the same time, after the passage of a few days, when Guthlac the man of blessed memory in his usual way was once keeping vigil at the dead of night in uninterrupted prayer, he suddenly saw the whole tiny cell filled with horrible troops of

26 veluð A. 27 faciae A. 28 zabolicum C_1. zabuliticum C_2VBHnD. zabolitium N. zabolitium E_1. i.e. adversarium D. diabolicum A_2E_2G. 29 *om.* E_2G. i.e. contempnens D. 30 *alt. to* consentiendo C_1A. 31 s. duobus D. 32 *ab.* þu A. 33 *om.* A_2E_2G. 34 *ab.* fa A. 35 ordeacii C_2VBHNE_1. ordeicei n. ordeicii D. 36 quot... C_2H. 37 vesceri C_1VBAH. sumere A_2E_2G. 38 *om.* E_1. 39 intelleg... C_1C_2VBN. 40 diversis A. 41 *ins.* per VB. 42 *ins.* illa A_2E_2G. 43 exinde C_1C_2VBAHNE_1nE_2G. 44 phan... AG. fantasmate n. 45 i.e. dimicandi D. 46 brachio C_1VBHD. 47 ans... *alt. to* as... C_1C_2. ass... NE_1. 48 *ins.* enim A_2E_2G. 49 vero C_1VB. 50-52 intermissionibus C_1. 51 intermissis VBHE_1DE_2. *ab.* asend A. 53 i.e. sereno N. i.e. sereno vel medio vel inactuoso D. 54 ecce A_2E_2G. 55 *om.* G.

inmundorum spirituum catervis[1] totam cellulam[2] suam
inpleri conspexit. Subeuntibus[3] enim ab [4]undique illis[5]
porta patebat[6]; nam per criptas[7] et cratulas intrantibus[8]
non iuncturae[9] valvarum, non foramina cratium[10] illis
ingressum negabant; [11]sed caelo terraque erumpentes,
spatium totius aeris fuscis nubibus tegebant[12]. Erant
enim[13] aspectu truces, forma terribiles, capitibus magnis,
collis[14] longis, macilenta[15] facie, lurido[16] vultu, squalida[17]
barba, auribus hispidis, fronte torva[18], trucibus oculis,
ore foetido, dentibus equineis, gutture flammivomo[19],
faucibus tortis[20], labro lato[21], vocibus horrisonis, comis[22]
obustis[23], buccula[24] crassa, pectore arduo, femoribus
scabris, genibus nodatis[25], cruribus[26] uncis, talo tumido,
plantis[27] aversis[28], ore patulo, clamoribus raucisonis[29].
Ita enim inmensis vagitibus[30] horrescere[31] audiebantur,
ut totam paene[32] a caelo[33] in terram intercapedinem[34]
clangisonis boatibus[35] inplerent. Nec mora[36], ingruentes[37]
inrumpentesque[38] domum ac[39] castellum[40], dicto citius
virum Dei[41] praefatum, [42]ligatis membris[43], extra cellulam[44] suam duxerunt, et adductum in atrae paludis coenosis
laticibus inmerserunt. Deinde[45] asportantes[46] illum per
paludis[47] asperrima loca[48] inter densissima veprium vimina
dilaceratis[49] membrorum[50] conpaginibus[51] trahebant.
Inter haec cum magnam[52] partem umbrosae noctis in
illis adflictionibus exigebant[53], sistere[54] illum paulisper
fecerunt[55], imperantes[56] sibi[57], ut de heremo discedisset[58].
Ille stabilita[59] mente tandem respondens[60] prophetico[61]
velut[62] ore psallebat: [63]Dominus[64] a dextris est mihi[65],

Ps. 15. 8

1 ab. þi A.   2 cellam HD.   3 subeuntes A.   4 om. A_2E_2G.
4–5 ill. und. G.   6 i.e. operiebatur D. patebant E_2.   7 i.e. simas
(for rimas?) N.   8 intrantes C_1VBA.   9 iunctura C_1C_2ANE$_1$n.
iuncturas VB.   10 cart... C_1. rimarum A_2E_2G. in marg. crates
[dicitur?] in quibus lutum portari solet N.   11–12 om. C_1AE_2G. ins.
in marg. B.   13 autem A_2E_2G.   14 collibus C_1C_2VNE$_1$n.   15 maci-
lante E_1.   i.e. macra vel pallida D.   16 lurida C_1.   i.e. contaminato
vel sordido D.   17 i.e. sordida vel polluta D.   18 i.e. interribilis D.
19 alt. from flammivoma C_1A.   20 tostis C_2ANE$_1$n. tornis G.
21 loto N.   22 ab. loc A.   23 conb... C_1. comb... VB.
exust... A_2E_2G.   24 bucilla C_2VBNE$_1$n. bucella AE_2G.
25 nudatis A_2E_2G.   26 ins. ad AE_2G.   27 planctis E_1.   28 ad-

foul spirits; for the door was open to them as they approached
from every quarter; as they entered through floor-holes and
crannies, neither the joints of the doorways nor the openings
in the wattle-work denied them entry, but, bursting forth from
the earth and sky, they covered the whole space beneath the
heavens with their dusky clouds. For they were ferocious in
appearance, terrible in shape with great heads, long necks, thin
faces, yellow complexions, filthy beards, shaggy ears, wild
foreheads, fierce eyes, foul mouths, horses' teeth, throats
vomiting flames, twisted jaws, thick lips, strident voices,
singed hair, fat cheeks, pigeon breasts, scabby thighs, knotty
knees, crooked legs, swollen ankles, splay feet, spreading
mouths, raucous cries. For they grew so terrible to hear with
their mighty shriekings that they filled almost the whole inter-
vening space between earth and heaven with their discordant
bellowings. Without delay they attacked and burst into his
home and castle, and quicker than words they bound the limbs
of the said man of God and took him out of the cell; and leading
him away, they plunged him into the muddy waters of the
black marsh. Then they carried him through the wildest parts
of the fen, and dragged him through the dense thickets of
brambles, tearing his limbs and all his body. Meanwhile, when
they had spent a great part of the gloomy night in these perse-
cutions, they made him stand up for a short time, commanding
him to depart from the desert. He however answered at last
with steadfast mind, singing as though with prophetic words:
'The Lord is at my right hand, lest I should be moved.' And

versis E₂.   29 ab. hasgrumelum C₂.   30 ab. þo A.   31 ab. hlyþan C₂.
32 ins. aerem A₂E₂G.   33 ins. usque C₁A₂E₂G.   34 intercrepidinem
C₁VBAH. ab. þes A. om. A₂E₂G.   35 i.e. clamoribus C₂N. tumultibus
A₂E₂G.   36 s. erat C₂N.   37 i.e. supervenientes D.   38 om.
C₂NE₁n. i.e. ingravescentes D. om. -que C₁.   39 a VB.   40 casellum
D.   41 om. HD.   42–43 men. lig. D.   44 cellam E₁.   45 s. eum
C₂N.   46 ass... C₁C₂N. ansportaverunt A. asportaverunt A₂E₂G.
47 om. AE₂G.   48 ins. paludis AE₂G.   49 add. -que A₂E₂G. delacer...
C₂NE₁.   50 menb... D.   51 compagibus D. i.e. iuncturis D.
52 in marg. in fine A₂.   53 peregissent A₂E₂G.   54 i.e. stare D.
55 ins. ac C₁VBAHE₂G.   56 i.e. precipientes D.   57 ei A₂E₂G.
58 discederet nDA₂E₂G.   59 stabili A₂E₂G.   60 respondit H.
60–62 vel. proph. A₂E₂G.   61 prof... V.   63–1 (p. 104) Dominus
mihi adiutor est, non C₁VB.   64 ins. mihi G.   65 michi D. om. G.

ne[1] *commovear*. Dein[2] iterum adsumentes[3], flagellis velut[4] ferreis eum[5] verberare[6] coeperunt[7]. Cum autem, [8]post innumerabilia[9] tormentorum genera, post flagellorum[10] ferreorum[11] verbera, illum inmota[12] mente, robusta fide in eo quod incoeperat[13], perstare[14] viderent, horridis alarum[15] stridoribus inter nubifera gelidi aeris spatia illum subvectare[16] coeperunt[17]. Cum[18] ergo ad ardua aeris[19] culmina adventasset[20], horrendum dictu! ecce septentrionalis[21] caeli[22] plaga fuscis[23] atrarum[24] nubium caliginibus nigrescere videbatur. Innumerabiles enim inmundorum spirituum alas[25] in[26] obviam illis[27] dehinc venire cerneres[28]. Coniunctis[29] itaque in unum turmis, cum inmenso clamore leves[30] in[31] auras iter vertentes, supra memoratum Christi famulum Guthlac [32]ad nefandas tartari fauces usque perducunt. Ille vero[33], fumigantes aestuantis inferni cavernas[34] prospectans[35], omnia tormenta, quae prius a malignis spiritibus perpessus est, tamquam non ipse pateretur[36], obliviscebatur[37]. Non solum enim fluctuantium flammarum ignivomos[38] gurgites illic turgescere cerneres[39], immo etiam sulphurei[40] glaciali grandine mixti[41] vortices[42], globosis[43] sparginibus[44] sidera[45] paene tangentes[46] videbantur; maligni ergo[47] spiritus inter favillantium voraginum[48] atras cavernas discurrentes[49], miserabili[50] fatu animas impiorum diversis cruciatuum[51] generibus torquebant[52]. Igitur vir Dei Guthlac, cum innumerabiles tormentorum species horresceret, satellitum sibi velut ex uno ore [53]turmae clamabant[54] dicentes: 'Ecce nobis

---

1 non C₂ANE₁n. nec H. 2 deinde C₁VB. et HD. 3 *ins.* eum A₂E₂G. 4 veluti C₁VBAE₂G. 5 *om.* A₂E₂G. 6 verberari C₁. 7 coeperant H. 8–9 inn. post A. 10 virgarum A₂E₂G. flagellarum C₁C₂VBAHNE₁n. 11 ferrearum C₁C₂VBAHNE₁n. 12 inmutata VB. 13 incip... C₁. ceperat A₂E₂G. 14 *ab.* permaneret N. 15 hal... C₁. 16 subvehere C₂ANE₁nE₂G. subvectere VB. i.e. elevare vel deportare D. 17 coeperant C₁. 18 dum HD. 19 *ins.* spatiosi A₂E₂G. 20 deventum est C₂HNE₁nD. deductus est A. deductus esset E₂G. 21 septen... C₁VBAHnD. septemtrionali E₂G. 22 *om.* AE₂G. 23 fusscis V. 24 atrorum C₁C₂VBANE₁nE₂G. 25 turmae A₂E₂ G. 26 *om.* E₂G. 27 *om.* D. 28 cerneret A. cernebat A₂E₂G. *ab.* mutavit personam patientis in personam legentis

once again they took whips like iron and began to beat him. When after innumerable kinds of torments, after beatings with iron whips, they saw him persist unmoved and showing a robust confidence in the enterprise he had undertaken, they began to drag him through the cloudy stretches of the freezing skies to the sound of the horrid beating of their wings. Now when he had reached the lofty summit of the sky, then, horrible to relate, lo! the region of the northern heavens seemed to grow dark with gloomy mists and black clouds. For there could be seen coming thence to meet them, innumerable squadrons of foul spirits. Thus with all their forces joined in one, they turned their way with immense uproar into the thin air, and carried the afore-named servant of Christ, Guthlac, to the accursed jaws of hell. When he indeed beheld the smoking caverns of the glowing infernal region, he forgot all the torments which he had patiently endured before at the hands of wicked spirits, as though he himself had not been the sufferer. For not only could one see there the fiery abyss swelling with surging flames, but even the sulphurous eddies of flame mixed with icy hail seemed almost to touch the stars with drops of spray; and evil spirits running about amid the black caverns and gloomy abysses tortured the souls of the wicked, victims of a wretched fate, with various kinds of torments. So when Guthlac, the man of God, was horrified at the innumerable varieties of torture, the crowds of attendant demons, as if with one voice, cried out and said: 'Lo, the power has been granted to us to thrust you into

C_2N.   29 cunctis C_1VB.   30 levas VBA. *om.* A_2E_2G.   31 *ins.* tenues A_2E_2G.   32 *om.* C_1AE_2G.   33 *ins.* cum videbat C_1VB. 34 catervas C_1C_2VBn.   35 *om.* C_1VB.   36 passus fuisset A_2E_2G. 37 oblivisceretur E_1.   38 ignivomas $C_1C_2VBAHNE_1nE_2$.   39 cerneret C_1VBA. cernebat A_2E_2G. *ab.* si praesens adesses N.   40 sulphureos C_1AHDE_2G. *in marg.* Tria sunt flumina inferni, Acheros quod sine gaudio interpretatur ex quo nascitur secundum Stix, id est tristitia, rursus ex ista oritur Cocitus quod luctus interpretatur C_2. [*This marginal gloss is only partly legible in C_2 owing to binders' cuts. But it occurs also in N at the point noted below where it is complete.*]   41 mixtos C_1AHDE_2G.   42 i.e. voragines aquae C_2N. fortices E_1.   43 globis HD.   44 turbinibus A_2E_2G. 45 sydera n.   46 tangere A_2E_2G.   47 autem G.   48 forag... C_1. 49 *ab.* yr A.   50 miserabile $C_1C_2NE_1n$.   51 cruciatum C_1.   52 *ch. title* Quomodo sanctus Bartholomeus illic sibi apparuit, reportare illum iussit D.   53-54 clam. turm. C_1VBAE_2G.

potestas data est [1]te trudere[2] in has poenas, et illic inter[3] atrocissimarum gehennarum tormenta[4] variis cruciatibus nobis te torquere commissum est[5]. En ignis, quem accendisti in delictis tuis, te consumere paratus est; en tibi patulis[6] hiatibus[7] igniflua Herebi[8] hostia[9] patescunt[10]; nunc Stigiae fibrae te vorare malunt[11], tibi quoque[12] aestivi[13] Acherontis[14] voragines horrendis faucibus hiscunt[15].' Illis haec et alia [16]plurima his[17] similia [18]dicentibus, vir Dei minas eorum despiciens[19], inmotis sensibus, stabili animo, sobria mente, respondens aiebat: 'Vae vobis[20], filii tenebrarum, semen Cain, *favilla*[21] *cineris*[22]. Si vestrae potentiae sit[23] istis me tradere[24] poenis, en praesto sum; ut quid falsivomis[25] pectoribus[26] [26a]vanas minas[27] depromitis[28]?'

Job 30. 19

XXXII. Illis vero[29] veluti ad trudendum illum in praesentium tormentorum gehennas[30] sese praecingentibus[31], ecce sanctus Bartholomaeus cum inmenso caelestis lucis splendore medias furvae[32] noctis infuso lumine interrumpens[33] tenebras, sese ab aethereis sedibus radiantis[34] Olimpi[35] coram illis aureo fulgore amictus obtulit[36]. Maligni ergo[37] spiritus non sustinentes caelestis splendoris fulgorem, frendere, fremere, [38]fugere[39], [39a]tremere[40], timere[41] coeperunt. Sanctus vero Guthlac adventum fidelissimi[42] auxiliatoris[43] sui[44] persentiens, spiritali[45] laetitia repletus, gavisus est[46].

XXXIII. Tunc deinde sanctus Bartholomaeus[47] catervis satellitum iubet, ut illum in locum suum cum magna quietudine, sine ulla offensionis molestia, reducerent. Nec mora[48], praeceptis apostolicis obtemperantes dicto citius

1-2 trud. te G.　　　3 in HD.　　　4 tormento HD.　　　5 i.e. licitum C₂N.　　concessum est A₂E₂G.　　　6 *ab.* manifestis N. 7 chiat... C₁.　　8 Erebi C₁VB.　　9 ostia C₂NE₁n.　　10 patebunt C₁ VB.　　11 mallunt VBA.　　habent A₂E₂G.　　12 -que A₂E₂G.　　13 i.e. estuantis vel ardentis D.　　14 *marginal gloss in* N *as in* C₂ (*see note* 40, *p.* 105).　　15 *ins.* sed HD.　　16-17 *om.* E₂.　　18-19 *ins. in marg.* E₁.　　20 *ins.* sit A₂E₂G.　　21 faville C₂NE₁n.　　22 cyneris N.　　23 est A₂E₂G.　　24 *alt. to* trudere H.　　25 falso A₂E₂G.　　26 de pectore A₂E₂G.

these pains; and we have been commissioned to torture you there with manifold punishments in the torment of the most cruel depths of hell. Behold! the fire which you have kindled by your lusts has been prepared to consume you. Behold! the fiery entrances of Erebus gape for you with yawning mouths. Behold! the bowels of Styx long to devour you and the hot gulfs of Acheron gape with dreadful jaws.' But as they said these and many other things like them, the man of God despised their threats, and with unshaken nerves, with steadfast heart and sober mind he answered them: 'Woe unto you, you sons of darkness, seed of Cain, you are but dust and ashes. If it is in your power to deliver me into these tortures, lo! I am ready; so why utter these empty threats from your lying throats?'

XXXII. Indeed just as they were preparing themselves as if to thrust him into hell and instant tortures, lo! St Bartholomew in boundless splendour of heavenly light broke into the midst of the swarthy darkness of night with outpoured radiance, and presented himself before them girt with golden brilliance from the heavenly dwellings of glorious Olympus. Now the evil spirits could not bear the glory of the heavenly splendour, but began to gnash their teeth, to howl and flee, to fear and tremble. Then truly St Guthlac, perceiving the arrival of his most faithful helper, rejoiced, being filled with spiritual bliss.

XXXIII. Then St Bartholomew commands the escorting bands to take Guthlac back to his own dwelling with the utmost quiet, none molesting or harming him. Straightway they obey the apostolic behests, and quicker than words they

26a–27 min. van. E₂.   28 no ch. title in C₁.   no break in C₂VBD.
29 ergo E₂.   30 gehennam A₂E₂G.   31 ab. circumvallantibus N.
32 ab. deor A.   33 inrump... VB.   i.e. dividens N.   34 i.e. re-
splendentis D.   35 Olimphi VBE₁D.   36 opt... VBHE₂.   ins.
tum A₂E₂G.   37 om. AE₂G.   38 om. D.   38–40 trem. fug. HD.
39 add. -que E₂.   39a–41 om. A₂E₂G.   42 ins. amici C₁VB.
43 add. -que C₁VB. sui amici AE₂G.   44 om. AE₂G.   45 spirituali n.
46 no ch. title in C₁.   no break in C₂VBNE₁n.   ch. title in D: Quomodo cum
immensa quietudine ad sedes suas ab immundis spiritibus reportabatur D.
47 Bath... C₁.   48 s. erat C₂N.

iussa[1] facessunt[2]. Nam illum revehentes cum nimia[3]

Virg. *Aen.*
I, 301

suavitate, velut quietissimo[4] *alarum remigio,* ita ut nec in curru[5] nec in navi modestius duci potuisset, subvolabant. Cum[6] vero ad medii aeris spatia devenissent[7], sonus psallentium convenienter audiebatur[8] dicens[9]:

Ps. 83. 8

Ibunt sancti *de virtute in virtutem* [10]et reliqua[11]. Inminente

Virg. *Aen.*
XI, 210

ergo aurora, cum sol nocturnas *caelo demoverat*[12] *umbras,* praefatus Christi[13] athleta[14], adepto de hostibus triumpho[15], in eodem statu, a quo prius translatus est, grates[16] Christo[17] persolvens[18], constitit[19]. Dein[20] cum solito more[21] matutinas[22] laudes Domino Iesu inpenderet, paulisper lumina devertens[23], a[24] sinistra stantes duos satellites lugentes[25], sibi prae ceteris aliis notos, conspicit[26]; quos cum interrogasset quid plorassent, responderunt: 'Vires nostras ubique per te fractas lugemus, et inertiam nostram adversus valetudinem[27] tuam ploramus[28]; non enim [29]te tangere[30] aut[31] propinquare[32] audemus.' Haec dicentes, vel*ut fum*us

Ps. 67. 2

a facie eius evanuerunt.

XXXIV. [33]*Quomodo fantasticas*[34] *turbas satellitum cantato primo versu sexagesimi septimi psalmi fugavit*[35]

Contigit itaque in diebus Coenredi [36]Merciorum regis[37], cum Brittones[38], infesti hostes Saxonici generis, bellis, [39]praedis, publicisque[40] vastationibus[41] Anglorum gentem deturbarent, quadam nocte, gallicinali[42] tempore, quo[43] more solito vir beatae memoriae Guthlac orationum vigiliis incumberet, extimplo[44], cum velut imaginato[45]

---

1 *ab.* precepta N.   2 perficiunt A₂E₂G.   i.e. perfecerunt N.
3 *in marg.* spiþ A.   4 quietissima E₁.   5 cursu VB.   6 dum HD.   7 devenirent C₂NE₁n.   8 s. dicens N.   9 dicentium VB. *om.* C₂ANE₁nE₂G.   10–11 *om.* C₁VBnD.   v.d.d.i. A₂. videbitur Deus Deorum in Syon E₂G.   12 *ab.* sequestraverat D. depelleret E₂G.   13 *om.* NE₁.   14 analeta VB. anthleta A. adletha D. s. Christi N.   15 tropheo C₁VB.   16 gentes E₁. 17 *om.* E₂.   18 *ins.* Christo E₂.   19 constetit C₁A. inventus est A₂E₂G.   20 deinde C₁VBD. diem N.   21 timore E₂. 22 matutinales AE₂G.   23 div... AnE₂G.   24 *ins.* manu A₂E₂G.   25 -que A₂E₂G.   26 conspexit G.   27 vali...

fulfil his commands. For they carried him back with the utmost gentleness and bore him up most quietly upon the oarage of their wings, so that he could not possibly have been conveyed more steadily in a chariot or a ship. And indeed when they had reached the spaces of mid-air the sound of voices was heard singing in unison and saying: 'The saints shall go from strength to strength', etc. So when dawn was at hand and the sun drove the shades of night from the sky, the same athlete of Christ, having won the victory over his enemies, stood giving thanks to Christ in the very spot from which he had been carried off. Afterwards when according to his custom he was occupied in his morning praises to the Lord Jesus, he turned his eyes for a moment and saw at his left hand two of the attendant spirits, whom he had noticed more than any of the others, standing and weeping: when he asked them why they wept they answered: 'We mourn for our strength which has been everywhere broken by you, and we bewail our lack of power against your strength; for we dare not touch you nor even approach you.' Having said these words they vanished like smoke from his presence.

XXXIV. *How by singing the first verse of the 67th psalm he put to flight the phantasmal bands of the devil's train*

Now it happened in the days of Coenred King of the Mercians, while the Britons the implacable enemies of the Saxon race, were troubling the English with their attacks, their pillaging, and their devastations of the people, on a certain night about the time of cockcrow, when Guthlac of blessed memory was as usual engaged in vigils and prayers, that he was suddenly

$C_1C_2Hn.$ soli... VB.   28 ploremus C_1.   29–30 tang. te G. 31 *ins.* tibi DA_2E_2G.   32 *ins.* ulterius A_2E_2G.   proquinquare C_1B.   s. tibi C_2N.   33–35 Quomodo fantasticas demonum turmas qui se Brittonicam (Brittan... D) exercitum simulavere orationibus fugavit C_2NE_1D.   34 fantasicas VB.   36 Kenredi C_2nE_2G.   Coinredi H.   Conredi D.   Kœnredi A_2.   36–37 reg. Merc. H.   37 *ins.* ut C_2VB.   38 Brytones C_2N. Brytotes E_1.   Britones nG.   39–40 pub. praed. E_1.   40 pupl... A. 41 vastantibus E_1.   42 gallicinii AE_2G.   43 cum DA_2E_2G. 44 extemplo n.   45 ymag... E_2G.

sopore opprimeretur, visum est sibi tumultuantis turbae[1] audisse clamores. Tunc dicto citius[2] levi[3] somno[4] expergefactus, extra cellulam, qua[5] sedebat, [6]egressus est[7], et *arrectis*[8] *auribus adstans*[9], verba loquentis vulgi Brittannicaque[10] agmina tectis[11] succedere agnoscit[12]; nam ille[13] aliorum temporum praeteritis voluminibus[14] inter illos[15] exulabat, quoadusque eorum strimulentas[16] loquelas [17]intelligere[18] valuit[19]. Nec mora; [20]per palustria[21] tectis subvenire certantes[22], eodem paene momento omnes *domus*[23] suas *flamma superante ardere*[24] conspicit; illum quoque[25] intercipientes[26] acutis hastarum[27] spiculis[28] in auras levare[29] coeperunt. Tum[30] vero vir Dei tandem hostis pellacis[31] millenis artibus millenas[32] formas persentiens, velut prophetico ore sexagesimi[33] septimi psalmi [34]primum versum[35] psallebat: *Exsurgat*[36] *Deus*, [37]et reliqua[38]; quo audito, dicto *velocius*[39] eodem [40]momento omnes daemoniorum[41] turmae[42] vel*ut fumus a facie eius* evanuerunt.

Virg. *Aen.*
II, 303

Virg. *Aen.*
II, 311

Ps. 67. 2
Vit. Ant.
c. 12

XXXV. *Quomodo*[43] *prophetico spiritu funestas*[44] *cogitationes* [45]*alicuius venientis*[46] *clerici*[47] *interimere se volentis noscebat*[48]

Post non multum temporis, cum vir vitae venerabilis Guthlac contra insidias lubrici hostis saepe certando triumphabat[49], ecce zabulus vires suas fractas conperiens, novas versutias[50] adversus[51] eum sub[52] toxico pectore versari[53] coepit. Erat enim quidam clericus nomine Beccel[54], qui se ipsum famulum fieri[55] tanti viri sponte

1 *ins.* se A₂E₂G.   2 *ins.* vir Dei C₁.   3 V *breaks off here.*
4 sompno G.   5 quam E₁.   6–7 egressit C₁C₂ANE₁n. *alt.*
in later hand to egressus est C₁n. egressus G.   8 erectus AE₂G.
9 astans nDE₂G.   10 Bret... C₁. Britton... AHDE₂. Brita...
B. Briton... G.   11 s. suis N.   12 cogn... C₂ANE₁nE₂G.
13 illa gens A₂E₂G.   14 excursibus A₂E₂G.   15 Anglos
A₂E₂G.   16 barbaras A₂E₂G. strimulantes C₂Nn. stimulantes E₁.
17–19 intellegeret C₁B.   18 intellegere C₂NE₁.   20 s. erat
C₂N.   20–22 *om.* C₁.   21 s. loca C₂N.   22 certans A₂E₂G.
23 domos C₁AE₂G.   24 *om.* A. *ins. ab.* A₂.   25 *om.* DA₂E₂G.

overcome by a dream-filled sleep, and it seemed to him that he heard the shouts of a tumultuous crowd. Then, quicker than words, he was aroused from his light sleep and went out of the cell in which he was sitting; standing, with ears alert, he recognized the words that the crowd were saying, and realized that British hosts were approaching his dwelling: for in years gone by he had been an exile among them, so that he was able to understand their sibilant speech. Straightway they strove to approach his dwelling through the marshes, and at almost the same moment he saw all his buildings burning, the flames mounting upwards: indeed they caught him too and began to lift him into the air on the sharp points of their spears. Then at length the man of God, perceiving the thousand-fold forms of this insidious foe and his thousand-fold tricks, sang the first verse of the sixty-seventh psalm as if prophetically, 'Let God arise', etc.: when they had heard this, at the same moment, quicker than words, all the hosts of demons vanished like smoke from his presence.

XXXV. *How by the spirit of prophecy he perceived the deadly intentions of a certain cleric, who had come wishing to slay him*

A short time afterwards when Guthlac, the man of venerable life, was frequently triumphing in the fight against the snares of the deceitful foe, lo ! the devil, who realized that his own strength was broken, began in his venomous heart to try new cunning against the saint. Now there was a certain cleric named Beccel who of his own accord offered himself to become

---

ins. vero C_1AHE_2G.   26 i.e. circumvallantes N.   intercientes HD.
27 astarum C_1B.   28 *ab.* or A.   29 *ab.* he A.   30 cum H.
31 invidi A_2E_2G.   32 *ab.* þus A.   33 sexagess... B.   34–35 vers. prim. H.   36 exurgat C_2BnE_2G.   37–38 *om.* A.   et dissipentur inimici eius C_1BnG.   7d.i.e.7.f.^1_q.o.e.a.f.e. A_2.   *ins.* et fugiant qui oderint eum a facie eius E_2G.   39 citius C_1BE_2.   40–41 momentorum E_1.
42 turbae $C_2ANE_1nE_2G$.   43 qualiter C_2NE_1D.   44 *om.* C_2NE_1D.
45–46 malignas C_2NE_1D.   47–48 cuiusdam intelligebat C_2NE_1D.
49 triumpharet A_2E_2G.   50 i.e. calliditates N.   51 *ab.* locu N.
52 *om.* A_2E_2G.   53 versare DA_2E_2G.   54 Becel H. Beccelmus D.
55 fore A_2E_2G.

obtulit[1] ac sub disciplinis ipsius caste Deo vivere proposuit. Cuius praecordia malignus spiritus ingressus, pestiferis vanae gloriae fastibus[2] illum inflare[3] coepit ac deinde, postquam tumidis[4] inanis fasti[5] flatibus [6]illum seduxit[7], admonere [8]ipsum quoque[9] exorsus est, ut dominum suum, sub cuius disciplinis Deo vivere initiavit, arrepta letali machera[10] necaret[11], hoc ipsius[12] animo[13] proponens, ut[14], et[15], si ipsum interimere[16] potuisset, locum ipsius postea, cum maxima regum principumque venerantia[17], habiturus[18] foret[19]. Quadam ergo die, cum praefatus clericus virum Dei Guthlacum, ut adsolebat, post bis denos[20] dierum cursus tonderare[21] devenisset, isdem, ingenti[22] dementia[23] vexatus, [24]viri Dei inmenso desiderio sanguinem sitiens[25], indubius illum occidere successit[26]. Tunc sanctus[27] Dei Guthlac, cui Dominus adsidue[28] futurorum praescientiam manifestabat, conperto novi[29] sceleris piaculo, illum sciscitari[30] coepit dicens; 'O mi Beccel[31], ut quid hebido sub pectore antiquum hostem occultas? Quare amari veneni mortiferas limphas[32] non vomis[33]? Scio enim te a maligno spiritu deceptum; quapropter flagitiosas[34] meditationes quas tibi generis humani hostilis criminator inseruit, ab illis convertendo, confitere.' Tum ille, cum se a maligno spiritu[35] seductum intellexisset[36], prosternens se ad pedes tanti viri Guthlaci, delictum suum lacrimabili voce confessus, supplex veniam orabat[37]. Itaque vir beatae memoriae Guthlac non solum illius culpae veniam indulsit[38], sed et[39] in futuris tribulationibus adiutorem illius se venturum[40] fore promisit.

1 opt... HE₂. 2 fascibus A₂E₂G. 3 inflammare C₁C₂BAE₂G. 4 tumidus H. 5 gloriae C₁B. fastus HD. i.e. iactantia N. 6 fascibus C₁. fastibus B. 6–7 sed. ill. C₁BA. 8–9 quoq. ips. C₁B. 10 machina C₁C₂ANE₁nE₂G. macera D. 11 necare H. necharet E₂. ins. exorsus C₁. ins. exorsus est A. 12 ipsum AE₂G. 13 ins. illius A₂E₂G. 14 quod AE₂G. 15 om. DA₂E₂G. 16 interrim... E₂. 17 veneratione A₂E₂G. 18 habiturum C₁B. om. n. 19 fore

the servant of so great a man, and proposed to live piously in God's service under his teaching. But an evil spirit entered his heart and began to puff him up with pestiferous arrogance and vainglory; then after his swollen and empty pride had seduced him with its vanity, he also began to urge him to take a death-dealing sword and slay the master under whose teaching he had begun to live in the service of God. The devil suggested to him that if he could slay him, he would afterwards live in Guthlac's dwelling and also enjoy the great veneration of kings and princes. So on a certain day when this same cleric had come to tonsure Guthlac the man of God, as he was accustomed to do every twenty days, he was seized with a violent madness, and thirsting with an overwhelming lust for the blood of the man of God, without hesitation he approached to slay him. Then Guthlac, the holy man of God, to whom the Lord continually gave foreknowledge of the future, realizing this new crime and guilt, began to question him, saying: 'O, my Beccel, why do you harbour the ancient foe in your foolish breast? Why do you not spew out the deadly draught of bitter poison? For I know that you have been deceived by an evil spirit; wherefore confess the criminal thoughts which the hostile accuser of the human race has instilled into your mind, by turning from them.' Then when Beccel realized that he had been seduced by an evil spirit, he threw himself at the feet of that great man Guthlac and, tearfully confessing his crime, he humbly prayed for pardon. Guthlac the man of blessed memory not only granted him pardon for his fault but also promised him that in future tribulations he would come to Beccel's aid.

sciret C₁B.   20 binos H.   21 tondere A₂E₂G.   22 i.e. magna
C₂N.   23 *ab.* witleas A.   24 *ins.* et A₂E₂G.   25 sentiens N.
26 cogitavit AE₂G.   27 *ins.* vir C₁B.   28 *ins.* interdum A₂E₂G.
29 novo E₂G.   30 sciscitare A.   31 Beccelme D.   32 lymph... B.
cogitationes A₂E₂G.   33 evom... A₂E₂G.   34 *ab.* fac A₂.   35 *om.*
E₂.   36 intellexit N.   37 rogabat E₂.   38 indulsisse fertur
AE₂G.   39 *om.* C₂BAHNE₁n. *ins. ab.* A₂.   40 futurum AE₂G.

XXXVI. *Quomodo nocte quadam maligni*[1] *spiritus in diversarum bestiarum formis illum terrebant*[2]

Verum[3] quia superius, quantum isdem [4]vir[5] venerabilis[6] Guthlac adversus veras [7]apertasque diabolicas[8] insidias valuit, explicavimus[9], nunc [10]quoque, quid[11] adversus simulaticias malignorum spirituum fraudes[12] praevaluit, exponemus[13]. Iisdem[14] fere temporibus, cum vir saepe memoratus quadam nocte in assiduis orationibus adsueto more perstaret, ingenti *sonitu* totam insulam qua sederet[15] tremere circum[16] putabat[17]; deinde, parvi temporis [18]intervallo[19] succedente[20], ecce subito velut concurrentium armentorum crepitum cum magno terrae tremore[21] domui succedere exaudiebat[22]. Nec mora[23], domum[24] ab[25] undique inrumpentes[26] variorum monstrorum diversas figuras introire prospicit[27]. Nam *leo* rugiens dentibus sanguineis morsus rabidos[28] inminebat[29]; *taurus* vero *mugit*ans[30], unguibus terram defodiens, [31]*cornu* cruentum[32] solo defigebat[33]; *urs*us denique[34] infrendens, validis ictibus brachia commutans[35], verbera promittebat; coluber quoque[36], *squamea coll*a porrigens, indicia atri veneni monstrabat, et ut brevi sermone[37] concludam, aper grunnitum, lupus ululatum, equus hinnitum, cervus axatum[38], serpens sibilum, bos balatum[39], corvus crocitum[40] ad turbandum veri Dei verum militem *horris*onis *voc*ibus stridebant[41]. Sanctus itaque Christi famulus, armato corde signo salutari, haec omnia fantasmatum[42] genera despiciens[43], his vocibus usus aiebat: 'O miserrime[44] Satana[45], manifestae sunt vires tuae; nonne[46] nunc miserarum[47]

Vit. Ant. c. 8

Virg. Aen. II, 218

---

1 maligant N.   2 *ins.* finis C₂.   3 sed B.   4–6 ven. vir. C₂NE₁n.   5 *om.* AHDE₂G.   7 feras AHDE₂G.   7–8 diaboli apertas B.   diaboli H.   diabolique apertas C₁AE₂.   diabolicasque G. diaboliticas C₂E₁.   9 i.e. narravimus C₂N.   10–11 quomodo B. 12 *ab.* qualiter C₁.   13 i.e. tractavimus C₂.   i.e. tractabimus N. 14 hisdem C₁BAHE₂G.   isdem C₂NE₁n.   15 sedebat D. 16 *om.* A₂E₂G.   17 persensit A₂E₂G.   18–20 succ. int. HD. 19 i.e. spatio C₁.   20 succedenti G.   21 motu AE₂G. 22 audiebat DA₂E₂G.   23 s. erat C₂N.   24 *om.* C₁BAE₂G. 25 *om.* A₂E₂G.   26 *ins.* domum B.   inter... G.   27 consp...

XXXVI. *How one night the evil spirit terrified him in the form of various beasts*

Since we have explained above how strong this same venerable Guthlac was against those snares of the devil which were real and open, we will now also show how he prevailed against the feigned deceits of the evil spirits. About this time, when the man we have often mentioned was spending a certain night in assiduous prayer, as was his custom, he thought that the whole island in which he was dwelling trembled all around with a tremendous clamour. Then after a short interval, lo ! suddenly he heard the noise as of a herd of beasts rushing together and approaching his dwelling with a mighty shaking of the earth. Straightway he saw manifold shapes of various monsters bursting into his house from all sides. Thus a roaring lion fiercely threatened to tear him with its bloody teeth: then a bellowing bull dug up the earth with its hoofs and drove its gory horn into the ground; or a bear, gnashing its teeth and striking violently with either paw alternately, threatened him with blows: a serpent, too, rearing its scaly neck, disclosed the threat of its black poison: to conclude briefly—the grunting of the boar, the howling of the wolf, the whinnying of the horse, the belling of the stag, the hissing of the serpent, the lowing of the ox, the croaking of the raven, made harsh and horrible noises to trouble the true soldier of the true God. And so the holy servant of Christ, arming his breast with the sign of salvation and despising all phantoms of this sort, uttered these words: 'O most wretched Satan, your strength is made manifest; for now do you not imitate the whinnying, the

C_1AE_2G. conspexit B.   28 rabido ore C_1B.   29 minitabat A_2E_2G.
i.e. ostendit N.   30 *ab.* hlopende A.   31–32 cru. corn. E_2.
33 figebat C_1AE_2G.   34 *om.* A_2E_2G.   35 commot... $C_1C_2BNE_1n$.
alt. from commot... A.   commovens E_2G.   36 *om.* A_2E_2G.   37 *ins.*
cuncta A_2E_2G.   38 anx... C_2n.   39 boatum C_1.   *ab.* hlo A.
40 croccitum C_1.   crucitum N.   *ins.* emittentes A_2E_2G.   41 strinebant
C_2NE_1n. s. sic N.   *ab.* scriccettan C_2.   perstrepebant A_2E_2G.   42 phan...
A.   43 disp... C_1.   44 miserrima C_1.   45 Satanan C_1.   Satan
C_2Nn.   Sathana A_2E_2G.   46 nam C_1B.   quippe A_2E_2G.   47 miseriarum C_1BH.

bestiarum hinnitus, grunnitus crocitusque imitaris, qui
ante[1] aeterno Deo te[2] simulare[3] temptasti? idcirco
impero tibi in nomine Iesu Christi, qui te[4] de caelo
damnavit[5], ut ab hoc tumultu desistas.' Nec mora[6],

Virg. *Aen.*
IV, 705 and
XII, 592

dicto citius universum[7] fantasma[8] *vacuas in auras recessit*[9].

XXXVII. *Qualiter corvus cartulam* [10]*inter undas*[11] *stagni dimisit*[12]; *nec illam*[13] *aquae laedere valuerunt*

Contigit quoque, sub cuiusdam temporis cursibus[14], cum
alius[15] Dei famulus ad colloquium venerabilis[16] viri Dei
Guthlaci[17] pervenisset, aliquot diebus in insula praefata
hospitari[18] coepit[19]. Quadam[20] autem die, membranas[21]
quasdam[22] scribens, cum ad finem scripturam suam[23]
deflexisset, extra domum recedens, quando[24] in quodam
oratorio orationibus incumberet[25], ecce quidam corvus,
accola eiusdem insulae[26], intrans domum praedicti hos-
pitis[27], ut cartulam[28] illic prospexit[29], rapido[30] forcipe[31]
arripuit; praefatus vero hospes[32], cum visus suos[33] forte
foris[34] divertisset[35], volantem alitem[36] cartulam[37] in [38]ore
suo[39] portantem prospicit[40], confestimque cum cartulam[41]
suam defuisse[42] conperit, ab alite corvo raptam fuisse
cognoscit. Forte[43] denique[44] eadem hora sanctus Guthlac
extra oratorium egrediebatur[45]; qui cum praefatum fratrem subita maestitia correptum prospiceret, consolari
illum coepit, pollicens ei cartulam suam cum Dei omni-

Hier. *Vita
Pauli*,
c. 16 (cf.
Matt.
10. 29)

potentis auxilio[46] sibi recuperari[47] posse[48], *sine cuius
potestate nec*[49] *folium arboris defluit nec unus passerum*
[50]*ad terram cadit*[51]. Inter[52] haec alitem[53] longe in austrum

1 *om.* n. coram G.   2 *om.* C_1.   3 assimilari C_2NE_1n.
assimilare B.   4 *ab.* C_1.   5 dampn... AHE_1DE_2G.   6 s. erat
C_2N.   7 universa HD.   8 phant... A. fantasmata D.   9 reces-
serunt HD.   10–11 *om.* C_1. in medio BD.   12 dimiserit D.
13 *ins.* orante Guhtlaco C_2.   *ins.* orante Guthlaco NE_1.   *ins.* orante
sancto Guthlaco D.   14 articulo A_2E_2G.   15 *ins.* quidam
A_2E_2G.   16 *om.* E_2.   17 *ins.* Wilfrið A. *ins.* nomine Wilfrithus
A_2E_2G.   18 hospitare C_1A. hospitatus est A_2E_2G.   19 *om.*
A_2E_2G.   20 qua H.   21 membranos $C_1C_2ANE_1$n. men-
brana BH. membranam D.   22 quosdam $C_1C_2ANE_1$n. quaedam

grunting and the croaking of miserable beasts, you who once attempted to liken yourself to the eternal God? Therefore I command you in the name of Jesus Christ who banished you from heaven, to desist from this tumult.' Forthwith, quicker than words, the whole apparition vanished into the empty air.

XXXVII. *How a jackdaw dropped a document into the midst of the pool and how the waters could not harm it*

It happened also in course of time that a certain servant of God came to talk with Guthlac the venerable man of God, and was lodged for some days in this same island. One day, as he was writing on some leaves of parchment, having brought his writing to an end, he left the house in order to pray in a certain oratory: whereupon a jackdaw that dwelt near by on the same island entered the house of this guest and, when it saw the document there, quickly seized it in its beak; the said guest, looking by chance out of doors, saw a bird flying off and carrying a document in its beak; immediately when he perceived that his own document was missing, he knew that it had been carried off by the jackdaw. It happened by chance that at the same time St Guthlac was leaving the oratory: he saw the said brother stricken with sudden sadness and began to console him, promising him that his document could be recovered with the help of Almighty God, without whose power not a leaf of a tree is blown down and no single sparrow falls to the ground. Meanwhile they saw the bird flying far to

BH. quandam D.   23 illam A_2E_2G.   24 *om.* AE_2G.   25 incumbebat cum A_2E_2G.   26 *om.* G.   27 *om.* G.   28 chartulam A. 29 s. eam C_2.   30 vel rabido C_2N.   *ins.* eam B.   31 i.e. bile C_2. ore A_2E_2G.   32 hospis C_1.   33 *om.* C_1B.   34 illuc A_2G. velut E_2.   foras D.   35 dev... $C_1C_2HNE_1nD$.   36 *ab.* et C_1. 37 *ins.* -que A_2E_2G.   38–39 suo ore A_2.   suo in ore E_2G.   40 prospexit E_2G.   41 chart... A.   42 s. eum N.   43 *om.* C_2NE_1n. 44 *om.* A_2E_2G.   45 s. forte N.   46 auxilios B.   auxiliis $C_1C_2NE_1n$. 47 recuperare $C_1C_2NE_1n$.   recuperandam E_2G.   48 *om.* E_2G. 49 *ab.* pro non N.   50–51 cadet ad terram C_1.   cadit ad terram B. 52 in H.   53 ales HD.

volantem[1] cernebant[2], cursumque[3] suum inter stagnosa[4]
paludis ligustra[5] deflectens, sese subito ab eorum obtutibus[6] velut evanescens abdidit[7]. Sanctus vero Guthlac
firmam fidem[8] firmo[9] pectore gestans, fratri praefato
praecepit, ut naviculam [10]in contiguo portu[11] positam
conscendisset[12], et ut[13] inter densas[14] harundinum con-
pagines[15], quo via sibi[16] monstraret[17], incederet[18]. Ille
autem, praeceptis sancti viri obtemperans[19], quo se trames[20]
ducebat, perrexit. Dein[21], cum ad aliquod stagnum[22]
haud[23] procul a praefata insula situm devenisset, conspicit
non longe in media planitie stagni[24] unam harundinem
curvato cacumine stantem, quae stagni[25] tremulis quassa-
batur[26] undique limphis; in cuius[27] fastigio aequiperatas[28],
scedulas[29] aequali lance pendentes[30], velut[31] ab humana
manu positas[32], cerneres[33]. Mirabile dictu! tangi, [34]non
tactae[35], contiguis[36] videbantur[37] ab undis. At ille frater
arripiens[38] de harundine[39] cartam[40], cum magna admira-
tione[41] grates Deo persolvens, venerantiam[42] validae fidei
de eo quod contigit venerabili viro Dei[43] Guthlaco con-
ferens, unde[44] egressus[45] domum reversus est; praefatus
vero Christi famulus Guthlac non sui meriti, quod contigit,
sed divinae[46] miserationis fuisse firmabat[47].

XXXVIII. *Quomodo nequitiam corvorum pertulit et qualiter
ad vocem illius aves[48] heremi et pisces paludis veniebant[49]*

Erant[50] igitur[51] in supradicta insula duo alites corvi,
[52]quorum[53] infesta[54] nequitia fuit, ita[55] ut[56], quicquid fran-

1 avolans HD.   2 cernentes AE₂G. cernitur HD. *ins.* qui
C₂NE₁n.   3 *om.* -que C₂BAHNE₁nE₂G.   4 *ab.* fennegan A.
5 lyg... C₁C₂BNE₁n. ligistra A. lygustria D. ligustria H. *i.e.*
flores N. *ab.* hopu A. *om.* A₂E₂G.   6 op... E₂. *i.e.* oculis A.
7 *i.e.* abscondit A.   8 *om.* C₁.   9 *ins.* in BHD.   10–11 cont. in
port. C₁B.   12 conscenderet AE₂G.   13 *om.* A₂E₂G.   14 *i.e.*
multiplices A.   15 conpages C₂BANE₁. compages nE₂G.
16 *om.* C₂NE₁n.   17 monstraretur B. s. sibi N.   18 *i.e.*
pergeret N.   19 opt... E₂.   20 tramis C₂NE₁n. *i.e.* callis N.
21 qui D.   22 stangnum B.   23 haut C₂ANDG.   24 stangni B.
25 stagna B. stagnis E₂.   26 *i.e.* movebatur N.   27 s. con-

the south; turning in amidst the growth in the marshy pools it was suddenly hidden from their gaze as though it had vanished away. St Guthlac, showing a firm faith and a firm heart, ordered the aforesaid brother to get into a boat which was lying by the neighbouring landing-place and to make his way amid the dense clumps of reeds by the path which would reveal itself to him. So he obeyed the commands of the saint and went whither the path led. Then when he had reached a certain pool not far from the same island he saw near by, in the middle of the pool, a reed standing with its top bent down and shaken on every side by the moving waters of the pond; on the very top could be seen the very leaves of parchment hanging exactly balanced as though they had been placed there by a human hand, and, marvellous to relate, they were apparently being touched by the waves around them and yet were intact. And the brother, snatching the document from the reed, gave thanks to God in much amazement, at the same time showing great respect for the steadfast faith of the venerable man of God Guthlac with regard to what had happened; and so departing thence he returned to his dwelling. This same servant of Christ, Guthlac, declared that what had happened was not due to his own merits but to the divine mercy.

XXXVIII. *How he endured the mischief of the jackdaws and how the birds of the desert and the fish of the marsh came to his call*

Now there were in this same island two jackdaws whose mischievous nature was such that whatever they could break,

spicit C_2N.   28 aequiparatas E_1n.   aequiperatam HD.   i.e. ponderatas N. 29 scedulam HD.   30 pendentem HD.   31 velud A.   32 positam HD.   33 cerneret C_1BA.   cernit E_2G.   add. -que A_2E_2G. 34 tangeri C_1.   tangere AE_2G.   ins. undas A_2E_2G.   ab. æthrinan A. 34-35 incontacta HD.   et intactae E_2.   36 contigua vicinis HD. 37 videbatur HD.   38 arripuit C_1B.   39 arund... B.   40 ins. et A_2E_2G.   41 adoratione B.   ab. vel mi B.   42 gratiam A_2E_2G. 43 om. C_2NE$_1$n.   44 om. A_2E_2G.   45 om. A_2E_2G.   46 divini C_1. 47 confirm... D.   48 aures N.   49 deven... N.   50 alt. from erat C_1.   51 om. A_2E_2G.   52-56 marked for omission in A_2 but not omitted in E_2G.   53 ins. adeo E_2G.   54 i.e. perversa N.   55 om. E_2G.

gere, mergere, diripere, rapere[1], contaminare[2] potuissent,
sine ullius rei[3] reverentia[4] damnantes[5] perderent. Nam
veluti cum familiaribus ausis intrantes domus[6], omnia
quaecumque[7] intus forisque[8] invenissent, velut[9] inprobi
praedones rapiebant. Supramemoratus autem Dei famulus, varias eorum iniurias perferens[10], longanimiter pio
pectore sufferebat, ut[11] non solum in hominibus exemplum
patientiae ipsius ostenderetur, sed etiam in volucribus et
in feris manifesta esset[12]. Erga [13]enim omnia[14] eximiae
caritatis[15] ipsius gratia abundabat[16], in tantum ut incultae
solitudinis volucres [17]et vagabundi coenosae[18] paludis[19]
pisces ad vocem ipsius veluti ad pastorem[20] ocius natantes
volantesque subvenirent[21]; de manu enim illius[22] victum,
prout uniuscuiusque natura indigebat[23], vesci[24] solebant[25].

*Non sol*um vero terrae *aeris*que *animalia* illius iussionibus
obtemperabant[26], immo etiam [27]aqua *aer*que[28] ipsi[29] veri[30]
Dei vero[31] famulo oboediebant. Nam *qui auctori omnium
creaturarum fideliter et*[32] integro spiritu *famulatur, non est
mirandum, si eius imperiis*[33] *ac votis*[34] *omnis creatura deserviat.
At*[35] *plerumque idcirco subiectae nobis creaturae dominium
perdimus*[36], *quia Domino* universorum *creatori*[37] *servire
negligimus*[38], secundum illud: '*Si oboedieritis*[39] *et audieritis
me, bona terrae comedetis',* [40]*et reliqua*[41]: item[42]: '*Si
abundaverit*[43] *fides* vestra *ut granum sinapis'* [44]*et reliqua*[45].

Bede,
V.pr.
c. 21

Isa. 1. 19
Matt.
17. 19

XXXIX. *Qualiter hirundines*[46] *eius*[47] *imperiis*[48] *obtemperabant*[49]

[50]Libet[51] etiam[52] beatissimi Dei famuli Guthlaci quoddam
spiritale[53] miraculum explicare[54]. Contigit enim[55] qua-

---

1 *ins.* vel E₂G.   2 con- *bis* E₁.   3 regi E₁.   4 i.e. verecundia N.   5 dampn... AHE₁DE₂G.   6 domos C₁A₂E₂G.
7 quaecunque n. quocumque G.   8 vel foris G.   9 veluti HD.
10 pertulens C₁A.   11 et N.   12 *ab.* ut N.   13–14 om.
en. A₂E₂G.   15 kar... HD.   16 hab... C₁C₂BANE₁G.
17–19 *om.* A₂E₂G.   18 cenosi C₁C₂BNE₁n.   19 *ins.* et A₂E₂G.
20 pastorum B.   21 deven... C₁BAHDE₂G.   22 ipsius AE₂G.
ins. sepe A₂E₂G.   23 indiebat B.   24 vescere C₁. vesceri A.
25 solebat D.   26 opt... E₂.   27 *om.* C₁AE₂G.   27–28 aer

drop into the water, tear in pieces, steal or defile they would destroy, damaging everything without any respect. For they ventured into houses with, as it were, daring familiarity, and seized everything they could find inside and out, like shameless robbers. This same servant of God bore their manifold injuries patiently and piously, so that the example of his patience was not only shown among men but was clear even among birds and wild beasts. For the grace of his excellent charity abounded to all creatures, so that even the birds of the untamed wilderness and the wandering fishes of the muddy marshes would come flying or swimming swiftly to his call as if to a shepherd; and they were even accustomed to take from his hand such food as the nature of each demanded. Not only indeed did the creatures of the earth and sky obey his commands, but also even the very water and the air obeyed the true servant of the true God. For if a man faithfully and wholeheartedly serves the Maker of all created things, it is no wonder though all creation should minister to his commands and wishes. But for the most part we lose dominion over the creation which was made subject to us, because we ourselves neglect to serve the Lord and Creator of all things, as it is said: 'If ye be willing and obedient ye shall eat the good of the land', and so on; and, 'If ye have faith as a grain of mustard seed', and so on.

XXXIX. *How the swallows obeyed his commands*

It is also pleasant to describe a spiritual miracle of Guthlac the most blessed servant of God. For it happened that on a certain

aqua G.   29 *om.* A₂E₂G.   30 *om.* C₂NE₁n.   31 *om.* E₂G.
32 ex HD.   33 inp... C₁.   34 vocibus C₂NE₁n.   35 ad B.
atque AE₂G. et HD.   36 perdidimus A.   37 ceatori E₁.   38 negleg... C₁C₂HNE₁n.   39 *ins.* mihi D.   40–41 *om.* nDA₂E₂G.
42 *ins.* apostolus C₁B.   43 hab... C₁C₂BANE₁G.   44–45 *om.* A₂E₂G.
44 *ins.* dicentibus monti huic transfer te et transferetur A₂.   *ins.* dicetis huic monti transfer te (transferre G) et transferretur E₂G.   46 hyrun... B.
ins. obtemperebant E₁.   46–48 imp. eius C₂.   47 *om.* NE₁.
49 obtemtarebant C₁. *om.* E₁.   50–54 *om.* A₂E₂G.   51 *ins.* nunc C₁B.
s. me C₂.   52 *ins.* mihi C₁B. s. etiam N.   53 spirituale n.   54 i.e.
narrare C₂N. i.e. manifestare A.   55 *om.* A₂E₂G. autem NE₁.

dam die, cum[1] quidam vir venerabilis, nomine Wilfrith[2],
iamdudum viro Dei Guthlaco spiritalis[3] amicitiae foedere
copulatus[4], ut adsolebat, cum eo loqueretur, forte [5]duae[6]
hirundines[7] subito domum intrantes, [8]velut[9] cum[10]
indicio[11] magnae[12] laetitiae[13] avino[14] forcipe[15] flexuosi[16]
gutturis carmen canentes, veluti ad[16a] adsuetas sedes devenissent[17], sese non haesitantes humeris viri Dei Guthlaci
inposuerunt, ac deinde, cantulis vocibus garrulantes[18],
brachiis genibus[19] pectorique illius insedebant[20]. Wilfrith[21]
vero stupefactus[22], efflagitata sermocinandi licentia, sciscitari[23] ab illo coepit, ut quid incultae solitudinis volucres,
humani successus[24] insueti[25], illam propiandi fiduciam
habuerunt[26]. Sanctus vero Guthlac e contra respondens[27]
aiebat: [28]'Nonne legisti[29], quia, qui Deo[30] puro spiritu
copulatur[31], omnia sibi in Deo coniunguntur[32]? et qui
ab hominibus cognosci denegat, agnosci a feris et frequentari ab angelis quaerit[33]? nam qui frequentatur[34] ab
hominibus, frequentari ab angelis nequit[35].' Tunc ad-
sumens[36] quandam ventinulam posuit[37] in ea[38] festucam;
quod cum alites prospicerent, velut[39] notato signo inbuti,
illic nidificare coeperunt. Cumque veluti unius horae
spatio transacto adgregatis quisquiliis nidum fundarent,
sanctus Guthlac, exsurgens[40], sub testudine tecti quo
sederet[41] ventinulam posuit; volucres vero, quasi adepto[42]
propriae mansionis loculo, illic manere coeperunt; non
enim sine licita[43] volentia viri Dei locum nidificandi sibi
eligere praesumebant, sed in unoquoque anno, petentes
mansionis indicium, ad virum Dei veniebant. *Nulli* ergo
absurdum[44] sit *a volucribus formam* oboedientiae *discere, cum
Salomon dicat*[45]: '*Vade*[46], *piger*[47], imitare *formicam, considera
vias eius et disce sapientiam illius.*'

Bede,
V. pr.
c. 20 (cf.
Prov. 6. 6)

---

1 ut dum E₂G.　　2 Wilfrið A.　Wilfriðus A₂.　Wilfrid H.　Wilfridus
nDE₂G.　　3 spirituales nG.　　4 *ins.* ita D.　　5–7 hir. du. H.
hyr. du. D.　　6 duo C₁.　　7 hyr... E₂.　　8–16a *om.* A₂E₂G.
9 veluð A.　　10 *om.* HD.　　11 *om.* C₁BAHD.　　12 magna
BHD.　　13 letitia BHD.　　14 avido H.　　15 i.e. bile C₂.
16 flexosi C₁C₂BANE₁n.　　17 adv... C₁B.　　18 gargul... C₁.
ab. pri N.　exultantes A₂E₂G.　　19 *ins.* -que HD.　　20 insid...
HE₂.　　21 Wilfrid C₁B.　　22 *ab.* p. A.　　23 sciscitare A.

day, while a venerable man named Wilfrid, who had long been bound by the bonds of spiritual friendship to Guthlac the man of God, was talking with him as was his custom, by chance two swallows suddenly entered his house: showing every sign of great joy, they opened their beaks and sang a song from their supple throats, as though they had arrived at their accustomed abode; without any hesitation they settled on the shoulders of the man of God Guthlac, and then chirping their little songs they settled on his arms, his knees, and his breast. Wilfrid was indeed amazed and, begging permission to speak, he began to ask how birds from the wild solitudes, unused to the approach of human beings, had the confidence to come near him. St Guthlac answered him and said: 'Have you not read how if a man is joined to God in purity of spirit, all things are united to him in God? and he who refuses to be acknowledged by men seeks the recognition of wild beasts and the visitations of angels; for he who is often visited by men cannot be often visited by angels.' Then, taking a certain basket he placed one straw in it; and when the birds perceived this, as though they had been instructed by a familiar sign, they began to build a nest in it. And after about an hour had passed, when they had gathered together odds and ends and established a nest, St Guthlac then placed the basket under the eaves of the dwelling in which he was sitting; and there the birds began to settle, having, as it were, acquired their own place of residence; but they did not presume to choose a nesting-place without the permission of the man of God; and each year they came and sought from the man of God a sign to tell them where they were to dwell. Therefore let it not seem absurd to anyone to learn the way of obedience from birds, since Solomon says: 'Go imitate the ant, O sluggard, consider her ways and learn her wisdom.'

24 successu C_1.   25 insuetae AE_2G.   26 habuerint D.   haberent E_2G.   27 respondit HD.   28 om. $AHDE_2G$.   28–29 om. AE_2G.   30 ins. inquit A_2E_2G.   31 copulabitur HD.   32 iunguntur AE_2G.   33 habet A_2E_2G.   34 frequentantur G.   35 querit D.   36 assumsit B.   37 ins. -que B.   38 eam C_2NE_1n.   39 velud A.   40 exurgens nDE_2G.   41 sederunt AE_2G.   42 i.e. invento N.   43 licentiae C_1.   licentia B.   44 obs... C_1BH. i.e. inconveniens N.   45 dicit C_2n.   46 ins. o AE_2G.   47 s. o N.

XL. *Quomodo domi sedens duas manicas* [1]*a corvis*[2] *praedatas intellexit et iterum restitutas fore in eadem hora praedixit*

Neque tacendum quoque[3] esse arbitror quoddam praefati viri providentiae miraculum. Erat itaque[4], sub eodem tempore, quidam exul de inclita Merciorum prole, vocabulo Æthelbald[5], qui quadam[6] die, ut adsolebat, virum Dei visitare malens[7], comite[8] praefato Wilfrith[9], adepta[10] rate, usque[11] insulam praedictam pervenit. Wilfrith vero ratis[12] de prora saltu[13] terram petens[14], ambas manicas suas in[15] puppi[16] dimisit; ac deinde ad colloquium [17]sancti[18] viri[19] venientes[20], postquam ad invicem se[21] salutaverunt[22], inter alia sermocinandi colloquia supramemoratus vir[23] beatae memoriae[24] Guthlac, cui Dominus absentia praesentabat[25], velut prophetiae[26] spiritu inflatus[27], cum domi sedisset et nihil[28] aliud excepto domus vestibulo prospicere potuisset, subito ab illis[29] sciscitari coepit, utrumne rem[30] aliquam[31] in navi dimisissent. Cui Wilfrith respondens duas manicas suas illic obliviscendo se[32] dimisisse[33] aiebat.

Gen.
41. 13
[34]Ille vero corvos suos tunc manicas possedisse, sicut *eventus rei probavit*, dicebat[35]. Nec mora[36], extra[37] domum egredientes, conspiciunt [38]corvicinae[39] sobolis[40] atrum[41] praedonem[42] in fastigio cuiusdam casae inprobo forcipe[43] manicam lacerare. Sanctus autem Guthlac alitem levi sermone conprimebat[44]; veluti criminis sui conscius esset, ales vero[45] manicam in culmine[46] casae relinquens[47], velut[48] fuga facta, occiduas in auras volabat. Wilfrithus[49] vero de culmine tecti in summitate virgae manicam deducere[50] fecit, ac deinde, conperiens tanti viri potentiae fuisse,

---

1-2 *om.* C₁.   3 *om.* A₂E₂G.   4 *om.* A₂E₂G.   5 Aethelbald C₂. Aeðelbald A.   Aeðelbaldus A₂.   Ethelbald H.   Ethelbaldus nD. Etdelbaldus E₂.   Edelbaldus G.   6 quadam HD.   7 mallens C₁BA.   volens A₂E₂G.   *ins.* cum C₁B.   8 *ab.* pro comitante N. 9 Wilfritho C₂HNEnDE₂G.   Wilfriðo A.   10 adepto C₁C₂BANE₁nE₂G.   11 *ins.* in A₂E₂G.   *ins.* ad D.   12 *om.* A₂E₂G.   13 *ab.* pro saltatu N.   14 pendens N.   15 *om.* C₁BHD.   16 pupi C₁B.   puppe A.   17-19 vir. sa. C₁. 18 *om.* AE₂G.   19 *ins.* Dei AE₂G.   20 veniens E₂.   21 *om.* G. 22 salutavere C₁AE₂G.   *ins.* se G.   23 *om.* C₁BAE₂G.   24 *ins.*

XL. *How, seated in his house, he perceived that two gloves were being carried off by jackdaws and how he predicted that they would be restored the same hour*

Nor do I think that one ought to be silent either about a miracle of foresight wrought by the same man. Now there was at that time a certain exile named Æthelbald of famous Mercian stock who on one occasion, when wishing according to his wont to visit the man of God accompanied by the aforesaid Wilfrid, took a boat and came to this same island. But Wilfrid jumped on to land from the prow of the boat and left both his gloves in the stern. Then they came and talked to the saint, after they had saluted one another. Now the Lord showed things that were absent to this man of blessed memory, Guthlac, filling him as with the spirit of prophecy; and so in the midst of their conversation, although he was seated in the house and could not see farther than the entrance, he suddenly began to ask them whether they had left anything in the ship. Wilfrid in reply said that he had forgetfully left his two gloves there. Guthlac declared that his jackdaws had possession of the gloves; and so it proved. Without any delay they leave the dwelling and see a black thief of the raven kind on the roof-top of a certain cottage tearing a glove with its mischievous beak. Thereupon St Guthlac restrained the bird with gentle words, and then, as if conscious of its ill-doing, it left the glove on the top of the cottage and like a fugitive fled westwards. So Wilfrid had the glove brought down from the top of the roof on the end of a stick; then, realizing that it was in the power of this

vir C_1BAE_2G. 25 monstrabat D. 26 prof... A. 27 afflatus AE_2G. 28 nil $C_1BAE_1nE_2G$. nichil HD. *ab.* s. eum C_2N. 29 aliis B. 30 ullam B. *ins.* ullam H. 31 ullam C_2NE_1n. 32 *om.* C_1D. 33 *ins.* se C_1D. 34–35 *in marg.* B. 36 s. erat C_2N. 37 V *begins again here.* 38–41 *marked for omission* A_2. 39 corvini VB. corvine HD. corvicini $C_1C_2ANE_1nG$. 40 generis G. 41 i.e. nigrum C_2N. 42 *ins.* corvum A_2E_2G. 43 ore A_2E_2G. 44 comprimit C_1. comprimens A. comprimeret A_2E_2G. i.e. corripuit N. 45 *om.* $C_1C_2AHNE_1nDE_2G$. 46 cuiusdam C_1VBAE_2G. 47 linquens C_2NE_1nD. liquens H. 48 veluti VB. 49 Wilfrid V. 50 afferri A_2E_2G.

alteram[1] sibi reddere sicut et illam, sollicitus de alterius manicae damno[2] fieri coepit. At vir Dei, illum [3]egrota mente[4] damnum[5] rei graviter pertulisse[6] sentiens, ludibundo[7] verborum famine illum consolari coepit, pollicens ei possibilitatis Dei fuisse, cito sibi rem perditam recuperari[8], si fides eorum[9] non titubasset. Nec plura[10]; [10a]inter haec[11] verba[12], ecce tres viri fratres [13]pulsato signo[14] ante portum[15] praefatae insulae steterunt, ad quos dicto velocius[16] sanctus Guthlac, ut adsolebat, hilari vultu successit[17]; nam semper gratia eximiae caritatis[18] in ore [19]ipsius et[20] vultu fulgebat. Salutatis vero fratribus, confestim unus eorum, inclinata[21] sibi cervice[22] efflagitata venia, forte[23] in via quandam manicam de uncis pedibus corvi demissam[24] invenisse se[25] fatebatur, [26]et manicam sibi ostendit[27]. Guthlac parumper subridens, de manu illius manicam tenuit et, admiratus divinae clementiae benignitatem, loquente[28] spiritu[29] gratias egit ac deinde salutatis illis, sicut ante promisit[30], Wilfritho manicam reddidit[31].

XLI. *Quomodo quendam per[32] quadriennium[33] a maligno spiritu vexatum pristinae saluti restituit*

Fuit itaque[34] in hisdem[35] fere temporibus in Orientalium[36] Anglorum terminis [37]quidam iuvenis[38], nomine Hwaetred[39], inclitae quidem[40], ut ferunt[41], sobolis[42]; qui cum[43] in[44] pietate[45] cotidiana[46] parentibus [47]iura inpenderet[48], quadam[49] die[50] domi sedens, subito illum nequam spiritus grassari[51] coepit. [52]In tantum[53] autem[54] inmensa dementia

---

1 i.e. manicam D. 2 dampno AHE_1DE_2G. 3–4 *om.* A_2E_2G.
5 dampnum AHE_1DE_2G. 6 perferre A_2E_2G. 7 blando A_2E_2G.
8 recuperare C_1AE_2G. 9 illorum E_2. 10 s. dico C_2N.
10a–12 locutus A_2E_2G. 11 *om.* C_1. *ins.* autem VB. 13–14 appulsi E_2G. 15 portam C_2NE_1n. 16 citius VBE_2. 17 secessit D. accessit A_2E_2G. 18 kari... H. 19–20 et ips. $C_1C_2VBAHNE_1nD$. 21 inclinato $C_1VBAHNE_1nDE_2$. 22 crevice C_1. capite HD. 23 *om.* A_2E_2G. 24 dim... C_1VBnE_2G. *ins.* se A_2E_2G. 25 *om.* $C_1VBAHDE_2G$. 26–27 quam cum eis ostendisset E_2G. 27 ostendens C_1A. 28 toto A_2E_2G. 29 spiritus C_1. 30 fecerat E_2G. 31 *ab.* vel promisit D.

great man to restore the other glove as he had done the first, Wilfrid began to be concerned about the loss of the other glove. But the man of God noticed that he was greatly troubled in mind by the loss, and began to console him, uttering playful words and promising him that it was within God's power quickly to restore to them the lost article, if their faith did not falter. To be brief, while they were still speaking, three brethren sounded the signal and appeared at the landing-place of this same island. St Guthlac, quicker than words, as was his custom, turned aside towards them with joyful countenance; for always the most excellent grace of charity shone in his face and speech. As soon as he had saluted the brethren one of them immediately bent his head to him and, having thus asked permission to speak, declared that he had found by chance on the way a certain glove dropped from the curved claws of a jackdaw, and showed him the glove. Guthlac smiled for a moment and, taking the glove from his hand, marvelled at the kindness of the divine clemency, and gave thanks in the spirit. Then, bidding the brethren farewell, he returned the glove to Wilfrid as he had previously promised.

XLI. *How he restored to health a certain man who had been vexed for four years by an evil spirit*

At about the same time, also, there was in the realm of the East Angles a certain young man called Hwætred, said to be of noble stock: while he was still at all times dutifully subject to his parents, on a certain day when he was sitting at home, suddenly an evil spirit began to attack him. He was affected with so great a madness that he tore his own limbs, so far as

32 *om.* C$_2$.   33 quadriennem C$_2$. quadriennium VBN. quadrigennium E$_1$.   34 *om.* A$_2$E$_2$G.   35 eisdem HD. isdem E$_1$n.   36 *ab.* est A. 37–38 iuv. quid E$_2$.   39 Hpatræd V. Hwetredus HD. Hwetred E$_1$. Wetredus A$_2$E$_2$G.   40 quidam E$_1$.   41 fertur AE$_2$G.   42 i.e. nativitatis D.   43 s. ille D.   44 *om.* C$_2$NE$_1$n.   45 cotidianae C$_1$VBNE$_1$nD. quotidianae C$_2$H.   46 pietatis C$_1$C$_2$VBHNE$_1$nD. 47–48 immineret A$_2$E$_2$G.   49 quodam C$_1$.   50 *ins.* se C$_1$. 51 *ab.* inpugnare C$_2$. i.e. inpugnare vel vexare vel corripere N. i.e. opprimere D. agitare A$_2$E$_2$G.   52–53 *om.* C$_1$.   54 enim AE$_2$G.

vexabatur[1] ita[2] ut membra sua propria ligno, ferro,
unguibus[3] dentibusque, prout potuit[4], laniaret[5]; non
solum enim[6] se ipsum crudeli vesania decerpebat[7], quin[8]
etiam omnes, quoscumque tangere[9] potuisset, inprobi
oris morsibus lacerabat. Eo[10] autem modo[11] insanire
coepit, ut eum[12] prohiberi[13] aut adligari [14]nullius ausibus
inpetraretur[15]. Nam quodam[16] tempore, congregata
multitudine, cum alii[17] illum [18]ligare temtarent[19], ar-
repto[20] limali[21] bipenne[22] tria [23]virorum corpora[24] leta-
bundis ictibus humo[25] sternens mori[26] coegit. At cum[27]
bis binis annorum cursibus[28] dira peste vesaniae[29] vastaretur [30]et exerti[31] macilentia[32] arido in corpore vires[33]
distaberent[34], tum demum a parentibus suis ad sacratas
[35]sedes[36] sanctorum[36a] adductus est, ut[37] a sacerdotibus
episcopisque sacratis[38] fontibus[39] lavaretur. Cum ergo nullus eorum pestiferum funesti[40] spiritus virus[41] extinguere
valuisset[42], tandem, exploratis reprobatisque omnium
remediorum stigmatibus[43], domum reversi sunt. Quadam
[44]vero[45] die[46], cum maesti parentes nati[47] mortem magis[48]
quam vitam optarent[49], fama volat[50] quendam heremitam
in [51]mediae[52] paludis[53] insula[54] Crugland[55] sedisse[56], cuius
rumor[57] diversis virtutum generibus fines [58]paene totius[59]
Brittanniae[60] longe lateque replebat. Quo conperto, [61]orto
mane[62], illuc[63] ducere vexatum certo [64]consilio parant.
Excussa[65] ergo opacae[66] noctis caligine, cum sol aureum
caelo[67] demoverat[68] ortum, ligatis membris[69] vexatum

1 *ab.* f A.   2 vel promisit D.   3 i.e. iugulis D.   4 *ab.*
potera A₂. poterat E₂G.   5 i.e. vulneraret D.   6 autem
C₁VBAE₂G.   7 decipiebat C₁C₂VBAHNE₁n. discerpebat E₂.
8 i.e. potuisset VB.   9 *alt. fr.* tangeri C₁.   10 hoc C₁VB.
11 forte A₂E₂G.   12 *ab.* aliquis N.   13 prohibere
C₁C₂ANE₁nDE₂G. s. a dementia D.   14 alligare C₁C₂ANE₁nDE₂G.
14–15 nullus auderet D. nullus valeret A₂E₂G.   16 autem C₁.
17 aliqui D.   18–19 tempt. lig. AE₂G.   19 temptabant C₁VB.
ab. inciperent C₂N.   20 arepto C₁. arrepta AHDE₂G.   21 i.e.
acuto B.   22 bipinne C₁VB. bipenni C₂NE₁n. bipenna A₂E₂G.
23 *ins.* cor VB. *later erased in* V.   23–24 corp. vir. A₂E₂G.
25 *om.* C₁.   26 morire C₁A.   27 *ins.* per quattuor annos
A₂E₂G.   28 *om.* A₂E₂G.   29 vesania C₁. *om.* A₂E₂G. *ab.* ab
vel N.   30 *ab.* æsceue N.   30–34 ei deficerent E₂G.   31 i.e.

he could, with wood and iron, with his nails and his teeth; and indeed not only did he wound himself with cruel madness, but all whom he could reach he fiercely bit and tore. He began to be so mad that no one could succeed by any efforts in checking him or binding him. On one occasion, indeed, a great number gathered together while some attempted to bind him, but he seized a well-filed double-winged axe and with deadly blows he felled three men to the ground and slew them. After he had been ravaged for the space of four years by the dread plague of madness, and his strength, once conspicuous, had melted away from his wasted body through emaciation, at last his parents took him to the holy places of the saints so that he might be washed in holy water by priests and bishops. But none of them could quench the pestiferous poison of the deadly spirit, and at length after every kind of application and remedy had been tried and rejected they returned home. One day, however, when his sorrowing parents were wishing that their son might die rather than live, a rumour came that there was a certain hermit who dwelt in the midst of the fen on an island called Crowland, whose fame for miracles of various kinds filled almost the whole of Britain, far and wide. When they had learned this, they prepared with firm resolution to take the tormented youth thither at daybreak. So when the sun had driven away the black mist of night and dispelled the golden dawn from the sky, taking the tormented boy with his limbs

aperta VBD.   exerta D.   exerte N.   s. cum N.   32 macell... C$_1$.
i.e. fame VBD.   33 *ab.* peor N.   34 distabuerunt C$_1$C$_2$ANE$_1$n.
distabuerent VBH.   35 *om.* A$_2$E$_2$G.   35–36*a* sanct. sed. HD.
36 pedes AE$_2$G.   37 uti C$_2$VBNE$_1$n.   38 sacro A$_2$E$_2$G.   39 fonte A$_2$E$_2$G.   40 *om.* E$_1$.   41 i.e. venenum VB.   42 i.e. potuisset VB.   43 *ab.* cicatricibus C$_2$N.   adhibitionibus AE$_2$G.   i.e. signis vel cauteribus D.   44–46 die ver. D.   45 namque HD.   47 i.e. filii VB.   48 plus C$_2$NE$_1$n.   49 expectarent A$_2$E$_2$G.   aptarent E$_1$.
50 pro volabat N.   51–53 pal. mediae G.   52 medii C$_1$C$_2$VBANE$_1$n.
54 *ins.* quae dicitur A$_2$E$_2$G.   55 Cruland C$_2$.   Cruglond VB.
56 con... C$_1$AE$_2$G.   57 i.e. fama VB.   58–59 tot. poene E$_2$.
60 Britan... C$_2$.   Brittan... A.   Britann... Hn.   61 *ins.* illuc VB.
61–62 *om.* C$_1$.   63 *om.* VB.   64 accepto A$_2$E$_2$G.   65 i.e. divisa N.
excusso E$_1$.   66 tenebrosae C$_2$N.   opacis E$_2$.   67 *om.* E$_2$.
68 devomerat VB.   depromeret A$_2$E$_2$G.   69 menbris B.

Virg. *Aen.*
V, 217

Virg. *Aen.*
IV, 130

Virg. *Aen.*
I, 371

ducentes, coeptum *iter rad*ere[1] coeperunt. Vesperascente[2] vero die, cum illuc[3] iter[4] divertissent[5], in quadam insula haud[6] procul a Crugland[7] noctem duxerunt[8], ac denique[9], *iubare*[10] *exorto*, ad[11] portum praedictae insulae subvenientes[12], pulsato[13] signo[14] colloquium tanti viri efflagitabant. Ille autem, more suo[15] eximiae caritatis[16] ardore fervescens[17], sese coram[18] illis obtulit[19]; et[20] cum[21] ipsi causam suam a primordio explicarent, vir Dei parentum sollicitudinem et vexatae humanitatis [22]labores miserescens[23], velut[24] paterno[25] pectore illis propitiari[26] coepit. Confestim enim, vexati manum[27] arripiens, intra oratorium suum duxit[28], et illic continuis trium[29] dierum[30] ieiuniis, flexis genibus[31], orare[32] coepit; tertia vero die, orto[33] sole, sacrati fontis undis abluit[34], et, inflans[35] in faciem eius spiritum salutis, omnem valitudinem[36] maligni spiritus [37]de illo[38] reppulit[39]. Ipse autem, velut qui de aestuantis gurgitis[40] fluctibus ad portum deducitur, longa suspiria *imo de pectore trahens*, ad[41] pristinae salutis[42] valitudinem[43] redditum[44] se esse intellexit; ab illo enim[45] tempore usque in diem exitus sui nullius molestiae inquietudinem ab inmundo spiritu pertulit.

XLII. *Quomodo comitem subzonam*[46] *suam*[47] *sibi donando ab inmundi spiritus infestatione dicto citius sanavit*[48]

Alio[49] quoque[50] tempore, cum praefati exulis Æthelbaldi[51] comes quidam, [52]vocabulo Ecga[53], ab inmundi spiritus validissima vexatione[54] miserabiliter grassaretur[55], ita ut

1 *ab.* arripere C₂. i.e. arripere vel inchoare N. i.e. carpere VB. vadere HD. agere A₂E₂G. 2 vesperes... C₁. 3 illic AE₂G. 4 *om.* A₂E₂G. 5 dev... C₂ND. rev... E₁. devertisset VB. 6 haut C₁C₂AnDG. aut V. i.e. non longe VB. 7 Cruland C₂H. Cruglond A. 8 *ab.* i.e. peregerunt VB. duxere AE₂G. 9 deinde HD. 10 i.e. splendore VB. die A₂E₂G. 11 *om.* E₂G. 12 i.e. de B. subeuntes A₂E₂G. 13 pulsantes E₂. 14 hostio A₂G. ostium E₂. 15 *ins.* solito HD. 16 kari... BH. 17 fervescens V. 18 *om.* A₂E₂G. 19 opt... VBHE₂G. 20 at VBAE₂G. 21 *bis* E₂. 22–23 mis. lab. G. 23 miserascens D. 24 velud A. pio E₂G. 25 de E₂G. 26 propitiare C₁A. 27 manus AE₂G. 28 *ins.* eum AE₂G. s. eum N.

bound, they made a start on their journey. When evening fell
they had reached a certain island off the way not far from
Crowland and spent the night there. Then when the sun rose
in its splendour, they approached the landing place of this said
island, and having struck the signal they begged for a talk with
the great man. But he, as was his custom, burning with the
flame of most excellent charity, presented himself before them;
when they had explained their case from the beginning, the
man of God, having pity on the anxiety of the parents and
the afflictions of tormented mankind, began to console them in
a fatherly manner. He immediately seized the hand of the tormented boy and led him into his oratory, and there prayed on
bended knees, fasting continually for three days. On the third
day at sunrise he washed him in the water of the sacred font
and, breathing into his face the breath of healing, he drove
away from him all the power of the evil spirit. And the youth,
like one who is brought into port out of the billows and the
boiling waves, heaved some deep sighs from the depth of his
bosom and realized that he had been restored to his former
health. Now from that time to the day of his death he suffered
no further molestations or trouble from an evil spirit.

XLII. *How quicker than words he healed the gesith from
the troubling of an unclean spirit by giving him his girdle*

At another time too a certain *gesith* of the before-mentioned
exile Æthelbald, named Ecga, was miserably attacked by the
extreme violence of an unclean spirit, so that he did not know

29 tribus C_1AHDE$_2$G. diebus VB.   30 diebus C_1AHDE$_2$G. tribus VB.
ins. persistens A$_2$E$_2$G.   31 *ins.* Deum A$_2$E$_2$.   32 *ins.* Deum G.
33 *ins.* iam HD.   34 s. eum N.   35 inflavit C_1. insufflans A$_2$E$_2$G.
36 i.e. firmitatem V. i.e. infirmitatem B.   37–38 *om.* A$_2$E$_2$G.
39 repellit C_1.   40 *ab.* f. A.   41 *om.* A$_2$E$_2$G.   42 saluti A$_2$E$_2$G.
43 i.e. fortitudinem VB.   44 reditum n.   45 autem A$_2$E$_2$G.
46 zonam VBD. zona C_2.   47 sua C_2.   48 sanuit C_1. sanaverit
VB.   49 *ins.* fuit VB.   50 s. fuit D.   51 Æðelbaldi C_2N.
Æþelbaldi VBn. Edilbaldi H. Adelbandi E$_1$. Aeðilbaldi A. Edelbaldi
E$_2$G.   52–53 *om.* A$_2$E$_2$G.   53 Egga C_1HD. Ecgga C_2NE$_1$n.
54 violentia C_2HNE$_1$nD. *ins.* vexatur et VB.   55 *ab.* inpugnaretur C_2.
i.e. inpugnaretur vel vexaretur N. *ab.* torqueretur A$_2$E$_2$G.

quid esset vel quo sederet vel quid [1]parabat[2] facere[3]
nesciret. Corporis autem[4] et membrorum[5] vigor [6]in-
laesus permansit[7], facultas vero loquendi, disputandi[8]
intelligendique[9] penitus defuit. Quadam[10] die[11] pro-
pinqui sui formidantes perpetuam vesaniam sibi venturam,
ad praefati viri Guthlaci[12] limina[13] duxerunt[14]; confestimque, ut se cingulo eius[15] succinxit[16], omnem amentiam
de[17] se ablatam animumque sibi integre[18] redditum persensit; se quoque[19] illo[20] cingulo semper praecingens,
usque in ultimum diem vitae suae nullam a Satana[21]
molestiam perpessus est.

XLIII. *Quomodo[22] cuiusdam abbatis ministrorum longe
repositorum[23] culpam[24] manifestando prodidit[25]*

Bede,
    V.pr.
c. 11 (cf.
Greg. dial.
II, 12)

Coepit etiam[26] *inter ista vir Dei* Guthlac *prophetiae spiritu
pollere, futura praedicere, praesentibus[27] absentia[28] narrare.*
Aliquibus enim diebus, cum[29] quidam abbas, ut adsolebat,
ad verbocinium[30] praefati viri devenire proposuit, incoepto[31] itinere duo ministri ipsius, simulata cuiusdam
causae[32] necessitate[33], abbatis licentiam poscebant, ut[34]
aliam viam, qua[35] causa[36] cogebat[37], devertissent[38]. Ille
autem, illis[39] concessa licentia, quo proposuit[40] perrexit;
ac[41] denique[42] adveniente[43] illo ad colloquium[44] viri Dei
Guthlaci, cum sese alterutrum divinarum scripturarum
haustibus[45] inebriarent, sanctus Guthlac inter alia ab illo
sciscitari coepit aiens[46]: 'Ut quid [47]duo isti[48] clerici (quos
vocabulo nuncupavit), ut adsolebant, huc te comitari
noluerunt?' Abbas autem illos, efflagitata licentia, alterius[49]
causae[50] necessitate[51] in alteram viam devertisse[52] dixit.

1–3 fac. par. C₂NE₁n.   2 pararet E₂G.   4 quidem A₂E₂G.
5 menb... DE₂.   6–7 perm. ill. AE₂G.   8 *ab.* meditandi C₂N.
9 intelleg... VB.   *ins.* ei A₂E₂G.   10 *ins.* ergo A₂E₂G.   11 *alt.*
to dies V.   12 *om.* C₂NE₁n.   13 *ins.* illum H.   *ab.* eum n.
14 *ab.* s. eum C₂N.   15 illius C₂HNE₁nD.   16 succinsit C₁.
17 a A₂E₂G.   18 ex integro C₁VB.   19 *ins.* -que A₂E₂G.
20 ille D.   21 Sath... DE₂.   22 qualiter C₂NE₁.   23 se
positorum C₂E₁. a se positorum ND.   24 occultum crimen

what he was or where he dwelt or what he was about to do. Although the strength of his body and limbs remained unharmed, yet his powers of speech, discussion, and understanding failed him entirely. One day his relatives, fearing that perpetual madness would come upon him, took him to the abode of this same Guthlac, and as soon as he bound himself with the saint's girdle, he felt that all his madness had disappeared and his mind had wholly returned to him; and also, because he always girded himself with that same girdle, he suffered no molestation from Satan to the last day of his life.

XLIII. *How he disclosed and made known the fault of the servants of a certain abbot though they were far away*

The man of God also began meanwhile to abound in the spirit of prophecy, to predict the future and to narrate absent things to those who were present. Now at a certain time an abbot had proposed to come and talk with the said man, as he was wont to do. When the journey was begun two of his servants, on the excuse of some pretended need, asked permission of the abbot to take another road for reasons of business. He gave them permission and proceeded on his way. But when he had arrived and was in conference with Guthlac, the man of God, and together they were drinking deep draughts from the holy Scriptures, St Guthlac began amongst other things to ask him: 'Why would not those two clerics (whom he named) accompany you hither as was their custom?' The abbot said that they had asked his permission and owing to other business

C₂NE₁D.   25 prodebat C₂NE₁.   i.e. manifestabat C₂.   26 autem G.   27 *ins.* presentia C₁NE₁.   28 absentibus C₁NE₁.   *ins.* presentibus A.   29 *om.* E₂G.   30 i.e. ad colloquium VB.   colloquium A₂E₂G.   31 *ins.* iam A₂E₂G.   *ins.* -que E₂G.   32 causa AE₂G.   33 necessitatis AE₂G.   34 *ins.* in A₂E₂G.   35 quam H.   36 *ab.* f. A.   37 agebat E₂.   dev... AnE₂G.   38 divertere possent A₂E₂G.   39 *om.* C₁.   40 prosuit A.   41 *om.* AE₂G.   42 deinde HD.   43 veniente HD.   44 *at top of folio* finis. Amen C₂.   45 sermonibus A₂E₂G.   46 dicens E₂.   47–48 isti duo C₁VBA₂E₂G.   49 cuiusdam C₁VB.   50 *ab.* f. A.   51 necessitatis VBG.   52 div... AnE₂G.

At[1] vero sanctus Guthlac, cui Dominus ex divina inspiratione absentia praesentabat, paulisper [2]demissa[3] fronte[4] subridens vultum deflexit. Abbas autem cum persensisset[5], quod viro Dei[6] aliter[7] praesentaretur, [8]obsecrans eum[9] in nomine Iesu[10] ut evidenter[11] monstraret[12], quod sibi de illis visum est, suppliciter rogabat. [13]Guthlac[14] vero, supplicibus obsecrationibus amici, qui sibi spiritali[15] foedere in Christo copulabatur[16], adnuens[17], iter eorum in[18] ordine sibi pandere coepit. Dicebat enim illos ad cuiusdam viduae casam devertisse[19] et, dum non[20] adhuc[21] tertia hora esset[22], in delicatis viduae fulcris[23] inebriari coepisse. Non solum ergo vir Dei iter illorum a primordio narrabat, quin etiam victum eorum et verba ex ordine monstrando explicavit[24]. Non [25]aliter enim[26] sibi[27] ex divino numine praesentabatur, quam ut[28] Helisaeo[29] cognitio furti facti[30] Giezi[31], Deo manifestante, monstratum est. In tantum enim[32] gratiae[33] divinae[34] *spiritus* [35]in eo[36] *polle*bat[37], ut *absentia*[38] [38a]*praesentibus* et futura praeteritis[39] ut praesentia arbitraretur[40]. Abbas itaque, perceptis salutaribus documentis viri[41] venerabilis Guthlaci, remeabili[42] cursu domum[43] migravit. Cum[44], ut adsolebant[45], duo [46]praefati clerici[47] ministerio[48] abbatis obviarent, omnes de domo[49], exceptis [50]illis duobus[51], discedere iussit; cumque in domo[52] sederent[53], ab illis abbas ubi moram hesternae[54] diei duxerint[55], sciscitabatur. Illi simulato pectore in alicuius amici sui casa[56] se[57] [57a]moratos esse[58] dicebant. Abbas autem illos fuisse in domo[59] viduae, quam[60] proprio vocabulo nuncupavit, alium[61] sibi nuntiasse aiebat[62]; illi contradicentes[63]

Cf.
II Kings
5. 25-7
Bede,
V.pr.
c. 11

1 ad B.   2–4 *om.* AE₂G.   3 dimisso C₁VB.   i.e. inclinata C₂N. dimissa H.   5 persensiset B.   6 *om.* E₂G.   7 *ins.* res A₂E₂G.   8–10 *om.* A₂E₂G.   9 *om.* VBAHD.   11 ab. manifeste C₂N.   12 monstraretur E₂.   13–16 *om.* A₂E₂G. 14 *ins.* consentit A.   15 spirituali n.   16 *ins.* at ille A₂E₂G. 17 *ab.* indicans C₂N.   18 ex A₂E₂G.   19 div... C₁NAE₂G. 20 *ins.* erat A.   *ins.* esset A₂E₂G.   21 *ins.* esset C₁VB.   22 *om.* C₁VB.   etiam AE₂G.   23 conviviis A₂E₂G.   fulchris H.   Fulcra sunt ornam ... lectorum dicta qui ... his fulcimur, id est susti ... quos thoros fulcia ... capud que reclina ... vulgus appellat ... *Note in marg. of* N, *only partly legible owing to cut edges.*   24 *ab.* narrabat C₂N.   25–26 en. al. Hn.   27 ibi N.   28 sicut A₂E₂G.

had gone by another road. But St Guthlac, to whom the
Lord by divine inspiration showed absent things as present,
bowed his head for a moment, and smiling turned his face away.
The abbot, having realized that the man of God had been given
a vision of something different, humbly besought him, praying
him in the name of Jesus to show him clearly what he had seen
concerning them. Guthlac, assenting to the humble petitions
of his friend to whom he was united in Christ by spiritual
bonds, began to describe their journey to him in order of events.
For he said that they had turned into the house of a certain
widow, and, though it was not yet the third hour, had begun to
drink deep draughts at the widow's luxurious table. So not only
did the man of God relate their journey from the beginning, but
he even described their food and conversation in detail. It was
shown him by the divine spirit in the same way as knowledge
of the theft committed by Gehazi was manifested to Elisha by
the revelation of the Lord. So greatly did the spirit of divine
grace abound in him that he discerned absent things by things
present, and future things by the past, as though they were
present. And so the abbot, having received the healthful instruction of the venerable man Guthlac, made his return journey
home. When, as was their custom, the two before-mentioned
clerics came to wait on the abbot, he ordered all to depart from
the house except these two. When they had sat down in the
house, the abbot asked them where they had lingered on the
previous day. They deceitfully asserted that they had lingered
in the house of a certain friend of theirs. But the abbot declared
that someone had told him that they had been in the house of
a widow whom he mentioned by name. They denied his words,

29 Heliae H. Helyseo E₂.   30 *ins.* ab A₂E₂G.   31 Iezi C₁. Gezi
C₂NE₁.   32 *ins.* in eo C₁VBAE₂G. *ins.* erat A₂E₂G.   33 gratia
C₂ANE₁nE₂G.   34 divina C₂NE₁n. divini A₂E₂G.   35–36 *om.*
C₁VBAE₂G.   37 *om.* AE₂G.   38 absentiam V.   38a–41 et futura
praesentibus indicaret A₂E₂G.   39 *om.* VBHD.   40 s. demonstraret N.
41 *ins.* Dei A₂.   42 celeri A₂E₂G. *ab.* hwyrf AH.   43 *ins.* suam D.
44 *ins.* -que A₂E₂G.   45 solebant AE₂G.   46–47 cler. pre. AE₂G.
48 *ab.* datur N.   49 domu C₂NE₁.   50–51 du. ill. HD.   52 domu
C₂NE₁.   53 sederet VB.   54 est... C₁.   55 duxerunt C₁C₂ ANE₁n.
56 causa V.   57 *om.* C₁AE₂G.   57a–58 morasse C₁VBAH.   59 domu
C₂NE₁.   60 *ins.* et A₂E₂G.   61 *ab.* oper A.   62 dicebat G.   63 *ab.* p A.

cum maxima procacitate illius[1] dicta negabant. Abbas
vero eorum inpudentiam[2] conprimens[3] nota signa monstrando culpam suam confiteri iussit[4]. Ipsi autem, cum
Acts 9. 5   *contra* [5]nota indicia[6] *calcitrare*[7] nequivissent[8], tandem[9]
se solo prementes[10] iter suum uno eodemque ordine, quo
vir Dei ante narravit, confessi sunt.

XLIV. *Quomodo duobus clericis ad se venientibus* [11]*flasculas*[12] *binas*[13], *quas in via abscondebant*[14], *monstravit*[15]

Venerunt quoque his[16] fere diebus de quodam monasterio
duo viri fratres, ut [17]sancti Guthlaci verba doctrinae[18]
audirent; [19]nam illo tempore tanti viri fama ubique notabunda[20] vagavit[21]. Deinde[22] cum[23] insulam devenissent,
habentes secum binas[24] flasculas[25] caelia[26] impletas[27], facto
consilio, illas[28] in via sub quodam[29] palustri sablone
absconderunt, ut, iterum revertentes, iter suum illa annona
relevarent[30]. Cumque praefati[31] fratres verbocinio[32]
venerabilis viri [33]potiti uterentur[34] [34a]et salutaribus praeceptis illos admoneret[35], hilari vultu leviter[36] subridens,
ludibri[37] famine[38] inter alia ab illis sciscitabatur dicens:
'Ut quid, filioli, huc portare noluistis binas[39] flasculas[40],
quas sub agrestis[41] glebae umbraculo abdidistis?' Quo
audito, illi[42] inmenso stupore perculsi se solo sternentes
veniam perpetrati criminis orabant. Sanctus vero Guthlac
sublevatis[43] eorum cervicibus[44] veniam indulsit, pacem
concessit, iter signavit[45].

1 illi G.   2 inpru... VBE₂G.   3 corripiens C₂N.   4 iusit A.
5–6 signa nota G.   6 signa AE₂.   7 recalc... C₂NE₁n.
8 nequissent C₁Hn. non possent AE₂G.   9 i.e. in fine C₂N.
10 sternentes A₂E₂G.   11–13 bin. flasc. D.   12 fascinas C₂.
flascones V. flasconas B.   14 absconderunt C₂NE₁D.   15 ludibri
verborum famine prophetice monstravit C₂NE₁D [*om.* prophetice NE₁].
16 is D. hiis G.   17–18 verb. doct. s. Guth. A₂E₂G.   19–22 *om.*
A₂E₂G.   20 *ab.* notanti simul D.   21 vagabatur D. *ab.* divulgata
est D.   23 *ins.* -que A₂E₂G.   24 bina A₂E₂G.   25 vasculos C₁.

contradicting him with the greatest impudence. But the abbot, restraining their shamelessness by showing them evident tokens, ordered them to confess their fault. They then, being unable to kick against the clear evidence, at length, casting themselves upon the ground, confessed every detail of their journey, exactly as the man of God had previously described it.

XLIV. *How he made known to two clerics who came to him, about the two flasks which they had each hidden by the wayside*

At about the same time two brethren came from a certain monastery in order to hear the teaching of St Guthlac, for at that time the fame of this great man had spread and become known everywhere. At the time when they reached the island they had each with them two flasks filled with beer; so they made a plan and hid them by the roadside in the marshy sand, in order that when they returned they might ease their journey with these supplies. And when these same brethren were enjoying the words of the venerable man and he was admonishing them with salutary teaching, with a gentle smile upon his cheerful face he playfully asked them in passing: 'My dear sons, why were you unwilling to bring hither the two flasks which each of you hid away in the darkness of the country soil?' When they heard this they were struck with intense amazement and, prostrating themselves on the ground, they begged his pardon for the offence they had committed. But St Guthlac raised them up, granted them pardon, gave them his peace and set them on their way.

vasculas VBA. vascula A_2E_2G.   26 i.e. cervisa C_2. cibis E_2G.
27 plenas C_1VB. impleta E_2G.   28 *om*. G. illa E_2.   29 *ab*. vel
a C_2. quadam NE_1.   30 revel... C_1. relevarentur VB.   31 prevati
C_1. prefatos E_2G.   32 colloquio A_2. *om*. E_2G.   33 vir E_2G.
33–34 potirentur A_2.   34a–35 salutaribus praeceptis admoneret E_2G.
35 s. eum C_2.   36 *om*. E_2. leniter G.   37 tali A_2E_2G.   38 *ins*.
verborum C_2NE_1n.   39 *om*. E_2.   40 fascinas C_1AG. sarcinas E_2.
41 agreste C_1C_2n.   42 *om*. AE_2G.   43 *ab*. f A.   44 animis
A_2E_2G.   45 i.e. benedixit VB.

XLV. Qualiter rumor virtutum ipsius fines[1] Brittanniae[2] pervagavit, vel quomodo comes quidam tactu[3] vestis illius sanatus est

Bede,
V.pr.
c. 22

Sub eisdem[4] quoque temporibus *ad virum Dei* Guthlacum *multi* diversorum ordinum gradus[5], abbates, fratres[6], comites, divites, [7]vexati, pauperes[8], *non solum de proximis* Merciorum *finibus*, verum *etiam de remotis*[9] Brittanniae[10] *partibus, fama nimirum*[11] *virtutum eius acciti*[12], confluebant[13], quos aut corporum egritudo aut inmundorum [14]spirituum infestatio[15] aut [16]*commissorum*[17] errorum professio, aut aliorum[18] quorumcumque[19] criminum *quibus* humanum genus adluitur [20]causa vexabat[21], prout[22] uniuscuiusque[23] necessitas[24] cogebat[25], *a tantae sanctitatis viro*[26] *consolandos fore sperabant*[27]. *Nec illos* vana *spes fefellit. Nam nullus ab illo*[28] egrotus sine remedio, nullus vexatus sine salute, nullus tristis *sine gaudio*, [29]*nullum*[30] taedium sine exortatione[31], nulla[32] maestitia sine *consolatione*, nulla anximonia[33] sine consilio ab illo[34] reversa est; sed vera caritate pollens, omnium labores cum omnibus unanimiter[35] pertulerat[36]. Contigit ergo[37], cum omnes e[38] diversis[39] partibus variis[40] causis ad tanti viri colloquium ab[41] undique confluebant[42], veniebat[43] inter alios quidam comes praedicti exulis[44] Æthelbaldi[45] Oba[46] nomine ad verbocinium[47] beati viri Guthlaci[48]; et[49] cum alia[50] die quaedam loca spinosa[51] perlustraret sincelli[52] agrestia rura gradiendo, inruit in quandam spinulam [53]sub incultae telluris[54] herbis latentem[55], quae[56] medilanium[57] plantae ipsius[58] infigens[59],

---

1 *om.* D.   2 Brittan... E[1].   3 tractu C[1].   4 isdem C[1]H. hisdem C[2]NE[1]n.   5 gradibus C[1].   *om.* A[2]E[2]G.   6 *om.* A[2]E[2]G. 7–8 pauperesque vex. A[2]E[2]G.   9 i.e. languoribus N.   10 Brittan... A.   11 *om.* A[2]E[2]G.   12 *ab.* advocati C[2]N.   excitati A[2]E[2]G. i.e. vocati D.   13 i.e. festinabant D.   14–17 *om.* C[1].   15 i.e. vastatio C[2]N.   16–18 *om.* A[2]E[2]G.   19 *ins.* professio C[1]VBA. *ins.* confessio A[2]E[2]G.   20 i.e. contaminatur C[2]N.   abluitur VB. i.e. deturpatur D.   20–21 ad hoc coegerat quoque A[2]E[2]G   *om.* HD. 22 vel varietas HD.   23 *ab. f.* A.   *ins.* vel HD.   24 necessitatis G. 25 *ins.* ut C[1].   26 *ins.* se C[2]NE[1]nA[2]E[2]G.   27 credebant C[1]VB.   sperarent AE[1]G.   *ab.* vel credebant A.   28 s. re-

XLV. *How the rumour of his miracles reached to the ends of Britain and how a certain gesith was healed by the touch of his garment*

During these times too, many people of various ranks crowded to see Guthlac the man of God—abbots, brethren, *gesithas*, rich men, the afflicted and the poor—not only from the neighbouring land of the Mercians, but also even from the remote parts of Britain, attracted indeed by the fame of his miracles. Those who were afflicted by sickness of body, by the possession of evil spirits, by the acknowledgement of sins committed, or by reason of any of the other wrongs by which the human race is surrounded, believed that according to their several necessities they would get consolation from a man of such sanctity; nor were they deceived by a vain hope. For no sick man went away from him without relief, no afflicted person without healing, no sad ones without joy, no weary ones without encouragement, no mourners without comfort, no anxious ones without counsel; but, as he abounded in true charity, he shared equally in the sufferings of them all. It chanced, therefore, when they all came together from all sides and from every district for various reasons to have speech with the great man, that there came amongst others a retainer of this same exile Æthelbald, named Ofa, to speak with the blessed Guthlac. One day he had been passing through some thorny places, while walking in the fields of a familiar friend, when he trod upon a thorn lying hidden under the grass of some uncultivated land:

versus est C_2N. 29–36 *om.* A_2E_2G. 30 s. fuit C_2N. 31 exhortatione C_2NE_1n. 32 s. fuit C_2N. 33 s. nullius hominis N. 34 yllo N. 35 i.e. cum uno animo vel concordia D. 36 pertulebat C_1. 37 ut A_2E_2G. 38 *om.* $C_1C_2ANE_1nE_2G$. 39 *ab.* ab vel N. 40 *ins.* ex A_2E_2G. 41 *om.* A_2E_2G. i.e. multis partibus D. 42 confluerent A_2E_2G. 43 veniret A_2E_2G. 44 *ab.* þe N. 45 Æþelbaldi V. Aeðelbaldi A. Ethelbaldi HE_2D. Edelbaldi E_2G. 46 Obba VB. 47 colloquium A_2E_2G. *ab.* hy A. 48 *om.* A_2E_2G. 49 *om.* VB. 50 alio $C_1VBAHDE_2G$. 51 spinea AHE_2G. 52 sincelle $C_1C_2VBNE_1n$. sine cella A. extra cellam A_2E_2G. sine celle HD. i.e. extra domo H. i.e. extra domum D. *ab.* secrete N. *ins.* per A_2E_2G. 53–54 a qua et graviter vulneratus A_2E_2G. 55 latitantem C_1AVBE_2G. 56 *om.* C_1VBAHE_2G. 57 mediumque E_2G. 58 eius C_1VB. 59 *ab.* hpol N.

tenus[1] talum[2] rumpendo totius pedis[3] cratem[4] perforavit. [5]Ille denique[6] contra vires coeptum iter carpens, ad insulam [7]praedictam, in qua[8] vir Dei [9]Domino militavit[10], laboriosissime[11] pervenit; et cum illic [12]noctem unam[13] exegisset[14], inflatico[15] tumore dimidia pars corporis ipsius[16] a lumbis tenus[17] plantam[18] turgescebat[19]. In tantum enim[20] novi[21] doloris molestia angebatur[22], ut sedere aut stare vel iacere nequisset[23]. Nam fervente membrorum[24] conpagine ab imis ossium medullis inmenso ardore coquebatur, ut morienti[25] similior quam languenti[26] videretur. Quod cum viro Dei Guthlaco nuntiaretur[27], illum ad se duci praecepit; ac deinde cum causam[28] vexationis suae[29] a primordio narraret, vir Dei Guthlac exuens se [30]luterio melote[31], in quo ille[32] orare solebat[33], ipsum circumdedit, confestimque dicto citius, postquam veste [34]tanti viri[35] se indutum persensit, eodem momento spinula, velut sagitta ab arcu demissa[36], statim[37] de pede ipsius detruditur[38], quousque procul quasi iaculata[39] institit[40], eademque hora[41] omnis[42] tumidi fervoris violentia[43] ex omnibus membrorum[44] ipsius conpaginibus secessit, [45]confestimque[46] exsurgens[47] pede reducto gradiri[48] coepit; et[49] postera die, allocuto[50] viro Dei Guthlaco, qui[51] totius sui corporis ex[52] unius membri[53] languore damnum[54] praestolabatur[55], hilari[56] animo sine ullius[57] valitudinis[58] molestia pergebat. Tunc omnes, qui testimonio virtutis[59] intererant, viri Dei valitudinem[60] fidei[61] mirantes[62], gloriam Domino[63] reddebant[64].

---

1 i.e. usque C₂. usque ad E₂G.　　2 talo D.　　3 om. E₂. 4 cutem E₂.　　5–6 attamen A₂E₂G.　　7–10 in marg. B. 8 ins. erat A₂E₂G.　9–10 om. AE₂G.　permansit HD.　11 laboriose AHDE₂G. vel laboriose N.　12 ille E₂.　12–13 un. noct. AE₂G.　14 ab. n. C₂. in marg. ðy A.　15 grandi A₂E₂G. 16 illius C₁VBAE₂G.　17 usque ad A₂E₂G.　18 planta D. 19 turgescens D.　20 ins. eum D.　21 om. C₁.　22 augebatur C₁C₂NE₁n. angebat D.　23 nequivisset E₂.　24 menb... B. 25 moriente C₁VB.　26 languente C₁VB.　27 ab. p A. 28 causas C₁VB. ins. suae AE₂G.　29 om. AE₂G.　30–31 melote sive cilicio A₂E₂G.　31 melotinae C₁VBAHD. alt. to meloti H.　32 om. A₂E₂G.　33 consueverat VB. 34–35 vir. tant. G.　36 dim... VBE₂.　37 om. A₂E₂G.

it stuck into the middle of his sole and in tearing it as far as the heel, pierced right through the framework of the foot. However he continued the journey he had begun though with difficulty, and after much toil reached that same island in which the man of God waged his war for the Lord. After he had spent one night there, half of his body was distended with a puffy swelling from the loins to the sole of the feet. And he was so sorely afflicted by the fresh pain that he was neither able to sit nor stand nor lie down. The joints of his limbs were inflamed, and he burned with an immense heat right to the very marrow of his bones, so that he seemed more like a dying than a sick man. When Guthlac, the man of God, was informed of this he commanded that the sick man should be brought to him; and when the latter had informed Guthlac of the cause of the trouble from the start, the man of God took off the sheepskin rug in which he was accustomed to pray and covered him with it. Immediately, quicker than words, at the very moment when he felt himself wrapped in the garment of the great man, the thorn was dislodged from his foot like an arrow loosed from a bow, and landed some distance away as though it had been thrown; and the same hour all the violence and heat of the swelling departed from every joint and limb, and immediately he arose and began to walk on his restored foot. The next day, after he had addressed Guthlac the man of God, he who had expected the destruction of his whole body as the result of the sickness in one limb, went on his way with cheerful mind and without any trouble about his health. Then all who were present to witness the miracle returned glory to the Lord, marvelling at the strong faith of the man of God.

38 detrisset C_1VB.   detrusa est C_2NE$_1$n.   exiliit A_2E_2G.   39 iacula C_1VB.   40 stetisset C_1VB.   stetit A_2E_2G.   41 ora V.   42 ins. lues E_2.   ins. dolor G.   43 om. AE$_2$G.   44 menb... B.   45 defluxit E_2.   46–49 om. A_2E_2G.   46 om. -que C_1VB.   ins. vero VB.   47 exurgens E_1nD.   48 gradire C_1BA.   gradi VD.   50 alloquuto H.   51 ab. þe N.   52 pro A_2E_2G.   53 menbri B.   54 i.e. periculum C_2N.   ab. hy A.   dampnum AHE$_1$DE$_2$G.   55 patiebatur C_1C_2VBNE$_1$n.   expectaverat A_2E_2G.   s. antea C_2N.   56 hyl... E_2.   57 illius E_2G.   ins. in A_2E_2G.   58 ab. pro egritudinis C_2.   i.e. egritudinis N.   59 ins. ipsius C_1VB.   ins. eius N.   60 om. A_2E_2G.   61 fidem A_2E_2G.   62 admir... AE$_2$G.   63 Deo G.   64 referebant E_2.

XLVI. *Qualiter[1] Wigfritho[2] verba, [3]quae illo absente promebat, providentiae spiritu sibi renarravit[4]*

[5]Nec me praeterire[6] silentio libet[7] quoddam miraculum praesagae[8] providentiae[9] venerabilis viri Guthlaci, cui ex divina donatione largitum est[10], ut verba absentium[11] quasi scripta videret cogitationesque praesentium velut locutas[12] cognosceret. Cum enim quidam episcopus Headda[13] nomine, quasi caelesti[14] consilio inbutus, ad colloquium venerabilis viri[15] Guthlaci veniret, habuit quidem[16] secum in comitatu suo virum[17] librarium, Wigfrithum[18] nomine, qui cum inter alios episcopi ministros equitabat[19], alii eorum coram illo de virtutibus et miraculis tanti[20] viri Guthlaci[21] mirari coeperunt, alii asperitatem[22] vitae ipsius et perseverentiam, virtutesque per illum[23] factas [24]ab ullo[25] alio ante inauditas[26] disputabant[27], alii in cuius virtute[28] miracula[29] illa quae[30] faciebat[31] dubitantes[32] erumpebant[33]; Wigfrith autem[34] se posse discernere et scire, utrum divinae religionis cultor esset aut[35] pseudo[36]-sanctitatis simulator, si umquam illum vidisset, pollicebatur[37]. Dicebat[38] enim[39] inter Scottorum se[40] populos habitasse[41] et illic[42] pseudo-anachoritas[43] diversarum religionum[44] simulatores vidisse, quos praedicere futura et[45] virtutes alias facere, quocumque numine[46] nesciens conperit[47]. Alios quoque illic fuisse narrabat[48] verae religionis cultores signis virtutibusque plurimis[49] pollentes, quos ille crebro adloqui[50], videre frequentareque solebat; ex quorum[51] experientia[52] aliorum religionem[53]

---

1 quomodo D.   2 Wigfrido C₁C₂VBNE₁D. Wilfrido E₂G. 3 *om.* V.   3–4 quae locutus illo absente renarraverit D.   4 *ins.* in ordinatione sancti Guthlaci anachoritae D.   5–6 non est praetereundum D.   7 debet H. *om.* D.   8 i.e. divine D. *ab.* ge-wittigre A.   9 *ab.* forescea A.   10 *om.* G.   11 i.e. visibilium D. 12 locuta C₂VBnD. auditas A₂E₂G. audita D.   13 Eadda VB. Hedda D.   14 caeleste C₁.   15 *om.* G.   16 quendam NE₁. 17 quendam A₂E₂G.   18 Wigfrid C₁. Wigfrið C₂VBANn. Wigfriðum A₂. Wigfridum HD. Wilfrid E₁. Wilfridum E₂G. 19 equitaret A₂E₂G.   20 sancti A₂E₂G.   21 *ins.* loqui et A₂E₂G. 22 i.e. duritiam C₂N.   23 ipsum AHDE₂G.   24–25 a nullo

XLVI. *How by the spirit of foresight he repeated to Wigfrith the words which he had uttered when absent*

Nor would I willingly pass over in silence a certain miracle of prophetic foresight wrought by the venerable man Guthlac, who was endowed with the divine gift of knowing the words of those absent as though he had seen them written down, and understanding the thoughts of those present as though they had been spoken. Now a certain bishop called Headda, as if imbued with heavenly counsel, came to speak with the venerable man Guthlac. Also he had in his retinue with him a secretary called Wigfrith, who was riding among the other servants of the bishop. Some of them began in his presence to marvel at the miracles and wonders of the great man Guthlac: some discussed the hardness of his life, his perseverance, and the miracles wrought by him and never before heard of in the case of anyone else: others gave vent to their doubts concerning the source of the power by which he performed those miracles. But Wigfrith promised that, if once he saw him, he would be able to discern and know whether he was a follower of the divine religion or a pretender to false sanctity. For he said he had lived amongst the Irish, and there had seen false hermits and pretenders of various religions, whom he found able to predict the future and to perform other miracles, but he knew not by what power. He said that there were others there who were followers of the true religion and abounded in many signs and miracles, whom he had been accustomed to speak with frequently, to see, and often to visit. From his experience

A_2E_2G.   26 auditas A_2E_2G.   27 praedicabant AE_2G.   28 *ins.* fecisset C_1VB.   29 s. faceret C_2N.   30 *om.* A_2E_2G.   31 faceret A_2E_2G.   32 dubitanter C_2.   33 erumebant C_2VBANE_1n.   i.e. eructebant C_2N.   inter se querebant AE_2G.   34 *om.* C_1VB.   35 an A_2E_2G.   36 *om.* A_2E_2G.   speudo E_1.   37 *ab.* behet A.   38 *ins.* se C_1VB.   39 *ins.* se $C_2A_2E_2G$.   40 *om.* $C_1C_2VBNE_1nA_2E_2G$.   41 habitare C_1VBA.   42 *ins.* se A.   43 pseudos anachoritas C_1VB.   *ins.* et A_2E_2G.   44 releg... C_1.   45 *om.* G.   46 i.e. potestate CN.   47 *ab.* invenit C_2N.   conperire N.   48 *ab.* s. Wigfriþ C_2. Wigfrið N.   49 *ins.* -que G.   50 alloquio NE_1.   51 *ins.* etiam A_2E_2G.   52 vel experimento C_1.   53 releg... C_1.

discernere se potuisse[1] promittebat. [2]Ergo cum[3] praedictus episcopus ad colloquium venerabilis viri Dei[4] Guthlaci pervenisset, fraternis salutationibus peractis, sese alterutrum haustibus[5] evangelici[6] nectaris[7] circumfundere[8] coeperunt. Erat autem in viro Dei Guthlaco divinae gratiae luculentia[9] in tantum, ut quicquid[10] praedicaret[11], velut ex angelico ore expressum[12] videretur. Erat in eo tantae sapientiae affluentia[13], ut quaecumque diceret[14], divinarum scripturarum exemplis firmaret.

XLVII. *Quomodo ab episcopo Headda officium sacerdotale acceperit*[15]

Ergo praedictus episcopus, postquam colloquiis illius potitus est[16] et melle dulciora praecepta sapientiae ipsius gustavit[17], ecce[18] repente in medio sermone submissa[19] cervice supplex adiurare [20]coepit illum[21], ut sacerdotale officium per eum susciperet. Guthlac vero, petitionibus[22] episcopi nolens[23] resistere, ocius se solo prosternens, volentiae[24] illius se[25] oboediturum esse promittit[26]. Episcopus autem ovanti[27] animo exsurgens[28], consecrata prius ecclesia, fidelem sacerdotem summo Deo sacravit[29]. Peractis ergo consecrationum obsequiis, rogatu summi pontificis contra rem solitam vir Dei illo die ad prandium[30] venire cogitur[31]. Adpositis ergo dapibus, priusquam[32] prandere[33] coeperunt, adspiciens[34] sanctus Guthlac praedictum fratrem Wigfrithum procul sedentem, inquit[35]: 'O frater Wigfrith, quomodo[36] tibi[37] nunc videtur[38] ille clericus[39], de quo hesterno die[40] iudicare promisisti?' Wigfrithus vero[41], haec miratus[42], confestim[43] exsur-

---

1 posse C₁VB. 2–3 cum ergo A₂E₂G. 4 *om.* VB.
5 doctrinis A₂E₂G. 6 evangelicae C₁VBA. 7 veritatis A₂E₂G. 8 recreare A₂E₂G. 9 i.e. claritas C₂N. i.e. lucis copia D. efficacia A₂E₂G. 10 quidquid A. 11 predicabat G.
12 i.e. manifestatum C₂N. 13 i.e. habundantia C₂N. i.e. abundantia D. 14 dixisset HD. 15 *no new chapter heading* C₁C₂VBNE₁. 16 i.e. melioratus vel ditatus D. 17 gustasset E₂G.
18 *om.* A₂E₂G. 19 submisso C₂VBNE₁n. i.e. humili vel inclinato D. 20–21 ill....coep.... C₂NE₁n. 21 episcopus

of these he promised that he could judge the religion of others. And so, when the same bishop had come to speak with the venerable man of God, Guthlac, and they had exchanged brotherly greetings, they began to pour out upon one another draughts of the gospel nectar. Now there was such a glory of divine grace in Guthlac, the man of God, that whatever he preached seemed as if uttered by the mouth of an angel. There was such an abundance of wisdom in him that, whatever he said, he confirmed by illustrations from the divine Scriptures.

XLVII. *How he received the office of priest from Bishop Headda*

So the said bishop, after he had had converse with him and had tasted of the teachings of his wisdom more sweet than honey, suddenly in the midst of his talk bowed his head, and began to beg and adjure Guthlac to receive priest's orders at his hand. Guthlac, indeed, was unwilling to refuse the bishop's petitions, and at once prostrated himself upon the ground and promised to be obedient to his wishes. The bishop rose up with joyful heart and, having first consecrated the church, dedicated him to the most high God as a faithful priest. When the service of ordination was over, at the request of the bishop and contrary to his custom, the man of God was compelled to come to a meal on that same day. So when the dishes were brought, and before they began to eat, St Guthlac, looking at the before-mentioned brother Wigfrith who was sitting some distance away, said to him: 'Brother Wigfrith, what do you now think of the cleric whom yesterday you promised to judge?' Wigfrith was amazed at this and, immediately rising, he prostrated himself

A₂E₂G.   22 petitioni C₁VB.   *ab.* b A.   23 nollens C₁VB.
24 voluntati A₂E₂G.   25 *om.* C₁VB.   26 promittebat C₁VBAE₂G.
27 i.e. gaudenti C₂VB.   i.e. leto vel hilari D.   28 surgens C₁VB.
exurgens nDE₂G.   29 consecravit V.   *ab.* vel a V.   consacravit B.
30–31 cog. ven. E₂.   32 postquam C₁C₂VBHDNE₁nG.   33 prandire
C₁A.   34 *ab.* intuens D.   35 dixit A₂E₂G.   inquid D.   36 quo V.
37–38 vid. nunc n.   38–39 cler. ille G.   40 *om.* G.   41–42 admiratus A₂E₂G.   43 *ab.* p A.

gens[1], [1a]se totum solo[2] tota mente prosternit, supplexque
veniam precatus, sese peccasse fatetur. Mirantibus[3] omnibus qui intererant, stupescere[4] ad invicem[5] coeperunt.
Sanctus[6] Guthlac dicebat: 'Conprobamini[7] alterutrum
sciscitantes[8], si quis vestrum mihi[9] nuntiavit[10].' Contigit
ergo[11] consecratio insulae Crugland[12] et constitutio[13] beati
Guthlaci in officium sacerdotale in autumnali[14] tempore,
[15]retro calculatis[16] quinque diebus ab illo die, quo missa[17]
sancti Bartholomaei [18]celebrari solet[19].

XLVIII. *Quomodo Ecgburge interroganti se respondisse
fertur heredem post se* [20]*venturum iam*[21] *paganum fuisse*

[22]Alterius denique temporis[23] praelabentibus[24] circulis[25],
reverentissima virgo virginum[26] Christi [27]et sponsarum[28]
Ecgburh[29] abbatissa, Adulfi[30] regis filia[31], ad[32] sublimium
meritorum[33] venerabilem virum Guthlacum sarcofagum[34]
plumbeum linteumque[35] in eo volutum[36] transmisit[37],
quo virum Dei post obitum circumdari rogabat, adiurans[38]
per nomen terribile [39]ac venerabile[40] superni regis, [41]seque
ad patibulum dominicae crucis erigens in indicium sup-
plicis[42] deprecationis[43] extensis palmis[44], ut in officium
praedictum vir Dei illud munus susciperet;[45] per nuntium
alterius fidelis fratris praecipiens, ut[46] hoc indicium coram
illo faceret[47], supplici rogatu[48] mittebat[49]. Addidit quoque
ut ab illo[50] sciscitaretur, quis loci illius post obitum heres
futurus foret. Qui cum sanctae virginis fidele munus
gratulanter[51] suscepisset, de eo, quod interrogatus[52] est[53],

1 exurgens C₂VnDE₂G.　　1a-2 solo se A₂E₂.　se solo G.　　2 i.e.
terra B.　　3 *ins.* -que VB.　*ins. itaque* VB.　　4 *ab.* fo A.
quique A₂E₂G.　　5 dicere A₂E₂G.　　6 *ins. itaque* VB.　*ins.*
vero HDE₂G.　　7 sciscitamini A₂E₂G.　　8 sciscitantibus A.
om. A₂E₂G.　　9 *ins.* haec C₂VBNE₁n.　*ins.* hoc A₂E₂G.　michi n.
10 s. haec D.　　11 *om.* C₁.　namque VB.　　12 Cruland C₂V.
Cruglond A.　Crouland D.　　13 ordinatio A₂E₂G.　　14 au-
tumpnali E₂G.　　15-16 calc. ret. A₂E₂G.　　16 calcatis C₁VB.
computatis C₂NE₁n.　i.e. enumeratis C₂N.　i.e. computatis D.
17 festum E₂G.　　18 *ins.* apostoli VBAE₂G.　　18-19 sol. cel. H.
20-21 iam vent. C₁VB.　　22-23 alio quoque tempore A₂E₂G.

with utter abandonment upon the ground and humbly prayed for pardon, confessing that he had sinned. All who were present wondered at this, and began to look at one another in amazement. St Guthlac said: 'Question one another and find out if anyone of you has told me of this.' Now the consecration of the island of Crowland and the ordination of the blessed Guthlac to the office of priest took place in the autumn, five days before the day on which it is customary to celebrate the feast of St Bartholomew.

XLVIII. *How when Ecgburh questioned him, he is said to have answered that his heir and successor was then a pagan*

On another occasion, some time after, the most reverend maiden Ecgburh, abbess of the virgins and brides of Christ and daughter of King Aldwulf, sent to Guthlac, that venerable man of high merit, a leaden coffin with a linen cloth folded up in it, and asked that the man of God might be wrapped therein after his death; she invoked him by the terrible and awful name of the heavenly king, with arms outstretched in the form of the cross of our Lord and with palms extended in token of humble prayer, that the man of God would receive the gift for this said purpose. She instructed another faithful brother that he should make this sign in Guthlac's presence, and sent him with this humble request. She also added that he should ask him who was to inherit that place after his death. When he had gratefully received the faithful gift of the holy virgin, he is said to have

23–25 *om.* A₂E₂G.   24 i.e. decurrentibus D.   26 *om.* A₂.
27–28 genetricis C₁VB.   *om.* C₂NE₁n.   *om.* A₂.   spiritualis genetrix E₂G.
29 Ecgburga A.   Egburh H.   Egcburg n.   Egcburcha D.   Edburga E₂G.
30 Adulfi E₁.   Alduulfi n.   Eldufi E₂.   31 *ins.* deduxit VB.
32–33 *om.* A₂E₂G.   34 sarcophagum n.   35 linth...
C₂VBHNE₁nDE₂G.   36 positum A₂E₂G.   37 *om.* C₁VBAHD.
misit A₂E₂G.   38 *ins.* eum A₂E₂G.   39–40 *om.* HD.   41–44 *om.*
A₂E₂G.   42 supplicibus C₁VB. supplici A.   43 deprecationibus
C₁VB.   45 suscipere A.   suscipere dignaretur A₂E₂G.   45–47 *om.*
A₂E₂G.   46 ait N.   48 *ins.* per nuntium A₂E₂G.   49 obsecrans
A₂E₂G.   50 *ins.* idem A₂E₂G.   51 i.e. gratulabundus D.   52 inter-
rogatur HD.   *ab.* vel interrogatus est D.   53 erat A₂E₂G.

respondisse fertur, illius loci heredem in gentili populo fuisse[1] necdum ad baptismatis lavacrum[2] devenisse, sed mox futurum fore dicebat; quod spiritu providentiae[3] **Gen.** dixisse[4] *eventus* futurae[5] *rei probavit.* Nam ipse Cissa[6], **41. 13** qui nunc nostris temporibus sedem[7] Guthlaci [8]viri Dei[9] possidet[10], post annos[11], ut et ipse narrare solet, lavacrum baptismatis in Brittannia[12] percepit[13].

XLIX. *Qualiter exulem[14] ad se venientem[15] consolatus est et regnum sibi mox futurum fore[16] praedixit*

[17]Non me[18] quoque supramemorati viri[19] Guthlaci vati- dico[20] pectore quoddam spiritale[21] praesagium narrare piget. Quodam[22] enim[23] tempore, cum exul ille, quem supra memoravimus, Æthelbald[24], huc illucque, perse- quente illum[25] Ceolredo[26] rege, in diversis nationibus iactaretur, alia[27] die, deficiente[28] virium [29]ipsius valitudine suorumque[30] inter dubia pericula, postquam exinanitae[31] vires defecere, tandem [32]ad colloquium[33] sancti viri[34] **Philo,** Guthlaci, ut adsolebat[35], pervenit, ut, quando[36] *humanum[37]* **quoted by** consilium defecisset, *divinum adesset.* Illo[38] vero cum beato **Gildas** viro[39] Guthlac loquente, vir Dei, velut divini oraculi[40] interpres[41], pandere [42]quae ventura essent sibi, ex ordine[43] coepit dicens: 'O mi puer, laborum tuorum non sum expers[44], miseriarum tuarum ab exordio vitae tuae non sum inscius; propterea misertus[45] calamitatis tuae rogavi Dominum, ut subveniret tibi in miseratione[46] sua[47], et exaudivit me et tribuit tibi dominationem gentis tuae et posuit[48] te principem populorum, et cervices inimicorum

---

1 adhuc esse et A₂E₂G.   2 lavarum E₁.   3 prophetiae A₂E₂G. 4 s. eum C₂N.   5 *om.* A₂E₂G.   6 Scissa DE₂.   7 *ins.* sancti AE₂G.   8 *om.* H.   8–9 *om.* D.   10 possedit H. 11 *ins.* aliquot E₂G.   12 Bryttannia C₁VB. Brit... C₂H. Brittan... A.   13 percepisset VB. *ab.* i.e. t B.   14 *ins.* Ethelbaldum D.   15 venienti C₂.   16 esse C₁VB. 17–18 nonne VBN.   19 *ins.* Dei G.   20 i.e. prophetico C₂D. i.e. profetico BN.   21 spirituale nE₂.   22 quoddam VB. 23 *om.* A₂E₂G.   24 Æthilbald C₁. Ethilbald H. Aeðelbald A.

answered her question by saying that he who was to inherit his place was still among the pagan people and had not yet approached the baptismal font, but it would soon come to pass; and that he had spoken thus by spiritual foresight, future events proved. For Cissa, who now in our times possesses the seat of Guthlac the man of God, some years afterwards received baptism in Britain, as he is accustomed to narrate.

XLIX. *How he consoled the exile when he came to him and foretold that the kingdom would soon be his*

It is no labour for me to relate a certain example of spiritual foresight on the part of the said man Guthlac, the result of his prophetic powers. Now at a certain time when that exile Æthelbald, whom we have mentioned above, was being driven hither and thither by King Ceolred and tossed about among divers peoples, one day amid doubts and dangers when his endurance and that of his followers was failing, and when his strength was utterly exhausted, he came at last to speak with the holy man Guthlac, as was his custom, in order that, when human counsels had failed, he might seek divine counsel. While he was conversing with the blessed Guthlac, the man of God, as if interpreting a divine oracle, began to reveal to him his future in detail, saying: 'O, my child, I am not without knowledge of your afflictions: I am not ignorant of your miseries from the beginning of your life: therefore, having had pity on your calamities, I have asked the Lord to help you in His pitifulness; and He has heard me, and has granted you to rule over your race and has made you chief over the peoples;

Athelbald E₁. Aethelbaldus D. Adelbaldus E₂. Edelbaldus G. 25 *om.* C₁VB. 26 Celredo A₂H. Coeolredo E₁. Cheldredo E₂. Celrodo G. 27 alio HD. aliqua A₂E₂G. 28 deficiens A₂E₂G. 29 viribus A₂E₂G. 29–32 *om.* A₂E₂G. 30 s. sociorum C₂N. 31 inanite C₁VB. i.e. evacuate vel exhauste D. 33–34 viri Dei E₂. 35 solebat AHDE₂G. 36 quia A₂E₂G. 37 *ins.* sibi A₂E₂G. 38 *ab.* p A. 39 *om.* E₂. 40 7 spa *in marg.* A. 41 *ins.* haec ei A₂E₂G. 42–43 *om.* AE₂G. 44 i.e. privatus D. 45 miseratus C₁C₂VBAHNE₁n. 46 vel in miseria tua VB. 47 tua C₁V. *ab.* vel sua V. 48 ponet AE₂G.

tuorum subtus calcaneum tuum rediget[1], et[2] possessiones
eorum possidebis[3], *et fugient[4] a facie tua qui te oderunt,
et terga eorum videbis, et gladius tuus vincet adversarios
tuos*. Et ideo confortare, quia *Dominus adiutor tuus est*;
patiens esto[5], *ne*[6] *declines*[7] *in consilium*[8] quod *non potest*[9]
stabiliri[10]. Non[11] *in praeda*[12] nec *in rapina* regnum tibi
dabitur, sed de manu Domini obtinebis[13]; exspecta[14] eum,
[15]cuius *dies defecerunt*[16], quia manus Domini opprimit[17]
illum, cuius spes *in maligno posita est*, et *dies illius velut
umbra pertransibunt*.' Haec et his[18] similia illo[19] dicente,
ex illo tempore Æthelbald [20]*spem suam*[21] *in Domino*[22]
posuit[23], *nec* vana *spes*[24] illum *fefellit, nam*[25] eodem modo[26],
ordine positioneque[27] omnia, quae [28]de illo[29] vir Dei
praedixerat, et[30] non[31] aliter[32], contigerunt[33], sicut praesentis [34]rei praesens effectus[35] conprobat[36].

L. *Quanta egrotus temtamenta pertulerit[37] aut[38] quid de sua commendaverit sepultura; quae novissima mandata[39] sorori commendaverit; [40]inter verba orationis spiritum quomodo emiserit[41]*

Verum quoniam humanum genus ab initio mortalis
miseriae cotidie[42] ad finem decurrit, mutatisque[43] temporibus generationes et regna mutantur[44], ad quem terminum[45] dominus et[46] servus, doctus et indoctus, iuvenis
et senex pari conditione demergitur[47], et licet meritis,
poenis praemiisque disiungamur[48], tamen nobis[49] omnibus[50] restat exitus idem. Nam *sicut mors in Adam* [51]data est[52],

Num.
10. 35
Ps. 27. 7
Ps. 26. 9
Ps. 20. 12

Ps. 89. 9
I John
5. 19;
Ps. 143.4;
Ps. 72. 28;
Bede,
V.pr.
c. 22

I Cor.
15. 22

1 i.e. revocabit vel retorquebit C₂N.   *ab*. restituet vel reponet D.
2 *ins*. possidebis E₂.   3 *om*. E₂.   4 fugiunt H.   5 *ab*.
inquit sanctus Athelbaldo D.   6 nec H.   7 declinas V.
ab. vel a B.   8 *ins*. belli A₂E₂G.   9 potes E₂G.
10 stabilire AE₂G.   11 *ins*. enim A₂E₂G.   12 i.e. vastatione D.
13 s. eam C₂N.   *ins*. illud A₂E₂G.   opt... HE₂G.   14 exp...
VnDE₂G.   *ab*. ergo A₂E₂G.   15–16 *om*. E₂G.   17 opprimet
HD.   i.e. pressabit vel quatiet D.   18 hiis G.   19 eo C₂NE₁n.
om. A.   ab eo A₂E₂G.   s. Guthlaco D.   20–21 *om*. C₁VBAE₂G.
22 *ins*. spem suam C₁VBAE₂G.   23 ponens C₁E₂.   vel posuit C₁.
24 *ab*. C₁.   25 *ins*. et G.   26 *om*. C₁VBH.   *ins*. et A₂E₂G.

and He will bow down the necks of your enemies beneath your heel and you shall own their possessions; those who hate you shall flee from your face and you shall see their backs; and your sword shall overcome your foes. And so be strong, for the Lord is your helper; be patient lest you turn to a purpose which you cannot perform. Not as booty nor as spoil shall the kingdom be granted you, but you shall obtain it from the hand of God; wait for him whose life has been shortened, because the hand of the Lord oppresses him whose hope lies in wickedness, and whose days shall pass away like a shadow.' After Guthlac had spoken such words as these to him, from that time Æthelbald placed his hope in the Lord. Nor did an idle hope deceive him; for all these things which the man of God had prophesied about him happened in this very way, in this very order and setting, and not otherwise, as the actual outcome of present events proves.

L. *How he endured temptations in his sickness and about his commands concerning his burial, of the last instructions entrusted to his sister and how while praying he yielded up his spirit*

But since the human race daily moves on from the beginning of mortal misery to its appointed end, and as times change, generations and kingdoms change too, so master and servant, learned and unlearned, young and old, are equally overwhelmed by the same end; and even though we may differ in our deserts, our punishments and rewards, yet for all of us the same latter end remains. For just as death was prescribed in Adam,

quoque D.   27 composito C₁VB. conpositioneque A. compositioneque HD.   *om.* A₂E₂G.   28–29 *om.* HD.   30 *om.* C₁VBADE₂G.   31 *om.* C₁VB. nec E₂G.   32 *om.* C₁VB. *ins.* sibi VB.   33 *ab.* curon A.   34 eventus C₁VBA.   34–35 eventus rei praesens AE₂G.   36 significat G.   37 pertulit C₁VB.   38 at C₁.   39 manda E₁.   40 commendam C₁. commendavit C₁C₂VBNE₁. *ins.* aut C₁VB.   40–41 *om.* D.   42 quot... H.   43 mot... NE₁.   *om.* -que D.   44 mot... H.   45 finem C₁VB.   46 *om.* C₁VB.   47 dilabitur A₂E₂G.   48 disiungemur VBA. disiungimur E₂G.   49 nos C₁VBH.   50 omnes C₁VBH.   51–52 est data AE₂G.

ita et in[1] omnes[2] dominabitur. Quisquis enim huius
vitae saporem gustaverit, amaritudinem mortis evitare
nequit[3]. Contigit ergo inter haec, postquam dilectus Dei
famulus[4] Guthlac ter quinis annorum[5] voluminibus[6]
devoto[7] famulatu[8] superni[9] regis[10] solitariam duxit[11]
vitam, ecce Dominus Iesus, cum[12] famulum suum de
laboriosa huius vitae servitute ad perpetuae beatitudinis
requiem adsumere voluisset[13], quadam die, cum in[14] oratorio suo orationibus vacans perstaret, subito[15] illum inti-
morum stimulatio[16] corripuit, statimque ut se subita[17]
infirmitate[18] diri languoris vir Dei arreptum persensit, confestim[19] manum Domini [20]ad se[21] missam cognovit. Tunc[22]
se ovante[23] spiritu ad perennis[24] regni gaudia praeparare
coepit. Septem enim[25] diebus dira egritudine decoctus,
octavo[26] die ad extrema pervenit. Siquidem quarta feria ante
Pascha[27] egrotare coepit, et iterum octavo[28] die, quarta feria,
quarto[29] etiam lumine[30] paschalis[31] festi, finita egritudine
[32]ad Dominum migravit[33]. Habitabat ergo[34] cum eo sub illo
tempore unus frater, Beccel[35] nomine, cuius relatione[36]
haec de obitu viri Dei Guthlaci descripsimus; qui cum illo
die inchoatae molestiae[37] ad eum veniret, coepit ille[38] virum
Dei, ut adsolebat, de aliis interrogare. Ille autem tarde
respondens[39], demum cum sermone suspirium traxit[40]. Cui
ipse frater inquiens[41] ait: 'Domine mi, quid novi tibi accidit?
an forte nocte hac ulla te[42] infirmitatis molestia[43] tetigit?'
At ille: 'Etiam', inquit[44], 'molestia me[45] tetigit nocte hac.'
Quem item interrogans[46] ait[47]: 'Scisne, pater mi, tuae
infirmitatis causam, aut[48] quem finem huius molestae
egritudinis esse putas?' Cui vir Dei respondens inquit[49]:
'Fili mi, languoris mei causa est, ut ab his[50] membris[51]

Bede,
V.pr.
c. 37

---

1 om. C₁VBA. 2 omnibus AE₂G. ins. filius eius AE₂G.
3 nequid D. chapter heading as above, here in D. 4 om. D.
5 annis AE₂G. 6 om. AE₂G. 7 i.e. obedientia D. 8 i.e.
servitio D. 9 superno AE₂G. 10 regi AE₂G. 11 duxerat
C₂NE₁n. 12 om. C₁VBAE₂G. 13 voluit C₁VB. volens
AE₂G. 14 om. C₁. 15 subita HD. 16 ab. sticel A.
17 ins. molestia AE₂G. 18 infirmitatis AE₂G. 19 ins. ad se
C₁VB. 20-21 om. C₁VB. 22 ins. -que G. 23 ovanti E₂G.
24 perhennis VBADE₂G. 25 denique A₂E₂G. 26 octava
HD. 27 Pasca N. 28 octava HD. 29 quarta AE₂G.

so it is to have dominion over all. And whoever has tasted the sweet things of this life, cannot avoid the bitterness of death. So it happened that after Guthlac, the beloved servant of the Lord, had led a solitary life for the space of fifteen years in devoted service to the heavenly King, the Lord Jesus willed to remove his servant from the toilsome servitude of this life to the rest of everlasting blessedness. So on a certain day, while he lingered in his oratory engaged in prayer, a spasm of his inward parts suddenly seized him and, as soon as the man of God felt himself attacked by a sudden illness and by a dreadful faintness, he at once recognized that the hand of God had been laid upon him. Then, with a triumphant spirit, he began to prepare himself for the joys of the everlasting kingdom. Now for seven days he was wasted by dire sickness and on the eighth day he reached his end. For he was taken ill on the Wednesday before Easter, and again on a Wednesday, on the eighth day, being the fourth day of the Easter festival, his illness came to an end and he went to be with the Lord. Now at that time there was a brother called Beccel living with him, and it is from his account that we have written this description of the death of Guthlac, the man of God. On the day when the illness first began, he came to Guthlac and, as was his custom, began to ask the man of God about certain things. He was slow in answering, and at last breathed a sigh as he spoke. The brother said to him: 'My lord, what new thing has happened to you? Perhaps some illness has touched you during the night?' He said: 'Yes, illness has touched me during the night.' Beccel further asked him: 'Father, do you know the cause of your illness, or do you know what the end of this trouble and sickness will be?' The man of God answered him: 'My son, the cause of my sickness is that my spirit is leaving this body;

---

30 die A₂E₂G.   31 pascalis B.   32–33 mig. ad Dom. E₂.
34 autem A₂E₂G.   35 Becel H. Beccelmus D.   36 i.e. narratione
D.   37 i.e. egritudinis D.   38 illum C₁C₂VBHNE₁nD om. E₂G.
39 respondit C₁VB.   40 duxit C₁VB.   41 om. A₂E₂G.   42 om.
A₂E₂G.   43 ins. te A₂E₂G. i.e. gravis D. molestie E₂.   44 inquid
C₁VBAD.   45 change of handwriting in A.   46 interrogavit C₁VB.
47 aut C₁. om. V.   48 at E₁.   49 inquid VBD.   50 iis n. is D.
hiis G.   51 menb... BE₂.

spiritus separetur[1]; finis autem[2] infirmitatis meae erit
octavus dies[3] ,in quo, *peracto huius vitae cursu,* debeo
dissolvi[4] *et esse cum Christo; expedit enim*[5], *sarcina carnis
abiecta, agnum Dei sequi.*' His auditis, praedictus frater
flens et gemens crebris lacrimarum rivulis[6] maestas genas
rigavit[7]. Quem vir Dei consolans ait: 'Fili mi, tristitiam
ne admittas; non enim mihi[8] labor est [9]ad Dominum
meum[10], cui servivi, in requiem venire aeternam.' Tantae
ergo fidei fuit, ut *mortem, quae cunctis* mortalibus timenda[11]
formidandaque videtur, ille vel*ut*[12] requiem aut[13] *praemium
laboris* iudicaret[14]. Interea, decursis quaternarum[15] dierum
articulis, dies Paschae pervenit[16]; in qua vir Dei contra[17]
vires exsurgens[18], immolato[19] dominici corporis sacrificio
et gustato sanguinis Christi libamine, praefato fratri
verbum Dei evangelizare[20] coepit, qui numquam ante
neque[21] post tam magnam profunditatem scientiae[22] ab
ullius ore[23] audisse testatur. Denique cum septimus dies
infirmitatis ipsius devenisset[24], praefatus frater illum *circa
horam sextam*[25] visitavit, *invenitque eum recumbentem in
angulo oratorii sui contra altare; nec* tamen tunc cum eo
loquebatur, quia pondus infirmitatis *facultatem loquendi*
exemit[26]. Denique, illo poscente, ut dicta sua[27] secum
dimitteret, antequam moreretur[28], vir Dei, cum[29] parumper a pariete fessos humeros levaret[30], suspirans aiebat:
'Fili mi, quia tempus[31] nunc propinquat, ultima mandata
mea intende. Postquam spiritus hoc corpusculum de-
seruerit, perge ad sororem meam Pegam[32], et dicas[33] illi[34],
quia ideo aspectum ipsius[35] in hoc saeculo vitavi, ut in
aeternum coram Patre nostro[36] in gaudio sempiterno [37]ad
invicem [38]videamur[39]. Dices[40] quoque, ut illa *corpus* meum
in*pon*at[41] *in sarcofago*[42] et *in sindone involv*at, *quam*[43] *mihi*

Phil. 1. 23
Hier. *Vita
Pauli,*
cc. 11–12

Greg. dial.
I, Prol.

Bede,
V.pr.
c. 39

1 reputetur C₂NE₁n.   2 *om.* C₁VB.   3 *om.* N.   4 disolvi
alt. to desolvi C₁. disolvi B.   desolvi A.   5 *om.* C₁VB.
6 rivis G.   7 rigabat AE₂G.   8 michi G.   9–10 a Domino
meo V.   11 *ins.* est AE₂G.   12 ut C₁VB.   12–13 *om.* G.
13 vel C₁VBAE₂G.   14 iudicare N.   15 quattuor A₂E₂G.
16 supervenit AE₂G.   17 vel ultra D.   18 exurgens
E₁nDE₂G.   19 *ins.* -que G.   20 evanzare B.   21 nec A₂E₂G.
22 *ins.* se HD.   23 *ins.* se E₂.   24 adven... A₂E₂G.

and the end of my sickness will be on the eighth day when, having finished the course of this life, I must be released and be with Christ; for it is fitting that I should put off the burden of the flesh and follow the Lamb of God.' At these words this same brother wept and sighed, bedewing his sad cheeks with floods of tears. But the man of God consoled him, saying: 'My son, do not give way to sadness, for it is no hardship to me to enter on eternal rest with my Lord whom I have served.' So great was his faith that death, which seems something to be feared and dreaded by all mortals, he considered to be, as it were, a rest and a reward for his labour. Meanwhile four days had passed away hour by hour, and Easter Day arrived. On it the man of God rose in spite of his weakness and, having offered the sacrifice of the Lord's body and tasted the outpoured blood of Christ, he began to preach the word of God to this same brother, who bears witness that never before nor since has he heard such profundity of wisdom from the mouth of any man. Finally, when the seventh day of the illness had arrived, the said brother visited him about the sixth hour and found him lying in the corner of his oratory opposite to the altar; but Guthlac did not speak to him then, because the weight of his affliction had deprived him of the power of speech. But when Beccel asked him to entrust his parting words to him before he died, the man of God raised his weary shoulders from the wall for a little while, and with a sigh said: 'My son, since my time now draws near, listen to my last commands. After my spirit has left this poor body, go to my sister Pega and tell her that I have in this life avoided her presence so that in eternity we may see one another in the presence of our Father amid eternal joys. Tell her also to place my body in the coffin and wrap it in the

25 septimam E₂.   26 *ch. heading in* D Quanta egrotus temptamenta pertulerit aut quomodo emiserit spiritum inter verba orationis.   27 *om.* C₁VB.   28 moriretur C₁VB.   29 *om.* C₁VB.   30 levavit V. 31 *ins.* meum A₂E₂G.   32 Pegan A.   Pegean C₁VB.   Pegian C₂NE₁n. 33 dices C₁VBAE₂G.   34 *om.* C₁VBA.   ei A₂E₂G.   35 illius C₁VBAE₂G.   36 *om.* C₁VB.   meo G.   *ins.* invicem A.   *ins.* invicem nos A₂E₂G.   37–38 *om.* A₂E₂G.   39 s. nos C₂N.   videamus VBAnE₂G. 40 dicas C₂NE₁n.   41 inponet C₁VBA.   ponat A₂E₂G.   42 sarco- fagum HD.   sarcoph... E₂.   43 quod C₁VB.

Ecgburh[1] *mittebat*[2]. *Nolui quidem vivens* ullo lineo[3] tegmine corpus meum tegere, *sed pro amore dilectae*[4] Christi virginis, *quae haec* munera *mihi*[5] mittebat[6], *ad volvendum*[7] *corpus meum*[8] *reservare curavi.*' *Audiens* autem *haec*[9] praefatus[10] frater[11] exorsus[12] inquit[13]: '*Obsecro*, [14]mi *pater*[15], *quia infirmitatem* tuam intelligo[16], *et moriturum te audio*, ut dicas mihi unum, de quo olim te interrogare non ausus diu sollicitabar[17]. Nam ab eo tempore, quo tecum, domine, habitare coeperam, te loquentem vespere et mane audiebam, nescio cum quo. Propterea adiuro te, ne me sollicitum[18] de hac re post obitum tuum dimittas.' Tunc vir Dei post temporis intervallum anhelans ait: 'Fili mi, de hac re [19]sollicitari[20] noli[21]; quod enim vivens ulli hominum indicare nolui, nunc tibi manifestabo. A secundo etenim[22] anno, quo hanc[23] heremum habitare coeperam, mane vespereque semper[24] angelum[25] consolationis meae[26] ad meum colloquium Dominus[27] mittebat, qui[28] mihi[29]

II Cor. 12. 4

misteria[30], *quae non licet homini* narrare[31], monstrabat, qui duritiam[32] laboris mei caelestibus oraculis sublevabat[33], qui [34]absentia mihi[35] monstrando ut praesentia praesentabat. O fili, haec dicta mea[36] conserva, nullique alii[37] nuntiaveris, nisi Pegae[38] aut Ecgberhto[39] anachoritae, si umquam in colloquium eius tibi[40] venire contigerit, [41]qui solus haec sic fuisse cognoscet[42].' Dixerat[43], et cervicem

Virg. *Aen.* I, 371

parieti flectens longa suspiria *imo* de *pectore tra*xit, refocillatoque[44] rursus[45] spiritu, cum parumper anhelaret[46], velut melliflui floris[47] odoratus de ore ipsius processisse[48] sentiebatur, ita ut [49]totam domum[50], qua sederet, nectareus[51]

---

1 Ecgburg C_1C_2BAn. Egburh H. Egburch D. Ecgburgis A_2G. Aedburgis E_2. *ins.* abbatissa VB. 2 misit A_2E_2G. 3 linteo C_1. lintheo V. lyntheo B. 4 *bis* E_2. 5 *om.* C_1C_2VBNE$_1$n. s. mihi C_2N. 6 mittere voluit A_2E_2G. 7 involv... A_2E_2G. 8 *om.* C_1. 9 *om.* C_1VB. hoc G. 10 praedictus C_1. 11 *ins.* ita A_2E_2G. 12 i.e. aec loquens D. 13 inquid C_1VBD. ait AE_2G. 14–15 pat. mi C_2HNE$_1$nD. 15 *ins.* te AHDE$_2$. 16 intellego C_1C_2VBNE$_1$n. 17 sollicitabam C_1VB. 18 i.e. curiosum C_2N. 19–21 nol. sol. AE_2G. 20 sollicitare C_1VB. 22 *om.* A_2E_2G. etiam C_1C_2VBANE$_1$n. 23 hoc C_1. *om.* C_2VBANE$_1$nE_2G. 24 *om.* G. 25 *om.* H. 26 *ins.* angelum H. 27 *ins.* mihi C_1VBAE$_2$G. 28 quo N. 29 *om.*

cloth which Ecgburh sent me. While I was alive I was unwilling to cover my body with any linen vestment, but out of
affection for the virgin beloved of Christ who sent me this gift,
I have taken care to keep it to wrap my body in.' When the
same brother heard this he began to say: 'I beseech you, father,
since I understand that you are ill, and I hear that you are like
to die, that you will tell me one thing which I have long been
troubled about but have not dared to ask you. From the time
I first began to live with you, my lord, I have heard you
talking, evening and morning, with someone, I know not
whom. Therefore I adjure you not to leave me troubled about
this matter after your death.' Then after an interval the man
of God said with a sigh: 'My son, do not be troubled about this
thing, which while I was alive I was unwilling to tell anyone;
but now I will make it clear to you. From the second year that
I began to inhabit this desert place, every morning and evening
the Lord has sent an angel to talk with me for my consolation,
who showed me mysteries which it is not lawful for man to
utter, who relieved the hardness of my toil with heavenly
oracles, and who revealed to me things which were absent as
though they were present. O, my son, keep these words of
mine and tell them to no one except to Pega or Ecgberht the
anchorite, if ever you should happen to converse with him, for
he alone will know that such things have happened to me.'
With these words he laid his head against the wall, heaved
a very deep sigh and revived his spirit again: after he had
breathed with difficulty for a short time, there seemed to pro-
ceed from his mouth the odour of sweet-smelling flowers, so
that the scent of nectar filled the whole building in which he

C_1VBAE$_2$G.   michi E$_1$.   30 myst... C$_2$nD.   31 *ins.* mihi AE$_2$G.
32 duritia E$_2$.   33 sublevavit C$_2$NE$_1$n.   34 *ins.* denique A$_2$E$_2$G.
34-35 mi. abs. A$_2$E$_2$G.   36 *om.* VB.   37 alio C$_1$C$_2$VBHNE$_1$n.
38 Pegiae C$_2$NE$_1$n.   39 Ecgberchto C$_1$.   Egberto H.   Egberchto D.
Ecgberto nE$_2$.   Egberto G.   40 te A$_2$E$_2$G.   41-42 *om.* A$_2$E$_2$G.
43 s. haec C$_2$ND.   *ins.* haec A$_2$E$_2$G.   44 refocila... C$_2$VBNE$_1$nD.   i.e.
se creato vel confortato D.   *om.* -que G.   45 *ins.* -que G.   46 ane-
laret E$_2$G.   47 roris C$_1$VB.   48 emanare A$_2$E$_2$G.   procedisse
C$_1$C$_2$VBAHNE$_1$n.   49-50 dom. tot. H.   50 *ins.* in G.
51 nectarius C$_2$NE$_1$n.

odor inflaret[1]. Nocte vero sequenti[2], cum praefatus
frater nocturnis vigiliis incumberet, igneo candore a
mediae[3] noctis spatio usque in auroram totam domum
circumsplendescere videbat. Oriente autem sole, vir Dei,
sublevatis parumper membris[4], velut[5] exsurgens[6], cum
supramemorato fratre loqui coepit dicens: 'Fili mi, prae-
para te[7] in[8] iter tuum pergere[9], nam[10] me nunc tempus
cogit[11] ab his[12] membris[13] dissolvi, et decursis huius vitae
terminis ad infinita gaudia spiritus [14]transtolli[15] malit[16].'

Bede,
V.pr.
c. 39

Dixit[17], et extendens manus ad altare, *munivit se com-*
munione corporis et sanguinis Christi, *atque elevatis oculis ad*
caelum extensisque in altum manibus, animam ad gaudia perpetuae exultationis[18] *emisit*[19]. Inter haec praefatus[20] frater
subito caelestis luminis splendore domum repleri tur-
remque[21] velut igneam a[22] terra in caelum erectam prospicit[23], in cuius splendoris conparatione, cum tunc sol
in medio caelo steterat[24], velut lucerna in die pallidescere[25]
videbatur. Cantantibus[26] quoque angelis[27] spatium totius
aeris detonari[28] audiebatur[29]; insulam etiam illam diversorum[30] aromatum odoriferis spiraminibus inflari[31]
cerneres[32]. Deinde supramemoratus frater inmensa[33] for-
midine tremefactus, eximii[34] splendoris coruscationem[35]
sustinere non valens, arrepta[36] navicula portum reliquit[37]
ac deinde, quo vir Dei praeceperat, coepto[38] itinere perrexit. Deveniens quoque[39] ad sanctam[40] Christi[41] virginem[42] Pegam[43], fraterna sibi mandata omnia[44] ex ordine
narravit. Illa vero, his[45] auditis, velut in praecipitium[46]
delapsa, se solo premens[47], inmensi maeroris[48] molestia

---

1 inflammaret C_1VB. repleret A_2E_2G. infunderet D.   2 sequente
C_1VBAE$_2$G.   3 medio C_2NE$_1$n. medii C_1VB.   4 menb... B.
5 *om.* A_2E_2G.   6 exurgens E$_1$nDE$_2$G.   7 *ins.* et VBA$_1E_2$G.
8 *om.* E$_2$.   9 perge C_1VBAHDE$_2$G.   10 iam D.   11 coegit
VB. *ins.* ut AE$_2$G.   12 is D. hiis E$_2$.   13 menb... B.
14–15 meus debeat transferri A_2E_2G.   15 transtuli C_1VBA.
transferri C_2NE$_1$n. i.e. transferri D.   16 *ab.* vel magis vult C_2N.
mallit VBA.   17 s. haec C_2N.   18 exaltationis G.   19 *ins.*
anno ab incarnatione Domini nostri DCCXV (*ab.* septingentesimo quinto
decimo) D. *extra chapter heading in* D. Qualiter turris illa ignea a
ministro illius visa sit et de angelico cantu et quomodo sepultus sit.
20 praedictus n.   21 turrimque HD.   22 e C_2HNE$_1$nD   23 *hand-*

sat. Now on that night, when the same brother was engaged
upon his nightly vigils, he saw the whole house lit up with
a fiery brightness from midnight until dawn. And when the
sun rose, the man of God, raising his body for a short time as
though he were getting up, spoke to the brother and said:
'My son, get ready for your journey, for now the time has
arrived for me to be loosed from the body; the end of my life
has come and my spirit is eager to be carried away to joys
without end.' He said these words and, stretching his hands
towards the altar, he fortified himself by the communion of
Christ's Body and Blood, then raising his eyes to heaven and
stretching out his hands aloft, he sent forth his spirit to the joys
of perpetual bliss. Meanwhile this same brother suddenly beheld the house filled with the splendour of heavenly light and
a tower as of fire stretching from earth to heaven, in comparison
with whose splendour the sun, though it was in mid heaven,
seemed to grow pale like a lamp in daylight. The whole air
was heard to thunder with angelic songs, while one would have
thought the island to be filled with the sweet scents of many
kinds of spices. Then that same brother, trembling with great
terror, was unable to bear the glitter of this marvellous splendour; so he took a boat and, leaving the landing-place, then
began the journey which the man of God had commanded
him. And finding the holy virgin of Christ Pega, he told her
in order all her brother's commands. When she heard them she
fell down in a headlong fall, and as she lay upon the ground she
withered away to the very marrow by the mighty affliction of

writing changes back to first hand A.   24 steterit C₂HNE₁n   *ab.* vel starqu C₂.
resplenderet A₂. splenderet E₂G.   25 pallescere C₂NnG.   palescere E₁.
26 cantibus C₂HNE₁nD.   27 angelicis C₂HNE₁nD.   28 detonare
AE₂G.   29 *ins.* insuper A₂E₂G. audiebat G.   30 diversarum C₁VB.
31 perfundi A₂E₂G.   32 cerneret C₁VBA. persensit A₂E₂G.   33 inmenso C₁C₂VBANE₁.   *alt. to* immensa n.   34 eximiae C₁VBA.
35 chorusc... H.   36 arepta E₁.   37 reliquid C₁VBDAE₂.
requirit C₂NE₁n.   38 certo C₂NE₁n.   39 ergo A₂E₂G.
40 *ins.* virginem A₂E₂G.   41 Dei C₁VB.   42 *om.* A₂E₂G.
43 Pegean C₁. Pegan VBA. Pegian C₂NE₁n.   44 omni
C₁C₂VBAHNE₁nE₂. *om.* G.   45 is D. hiis G.   46 i.e. in
deiectionem D.   47 sternens A₂E₂G. i.e. strenuens D.   48 i.e.
tristicie D. memoris G.

medullitus[1] emarcuit[2], lingua[3] siluit, [4]labrum obmutuit[5], omnique vivali[6] vigore velut exanimis evanuit[7]. Post vero [8]interventum temporis[9], ceu somno[10] expergefacta, [11]imis de pectoris[12] fibris[13] longa suspiria trahens, arbitrio omnipotentis[14] grates[15] egit. Postera vero die, secundum praecepta[16] beati viri[17] insulam[18] devenientes, totum locum omnesque[19] domus[20] velut ambrosio[21] odore repletas[22] invenerunt. Illa vero[23] Dei famula trium dierum spatiis fraternum spiritum divinis laudibus caelo commendans[24], tertia die[25] secundum praeceptum illius felicia membra in oratorio suo[26] humo tecta [27]condiderat[28].

LI. *Qualiter corpus ipsius sine corruptione post duodecim menses repertum est*

Bede,
V.pr.
c. 42

Volens autem[29] divina pietas *latius monstrare, quanta in gloria* vir sanctus[30] *post* obitum *viveret, cuius ante mortem vita* sublimibus crebrisque miraculorum indiciis *populis, tribubus*[31], *gentibus late ubique fulgebat, addidit quoque*[32] *aeternae commemorationis indicium. Transactis enim*[33] *sepulturae* eius *bis senis mensium orbibus*[34], *inmisit*[35] Deus[36] *in animum* sororis ipsius[37], *ut* fraternum corpus alio sepulchro[38] *reconderet. Adgregatis ergo fratribus presbiterisque*[39], *necnon et aliis ecclesiasticis gradibus, die* exitus ipsius *aperientes sepulchrum*[40], *invenerunt* [41]corpus totum[42] *integrum, quasi adhuc viveret, et lentis*[43] *artuum flexibus*[44] *multo potius dormienti quam mortuo similius videbatur. Sed et vestimenta*[45] *omnia, quibus involutum*[46] erat, [47]non solum[48] intemerata, verum etiam antiqua novitate et pristino*[49] candore splendebant. Quod

---

1 i.e. intimet vel evisceruntur D.   2 i.e. elanguit D.   3 linguam V.   4 soluit E₂.   4–5 *om.* A₂E₂G.   6 vitali A₂E₂G.   7 *hand changes in* C₁.   8–9 temp. int. C₁VB.   *om.* A₂E₂G.   10 sompno G.   11–12 imo de pectore A₂E₂G.   12 pectore VBH.   13 fissuris C₂NE₁n. *om.* A₂E₂G. i.e. divisionibus N. i.e. e visceribus D.   14 potentis HADE₂G.   15 gratias AE₂G.   16 praeceptum AE₂G.   17 *ins.* in A₂E₂G.   18 *ins.* ambo A₂E₂G.   19 *om.* -que C₁VBAE₂G.   20 domos C₁VBAE₂G.   21 ambrosiano C₂NE₁n. ambrosiae D. i.e. dulci D.   22 repletum C₁VB.   23 viri C₁. veri VB.   24 commendavit

her grief; her tongue was silent, her lips were mute, and she lost all life and strength, just as if she were dead. After an interval she aroused herself as though from sleep and, heaving deep sighs from the very bottom of her heart, she gave thanks for the Almighty's judgement. On the next day they came to the island in accordance with the commands of the blessed man, and found the whole place and all the dwellings filled with a sort of ambrosial odour. The handmaiden of God spent three days in commending the spirit of her brother to heaven with divine praises, and on the third day in accordance with his command she buried his blessed limbs in his oratory, covering them with earth.

LI. *How twelve months afterwards his body was found without corruption*

But the divine compassion wished to show still further in what glory the holy man lived after his death, whose life had shone forth before his death by frequent and sublime signs and miracles to peoples, tribes and nations far and wide: so He added a proof of His eternal remembrance. Twelve months after his burial God put it into the heart of his sister to place her brother's body in another sepulchre. So, having gathered together the brethren and the priests, as well as other ecclesiastical ranks, they opened the sepulchre on the anniversary of his death, and found his body whole as if it were still alive, and the joints of his limbs flexible and much more like those of a sleeping than a dead man. Moreover all his garments in which he had been wrapped were not only undefiled but shone with all their former newness and original brightness. When those who were

C_1VB. commendabat C_2NE$_1$n. 25 *om.* VB. 26–27 tect. hum. G.
28 conderunt C_1VBA. condiderunt C_2NE$_1$n. recondidit A_2E_2G. i.e. sepeliebat D. 29 itaque C_1VB. 30 Dei E_2. 31 *ins.* et A_2E_2G.
32 *om.* C_2NE$_1$n. 33 autem C_1VB. 34 diebus A_2E_2G. 35 s. divina pietas N. 36 *om.* C_2NE$_1$n. 37 eius AE$_2$G. 38 sepulcro G.
39 *om.* -que A_2E_2G. 40 sepulcrum E_2G. 41–42 tot. corp. C_1VBAE$_2$G. 43 *ab.* i.e. habundantibus N. 43–44 liβepacum N.
44 coloribus A_2E_2G. 45 *ab.* videbantur C_2N. 46 involutus HD.
47–48 *om.* VB. 49 pristina C_1VB.

ubi, [1]qui intererant, prospexerunt, statim stupefacti *trementes steterunt, adeo ut vix* fari[2] *potuissent, vix miraculum intueri auderent, et vix ipsi*[3] *quid agerent nossent.* Quod ubi [4]Christi famula[5] Pega[6] prospexit[7], spiritali[8] gaudio[9] commota[10] sacratum[11] corpus cum divinarum [12]laudum venerantia[13] in sindone, quam eo vivente Ecgberht anachorita[14] in hoc officium mittebat[15], revolvit; [16]sed et[17] sarcofagum[18]non[19]humo[20]terrae condidit, immo[21]etiam[22] in[23] memoriale quoddam posuit, quod[24] nunc ab[25] Æthelbaldo[26] rege miris ornamentorum structuris in venerantiam[27] divinae potentiae aedificatum conspicimus, ubi triumphale corpus tanti viri usque in hodierni[28] temporis cursum feliciter pausat,[29] per cuius[30] intercessionem miserationis divinae indulgentiam, quisquis integra fide pulsaverit, inpetrabit. O virum beatae memoriae, o magistrum divinae gratiae, o *vas electionis*, o medicum salutis, o praeconem veritatis, o thesaurum sapientiae ! o *quanta gravitas*[31], *quanta*[32] *dignitas in verbis et*[33] *confabulation*ibus illius erat ! *quam alacer*[34], *quam efficax*[35] in discernendis[36] causis fuit ! *quam in absolvendis* [37]*scripturarum quaestionibus*[38] *promtus*[39] *et facilis !* [40]*quam inremisso*[41] *famulatu*[42] Deo servierat[43], in tantum, ut *numquam in illius ore nisi Christus, numquam in illius corde nisi pietas, nihil*[44] *in ipsius*[45] *animo nisi caritas, nisi pax, nisi misericordia, nisi indulgentia perstabat*[46]. *Nemo vidit illum iratum, nemo elatum*[47], *nemo superbum, nemo commotum*[48], *nullus maerentem*[49]; sed *unus*[50] *idemque*[51] *semper*[52] permanens, *laetitiam in vultu*, gratiam in ore, suavitatem in mente, prudentiam in pectore, humilitatem in corde *praeferebat*[53], ita ut *extra*[54] humanam *naturam* notis ignotisque esse[55] *videretur.*

Acts 9. 15

Sulpicius
Severus,
Vita S.
Martini,
c. 25, 6

c. 27, 2

c. 27, 1

1 cum C₁VB.   1–4 *om.* E₂.   2 i.e. loqui D.   3 ipsius N.
4 cum C₁VB.   4–5 fam. Chr. AE₂G.   6 Pege C₁VB.   Pegia
C₂NE₁n.   7 perspexit C₁VB.   8 spirituali nE₂G.   9 *ins.* repleta
C₁VBAE₂G. *ins.* et A₂E₂G.   10 commotata NE₁.   *ab.* vel repleta N.
alt. from commotata *to* commut... C₂.   commutata n.   *om.* VB.
11 sacrum E₂G.   12 divinorum C₁BANE₁.   *alt. to* divinarum C₂.
12–13 ven. laud. HD.   14 ancho... C₁A.   15 miserat A₂E₂G.
16–17 *om.* A₂E₂G.   18 *ins.* vero A₂E₂G.   sarcophagum nE₂.   19 *ins.*
solum C₁VB.   *ins.* in E₂.   20 humum C₁VB.   21 *om.* A₂E₂G.
22 sed A₂E₂G.   23 *om.* C₁VB.   24 s. sarcophagum D.   25 *om.*

present saw this, they immediately stood trembling and amazed, so that they could scarcely speak or even venture to look upon the miracle, and hardly knew what to do. When Pega, the handmaiden of Christ, saw this, she was stirred with spiritual joy, and again wrapped the sacred body with veneration and divine praises in the cloth which the anchorite Ecgberht had sent him for that purpose while he was still alive; however, she did not hide the coffin in the ground, but placed it instead in a certain monument; and now, built around it, we behold wonderful structures and ornamentations put up by King Æthelbald in honour of the divine power: here the triumphant body of the great man rests in blessedness until this present time: and by his intercession whoever makes urgent request with absolute faith gains the grace of divine mercy. O man of blessed memory! O master of divine grace! O chosen vessel! O physician of salvation! O herald of the truth! O treasure of wisdom! What gravity, what dignity, in words and conversation was his! how swift and competent he was in pleading causes! how quick and ready in solving the problems of Scripture! how he served God with unremitting service, so that never was any name on his lips but the name of Christ, never anything in his heart but piety; nothing but charity, nothing but peace, mercy and tenderness was found in his spirit. No one saw him angry, puffed up, proud, ruffled or gloomy; but he was always the same, and showed joy in his face, grace in his lips, sweetness in his mind, prudence in his breast, humility in his heart, so that he seemed both to known and unknown to be more than human by nature.

C_2n.   26 Æþelrædo VB. Ethelbaldo H. Eþelbaldo N. Aeðelbaldo A. Edelbaldo E_2. Adelbaldo G.   27 reverentiam AE_2G. i.e. in honorem D. 28 hodiernum C_2NE_1n.   29–30 et per eius A_2E_2G.   31 gravitatis C_1VB. 32 om. VB.   33 ins. in G.   34 ab. promptus C_2N.   35 ab. agilis vel capax C_2N. i.e. agilis vel acutus D. ab. glau A.   36 i.e. divisis N. 37 obs... C_1. i.e. deliberandis D.   37–38 quaest. script. C_1VBAG. 39 promptus C_1C_2VBNE_1nE_2G. s. erat N.   40–46 om. A_2E_2G.   41 i.e. dissolubili vel insegni D.   42 famulato A.   43 serviebat A. serviret C_1C_2VBHNE_1nE_2G.   44 nichil E_1nD.   45 illius D.   47 elevatum AHDG. commotum E_2.   48 elevatum E_2.   49 mergentem N.   50 unius E_2. 51 idem G.   52 om. E_2. add. -que G.   53 prof... C_1VB. preparabat C_2NE_1n. vel proferabat N.   54 vel extra D.   55 om. C_1VB.

LII. *Qualiter post obitum suum Æthelbaldo se ostendit et quae ventura essent sibi per signa manifestavit*

Postquam ergo praefatus exul Æthelbald in longinquis[1] regionibus habitans obitum beati patris Guthlaci audivit, qui ante solus refugium et consolatio laborum illius[2] erat, subita[3] arreptus[4] maestitia[5] ad corpus ipsius pervenit, sperans in Domino daturum[6] sibi refocillationem[7] aliquam laboris sui per intercessionem [8]tanti viri[9] Guthlaci. Qui cum ad sepulchrum[10] illius[11] successisset[12], lacrimans aiebat: 'Pater mi, tu scis miserias meas, tu semper adiutor mei[13] fuisti[14], te vivente non desperabam[15] in angustiis[16],

Cf. Ps. 80. 8

adfuisti mihi[17] in periculis multis; per te invocabam Dominum, et liberavit me; modo quo vertam faciem meam, unde erit auxilium mihi[18], aut[19] quis consiliabitur[20] mecum[21], pater optime[22], si me dereliqueris, [23]quis me

Ps. 30. 15; Bede, *V.pr.* c. 22

consolabitur[24]? *in te spera*bam, *nec* me *spes fefellit.*' Haec et [25]alia multa[26] proloquens, sese[27] solo[28] sternebat, et supplex orans crebris lacrimarum fluentis totum vultum rigabat. Nocturnis autem[29] adpropiantibus umbris, cum in quadam[30] casula[31], qua ante, vivente Guthlaco, hospitari[32] solebat, pernoctans maestam mentem huc illucque[33] iactabat[34], parumper nocturnis orationibus transmissis[35], cum [36]lumina levi[37] somno[38] dimitteret[39], subito expergefactus, totam cellulam in qua quiescebat[40] inmensi luminis

Gen. 15. 1 Deut. 31. 7 Ps. 77. 35 Num. 21. 3

splendore circumfulgescere vidit; et cum ab[41] ignota visione terreretur, extimplo beatum Guthlacum coram[42] adstantem[43] angelico splendore amictum prospicit[44] dicentem[45] ei[46]: '*Noli timere, robustus esto,* quia *Deus adiutor* [47]tuus *est*[48]; propterea[49] veni ad te, quia *Dominus*[50] per

---

1 *ab.* fyr A. 2 ipsius C₂AHNE₁nDE₂G. 3 *om.* C₁VB.
4 corr... C₁VB. *ins.* subita C₁VB. 5 mestia VB. 6 dari
C₂NE₁n. dandam A₂E₂G. 7 refocil... C₁C₂VBHNE₁n.
8–9 sancti E₂. 10 sepulcrum G. 11 ipsius HD. *om.* VB.
12 *ab.* pervenisset C₂D. successit A. accessisset A₂E₂G. 13 meus
C₁VBAE₂G. 14 *om.* C₁. 15 disp... C₁A. *ins.* quia E₂G.
16 *ins.* meis VB. 17 *om.* C₁VB. michi nG. 18 michi G.
19 a A. *ab.* A₂. at E₁. 20 consolabitur HD. 21 *erase* -cum
C₁A₂. *om.* -cum HDE₂G. *ins.* et quis HD. 22 obt... C₁. *ins.*

LII. *How after his death he showed himself to Æthelbald and by signs revealed to him what was to come to pass*

Now when the same exile Æthelbald, dwelling in distant parts, heard of the death of the blessed father Guthlac, who alone had been his refuge and consolation in his affliction, he was seized with sudden grief and came to the saint's body, hoping in the Lord that he would grant him some respite from his affliction by the intercession of that great man Guthlac. Having approached the sepulchre, he said tearfully: 'My father, you know my wretchedness, you have always been my helper; while you were alive, I did not despair when in trouble, and you stood by me in many dangers: through you I called upon the Lord, and He freed me. But now whither shall I turn my face? Whence shall come help, and who, most excellent father, will give me counsel; who will console me if you leave me? In you have I hoped and the hope has not failed me.' With these and many other such words he stretched himself on the ground in humble prayer, and bedewed his whole face with continual floods of tears. When the shades of evening fell, he spent the night in a certain hut in which he used to stay when Guthlac was alive, his sorrowing mind tossing hither and thither. Shortly after, when his nightly prayers were finished and he had closed his eyes in light slumbers, he was suddenly aroused, and saw the whole cell in which he was resting lit up with the splendour of a mighty light. As he lay terrified by this same vision, he suddenly saw the blessed Guthlac standing before him robed in angelic splendour, while he said to him: 'Fear not, be strong, for God is your helper. I have come to you because the Lord has heard your prayers through my inter-

mihi consiliabitur HD.   23 dereliquis C₁.   derelinquis VBAE₂G. 23–24 *om.* A₂HDE₂G.   25 *ins.* his similia VB.   25–26 mult. al. C₁C₂HNE₁n. 27 se HD.   28 *om.* C₂E₁n.   *ins.* ab N.   29 *om.* C₁VB.   30 quandam VB.   31 casulam VB.   32 hospitare C₁VBA.   33 *ins.* cogitando E₂G. 34 iactabatur H.   iactaret A₂E₂G.   35 intermissis A₂E₂G.   36–37 luminalem H.   38 sompno E₂G.   39 demitt… C₂NE₁n.   40 *ins.* in D. 41 *om.* E₂.   42 *ins.* se E₂.   43 *ins.* vidit AE₂G.   44 *om.* A.   *ins.* et A₂E₂G.   45 dicens C₁VB.   46 *om.* A₂E₂G.   47–48 est tuus HD. 49 *ins.* enim A₂E₂G.   50 *om.* VB.

intercessionem meam[1] *exaudivit preces* tuas. Noli tristari[2],
dies enim miseriarum[3] tuarum[4] praeterierunt, et finis
laborum tuorum adest[5]; nam priusquam sol bis senis
voluminibus annilem[6] circumvolverit orbem, sceptris[7]
regni donaberis[8].' Non solum autem[9], ut ferunt[10],
regnum[11] sibi prophetavit, sed et longitudinem dierum
suorum[12] et finem vitae suae sibi in[13] ordine[14] manifestavit. Ille vero [15]e contra[16] dicebat[17]: 'Domine[18], *quod
signum* mihi *erit*, quia omnia sic eveniant[19]?' Guthlac
respondit: '*Signum* [20]tibi *hoc*[21] erit; cum crastina dies
advenerit, antequam [22]tertia hora[23] fiat, his[24] qui in [25]hoc
loco[26] habitant[27], unde non sperant, solatia alimentorum
donabuntur.'[28]Haec dicens [29]sanctus vir[30], lux quae coram[31]
apparuit[32] ab [33]oculis illius[34] recessit. Nec mora, dicta[35]
effecta[36] secuta[37] sunt; nam priusquam tertia [38]diei hora[39]
propinquasset[40], signum in portu[41] pulsatum[42] audierunt
hominesque[43] illic insperata[44] solatia portantes conspiciunt.
Exin ipse, omnia quae sibi dicta erant[45] recordans, in-
dubitata[46] spe[47] futura[48] fore credebat [49]fidemque inseduci-
bilem[50] in vaticiniis[51] viri Dei defixit[52]; nec [53]illum fides[54]
fefellit. Ex illo enim tempore usque in hodiernum diem[55]
infulata[56] regni ipsius felicitas per tempora consequentia[57]
de die in diem crescebat.

Mark 13.4
Luke 2.12

LIII. *Qualiter caecus*[58] *quidam post obitum ipsius per
sacratum*[59] *ante*[60] *salem sanatus est*

Nec etiam defuncto ac sepulto Christi famulo Guthlaco
signa virtutum ac sanitatum, quae per illum[61] viventem

1 *ins.* Dominus VB.   2 tristificari C₁VBDE₂G.   contristari E₂.
3 miseriae C₁VBAHDE₂G.   4 tuae C₁VBAHDE₂G.   5 iam
advenit HD.   6 annalem C₂nA₂E₂G.   *ab.* gear A.   7 sceptrum
C₁VB.   8 dominaberis C₁VBHD.   9 *ins.* haec VB.
10 fertur AE₂G.   fecerunt N.   11 *om.* C₁VB.   12 suarum
C₂NE₁n.   13 ex A₂E₂G.   14 *ins.* in D.   15-16 *om.*
A₂E₂G.   17 *ab.* cwæþ A.   18 *ins.* mi C₂NE₁n.   19 *ins.*
sanctus VB.   evenient H.   20-21 hoc tibi C₂NE₁n.   22-23 hor.
tert. AE₂G.   24 is D.   hiis G.   25-26 loco hoc AE₂G.
27 habitabant H.   *alt. from* habitabant D.   28-29 hec eo dicente

cession. Do not be sad, for the days of your miseries have passed away, and the end of your afflictions is at hand: for before the sun has passed through its yearly course in twelve revolutions you shall be given the sceptre of your kingdom.' It is related that he not merely prophesied to him about his kingdom, but also revealed to him in order the length of his days and the end of his life. On the other hand Æthelbald said: 'My lord, what sign will there be to me that all these things will happen thus?' Guthlac answered: 'This shall be a sign to you: when tomorrow comes, before the third hour, food will be given to relieve those who dwell in this place, from an unhoped-for source.' As the holy man uttered these words, the light which had appeared before him departed from his sight. The event followed the words without delay; for before the third hour of the day had arrived, they heard the signal sounded at the landing-stage, and they saw some men bringing thither unhoped-for food. Then Æthelbald, remembering all the things which had been said to him, believed with unwavering faith that they would happen, and placed unshakeable confidence in the prophecies of the man of God: nor did his faith deceive him. For from that time until the present day, his happiness as king over his realm has grown in succeeding years from day to day.

LIII. *How a blind man, after the saint's death, was healed by salt previously consecrated*

But even when the servant of Christ was dead and buried, the signs of miracles and of healing which the Lord had granted

A₂E₂G.   29 *ab.* s. erat C₂N.   29–30 *om.* C₁VBAHDE₂G.   31 i.e. manifeste N. *ins.* eo E₂.   32 apar... V.   33–34 oculis eius AE₂G. illius oc. H.   34 *ins.* Æthelbaldi C₂n.   *ab.* s. Æthelbaldi N.   35 *s.* Guthlaci N.   36 *ab.* gepor (?) A.   37 sequuta H.   38–39 hor. die. H. 40 approp... G.   41 porta C₂NE₁n.   42 pulsato VB.   43 -quae C₁. 44 insperate B.   45 sunt AE₂G.   46 indubitate C₁. *alt. from* indubita AH. *ins.* fide C₁VBAE₂G.   47 spei AE₂G.   48 futurae AE₂G.   49–52 *om.* A₂E₂G.   50 i.e. intitubantem N.   51 vaticinis C₁. 53–54 fid. ill. AE₂G.   55 *om.* E₂G.   56 *ab.* decorata C₂. i.e. decorata vel honorata N.   57 sequentia A₂E₂G.   58 *om.* VB. 59 sacratam C₂.   60 ab eo C₂N.   61 *om.* A₂E₂G.

Dominus hominibus donabat, per [1]invocationem intercessionis[2] ipsius [3]ubique candescere[4] praesentem [5]ad usque[6] diem[7] cessaverunt[8], ut qui vivens pomposis[9] virtutum rumoribus se elevare noluit[10], quanti meriti vel quantae valitudinis erat[11] post obitum suum per plurima miraculorum trophea[12] monstraretur. Erat namque[13] quidam vir[14] paterfamilias in provincia Wissa[15], cuius oculi bis senis mensium orbibus[16], adempto visendi[17] lumine[18], fulvis albuginis nubibus tegebantur[19], ita ut splendentis diei lumina a furvae[20] noctis caligine secernere[21] nequiret. [22]Qui cum[23], reprobatis pigmentorum fomentis[24], medendi salutem desperaret, [25]perpetuamque sibi [26]luminis orfanitatem[27] inminere conperit[28], tandem invento salubri consilio, ad corpus sacratissimum viri[29] Dei Guthlaci se[30] duci rogavit dicens: ' *Scio certe et confido, quia si aliquid de rebus* ab eo *sacratis*[31] *lumina mea tetigerit, cito sanabor*, et visus oculorum meorum mihi[32] reddetur[33].' Amici autem illius ut ipse rogaverat fecerunt; duxerunt quidem illum ad portum insulae Crugland[34] et illic [35]ascensa[36] navi[37], devenientes[38] insulam, adpetierunt[39] colloquium venerabilis [40]Christi virginis[41] Pegae[42]; quae ferventis[43] fidei illius spem indubiam[44] conperiens, intra oratorium quo[45] corpus beati[46] Guthlaci recumberet[47], duci[48] permisit. Illa [49]quoque partem[50] glutinati[51] salis a sancto Guthlaco[52] ante consecratam arripiens, in aquam offertoriam[53] levi rasura mittebat[54]; ipsam[55] denique[56] aquam, cum intra palpebras[57] caeci guttatim stillaret, mirabile dictu! ad primum tactum primae guttae, detrusis caecitatis nubibus, oculis infusum lumen redditum est; priusquam enim alterius oculi

Bede,
V.pr.
c. 23

1-2 intercessionem invocationemque E₂.   2 intercessionem A.
ins. -que A₂G.   3 illius HG.   3-4 presbiteri usque in A₂E₂G.
5-6 *om.* A₂E₂G.   7 *ins.* non E₂.   8 cesa... C₁.   9 *ab.* ornamentosis C₂N.   10 despexit A₂E₂G.   11 esset A₂E₂G.
12 *ab.* sigeas N.   13 autem N.   14 *om.* H.   15 Wisa HD.
vivissa N.   16 curriculis A₂E₂G.   17 videndi AE₂G.
18 numine C₁C₂ANE₁n. *ab.* vel lumine C₂.   19 fugebantur.
alt. to fugabantur C₁.   20 tetrae A₂E₂G.   21 *ab.* deliberare
C₂N.   22 nequivissent VB.   22-23 *illegible in* A.   24 favomentis D.   i.e. adiutoris vel auxiliis D.   25 disp... C₁.
25-28 *om.* A₂E₂G.   26-27 orf. lum. A.   27 orbanitatem

to men through him in his lifetime, did not cease to shine every-where by means of his invocation and intercession right up to the present day. When he was alive, he did not wish to exalt himself by boastful stories of miracles, and yet the greatness of his merits and his strength were proved after his death by many miraculous trophies. For there was a certain father of a family in the province of Wissa, whose eyes had been covered by yellowish clouds of film and deprived of light and vision for twelve months, so that he could not distinguish between the light of a radiant day and the darkness of black night. And despairing of healing it by useless fomentations and juices, he found himself threatened with the perpetual deprivation of sight. At length he hit upon a wholesome plan and asked to be taken to the most sacred body of Guthlac, the man of God, saying: 'I know well and believe that if some object consecrated by him touches my eyes, I shall be quickly healed and the sight of my eyes will be restored to me.' So his friends did as he asked and, boarding a boat, they came to the island and bringing him to the landing-place of that island of Crowland, there sought out Pega, the reverend virgin of Christ. She, recognizing his undoubting hope and fervent faith, allowed him to be led into the oratory in which the body of the blessed Guthlac lay. She also took a piece of glutinous salt which had previously been consecrated by St Guthlac and, grating it lightly, let the scrapings fall into consecrated water. She made this water drip, drop by drop, under the blind man's eyelids and, marvellous to relate, at the first touch of the first drop, the clouds of blindness were scattered and the light returned, pouring into his eyes. Now, before the healing water had been poured into

C_2VNE_1n. *ab.* privationem C_2N. orphan... HD. 29 vir C_1. 30 *om.* C_1AE_2G. 31 sacrificatis C_1AHDE_2G. sanctificatis A_2. 32 michi G. 33 reddet n. 34 Cruglond A. Cruglod B. Crouland D. quae Cruland dicitur A_2E_2G. 35-37 nav. asc. HD. 36 assc... VB. 38 *ins.* in A_2E_2G. 39 adpeterunt A. appetiverunt D. petierunt A_2E_2G. 40-41 virg. Christ. HD. 42 Pegiae $C_1C_2BNE_1n$. *alt. from* Pegiae V. 43 verventis C_1. 44 indubitam C_1VBAHD. indubitatam $C_2NE_1nA_2E_2G$. 45 qua C_1. 46 *om.* V. 47 recumbebat A_2E_2G. 48 s. eum C_2N. 49-50 *illegible in* A. 51 glutinam C_1VBHD. glutina A. *om.* A_2E_2G. 52 *ins.* paulo E_2G. 53 oportorium C_1. opertoriam VBHD. 54 misit A_2E_2G. 55 *ins.* -que A_2E_2G. 56 deinde A_2E_2G. 57 palpebris N.

palpebris salutaris limpha[1] infunderetur, quicquid domi[2] esset [3]in ordine[4] narrabat, visumque sibi in[5] eodem momento donatum[6] fatebatur[7]. Deinde[8], postquam diu clausas gratia[9] per gratiam frontis[10] reclusit fenestras, cognovit inventum olim quod perdidit lumen, dux se ducentibus factus est revertens[11] rursus[12]. Exin ubi lucem de fonte luminis hausit, ibat quo venerat, nec sic[13] reversus[14] ut erat, viditque videntes[15] quos prius videre negavit, *grates* Deo *persolvens dignas*, quas[16] nullus[17] reddere nescit[18].

Virg. *Aen.*
1, 600

1 limphe E₂. 2 in domo C₂NHD. in ea domo A₂E₂G.
3-4 *om.* A₂E₂G. 5 *om.* A₂E₂G. 6 *ab.* esse C₂. redon...
A₂E₂G. 7 *omission mark in* A₂. E₂ *and* G *end here with:* Ad laudem et gloriam summi Dei qui est mirabilis in sanctis suis, qui vivit et regnat in saecula saeculorum. Amen. Explicit vita sancti Gudlaci confessoris. (*The last sentence only partly legible in* G *owing to cut margin.*)
s. eo N. 8 dein A. H *ends here.* 9 *om.* A. i.e. Deus C₂D.
10 fontis A. 11 reversus C₁VB. 12 rursum C₁VB.

the lid of his other eye, he described in detail all that was in the house, and said that sight had at that moment been given to him. Then after grace had, by grace, opened the windows of his head which had been so long closed, he realized that the light which he had once lost was found, and returning home he became a guide to those who were his guides. And when he had drawn light from the fountain of light, he went back to the place whence he had come; but he did not return as he was before, for he saw those who saw him and whom he once said he could not see. And he returned fitting thanks to God, such as none could fail to give.

13 s. erat C₂N.   14 *ins.* est C₁A.   15 *ins.* eum A.   16 s. scit C₂.
17 ullus C₁V.   18 Explicit liber sancti Guthlaci anachoritae C₂N. Explicit vita sancti Guthlaci confessoris n.   *ins.* Omnipotens aeterne Deus qui omnes sanctos tuos cum mensura probas, et sine mensura glorificas, concede quaesumus ut gloriosi sacerdotis tui Guþlaci precatu vitam consequi mereamur perpetuam et dispiciendo calcare presentem, et ut per illius merita et intercessiones de tuis preceptis salutaribus muniamur et a nostris peccatis plurimis in hoc mundo abluamur. Finit vita B. D *continues with extracts from Ordericus Vitalis*, I, iv, cc. 15 *and* 16.

NOTES

NOTES

PROLOGUE (p. 60)

The prologue follows the usual pattern of introduction to saints' lives written after the Antonian model. The writer expresses his complete unworthiness and inability to write the life of his saint, but claims that he is fulfilling a pious duty in his rustic style. (Cf. E. R. Curtius, *European Literature and the Latin Middle Ages*, London, 1953, pp. 83 ff., 149 f., 411, 460; *Two Lives*, p. 310.) Felix had the prologue of the *V.pr.* before him as he wrote it and actually quotes it. He also quotes from the usual sources: Sulpicius, *Vita S. Martini*, Evagrius's translation of Athanasius, *Vita Antonii*, and also from the *Vita S. Martini*. In addition he quotes from Aldhelm, *De metris*. For the influence of Aldhelm on his style, see Introduction, pp. 17 ff.

Ælfwald. See Introduction, p. 15.

Catholicae congregationis vernaculus. This expression is a mere borrowing from Aldhelm so that it is not possible to assume from this, as Gonser does (p. 14), that the monastery to which Felix belonged had accepted the Roman allegiance.

Guthlac. The name is interpreted by Felix as meaning *belli donum*. It is more probable that *lac* should be interpreted as 'play' (cf. O.N. *leikr*), in which case it might be interpreted as 'battle-play', cf. *beadulac*, *heaðolac*, and the proper name *Hygelac*, all from Beowulf, or *Hadulac*, Bishop of Elmham, mentioned by Bede, *H.ecc.* v, 23. In all these instances it means 'play'. See Bosworth-Toller, *s.v.* 'lac'. In later times also, owing to the influence of the form 'Goodlake' and similar forms, as in the South English Legendary (see Introduction, p. 24), it was interpreted as 'good gift'.

A piscatoribus.... This phrase borrowed from the preface of the *Vita Martini* became a commonplace of hagiological literature; cf. H. Gunter, *Die christlichen Legenden des Abendlandes*, Heidelberg, 1910, pp. 167 and 223, n. 4.

Gregorii dicta. The words in all MSS. except D are wrongly attributed to St Jerome. See p. 61, n. 27,

Donatus. Aelius Donatus was a celebrated grammarian who taught St Jerome rhetoric. He flourished in the middle of the fourth century. It was probably the association of Donatus with Jerome which led to the wrong attribution of the quotation to that saint. His *Ars grammatica* was widely used all through the Middle Ages, and the word 'donat' came to have the meaning of any introductory treatise. See *N.E.D. s.v.* 'donat'.

Wilfrid and Cissa. The appeal to witnesses is in accordance with the Antonian tradition, followed also by Bede. The two witnesses mentioned here are again appealed to at the beginning of c. XXVIII which introduces the second part of the Life. Wilfrid is described as an abbot in the prologue but not in the other contexts in which his name occurs. Seeing that Wilfrid is described in c. XXVIII as a 'frequentator', it is presumably the same man. In c. XXXIX he is described as being a 'venerable man who had long been bound by the bonds of spiritual friendship' with the saint. This is the occasion on which he is much struck by the incident of the swallows and of their affection for the saint. In the next chapter (c. XL) he recovers the gloves carried off by jackdaws, through Guthlac's intervention. There is no reason for supposing that he is the *Uilfrith presbiter* mentioned in the list of abbots on fo. 15 b of the Durham *Liber Vitae*. The name is not uncommon and in fact occurs several times elsewhere in the *Liber*.

Cissa is mentioned again in c. XLVIII, where in answer to Abbess Ecgburh's enquiries, Guthlac names him as his successor in the hermitage. He is there described as being 'still among the pagan people' and as not yet having 'approached the baptismal font'. In the same passage Felix describes him as still inhabiting Guthlac's cell. The name Cissa is found occasionally in place-names such as Chichester in Sussex, Chisbury and Chiserbury in Wiltshire, and Chisworth in Derbyshire. It is also the name of one of the sons of Aelli, founder of the kingdom of the South Saxons in the late fifth century (*A.S.C. s.a.* 477). It is tempting to guess that Cissa may himself have been a South Saxon, for they were the last of the English tribes to be converted, being evangelized by St Wilfrid in 681–6. On the other hand, the story of the healing of the East Angle, Hwætred, in c. XLI, would seem to suggest that there were still pagans even among that race in the time of Guthlac. The Pseudo-Ingulf describes him (*Historia Ingulphi*, p. 5) as a man of noble birth who once exercised great influence in secular affairs, but actually nothing is known of him except what Felix tells us. The Pseudo-Ingulf's statement that, like Tatwine, Beccel, and Ecgberht, he occupied a cell near the saint, during the latter's lifetime (*ibid.* p. 5), is apparently based on no other evidence than the mere mention of their names in the Life. At any rate Cissa was, like Wilfrid, a 'frequentator' of the saint. The name occurs in the Durham *Liber Vitae* under the list of 'clerici' on fo. 24 b.

In the 'Resting places of the English Saints' there is a reference to a certain Saint Cissa, associated with the other saints whose relics were translated to Thorney in 973 by Bishop Æthelwold of Winchester when he refounded the monastery there (*V.C.H. Cambridge*, II, p. 210; F. Liebermann, *Die Heiligen Englands*, p. 16). It was these saints whom William of Malmesbury refused to mention because their names were so barbarous (*Gesta Pontificum*, ed. N. E. S. A. Hamilton, R.S. 1870, p. 327 and n. 4; cf. also W. Levison, *Das Werden der Ursula-Legende*, pp. 55 and 56, nn. 1 and 2). The relics of a 'Sancti Cissi anachorite' occur in a list of Thorney relics of about the twelfth century in B.M. Add. MS. 40,000 (*English Kalendars after 1100*, I,

p. 129). But no Saint Cissa is found either in the mid eleventh-century Crowland calendar (see above, p. 10) nor in the fourteenth-century Deeping calendar which probably represents the lost Thorney calendar (*ibid.*).

CHAPTER I (p. 72)

Rex Anglorum. This title was applied in charters to Æthelbald and to Offa his successor, but it is clear from this passage that the title was used of Æthelred too. Boniface speaks of Æthelbald as 'inclita Anglorum imperii sceptra gubernanti' (Boniface, *Ep.* 73, ed. Tangl, p. 146) though it is only fair to note that he is merely adapting Aldhelm's description of Aldfrith (Aldhelm, p. 61). In one at least of his charters he is styled 'rex Britanniae' and again in the same charter 'rex non solum Marcersium sed et omnium provinciarum quae generale nomine Sutangli dicuntur'. (See W. de G. Birch, *Cartularium Saxonicum*, 154.) As Stenton says, 'at the height of his power, Aethelbald was head of a confederation which included Kent, Wessex and every other kingdom between the Humber and the Channel' (Stenton, pp. 202 ff.; see also F. M. Stenton, 'The supremacy of the Mercian kings', *E.H.R.* XXXIII (1918), pp. 433 ff.). It would seem therefore that Ælfwald to whom the prologue is addressed was a subject king (D. Whitelock, *English Historical Documents c. 500–1042* (London, 1955), p. 453).

Penwalh. In both H and D, the form of the name is Penwald. This latter is the name of a Mercian moneyer found on a coin of Offa (C. F. Keary, *Catalogue of English Coins in the British Museum: Anglo-Saxon Series*, I, London, 1887, p. 28). No other example of either form of the name seems to be forthcoming. There is very little foundation for Sir John Rhys's suggestion that it is a Celtic name. The termination is almost certainly O.E. *wealh* which, though it means a foreigner or a Welshman is frequently found as the second element of O.E. names, so frequently in fact as to make it unlikely that the element was used only in the case of foreigners. Penwalh is in fact descended from the Mercian royal house, though he nevertheless lives in the district of the Middle Angles (cf. Introduction, p. 3; Stenton pp. 42–4, 301; Chadwick, *O.E.N.* p. 10). It is possible that he may have been ealdorman over some section of them. Bede, for instance, refers to a 'princeps' of the South Gyrwe (*H.ecc.* IV, 19) or as the O.E. version translates it 'Suðgyrwa aldormon'.

CHAPTER II (p. 74)

Icles. The form is the genitive case of Icel. He was presumably the first of the Mercian race to rule in England. His father Eomer is mentioned in *Beowulf*, l. 1960 (cf. *A.S.C. s.a.* 755, Plummer, I, p. 50, II, p. 6; Chadwick, *O.E.N.* pp. 15 ff.). In the Old English translation, Penwalh is said to belong to the race of the Iclingas. A curious memory of this survived in Crowland until last century. The supposed site of the saint's cell, Anchor Church hill, was until 1866 in the possession of a family called Hickling who protected it with almost superstitious care (cf. Rev. Canon Edward Moore, 'St Guthlac and Croyland', *Journal of the British Archaeological Association*, xxxv (1879), p. 133). The name Icel is preserved in Ickleford, Herts, Icklesham, Sussex, and Ickleton, Cambs. See E. Ekwall, *Oxford Dictionary of Place-names* (Oxford, 1936), p. 249.

CHAPTER III (p. 74)

Tette. This is also the name of a sister of Ine, king of Wessex, who was abbess of Wimborne and flourished about 700. See *D.C.B.*, *s.v.* Tetta.

CHAPTER IV (p. 74)

Epidendarum. This extraordinary word seems to be based on the form 'epido' which is glossed in the *Hermeneumata Codicis Vaticani Reg. Christ. 1260* as meaning 'inter ventrem et umbilicum' (*Corpus Glossariorum Latinorum*, ed. G. Loewe and G. Goetz, Leipzig, 1892, III, p. 600, 1, 38).

CHAPTER V (p. 74)

Guthlac's birth. Miracles are regularly associated with the birth of the saint. A miraculous light is seen at Wilfrid's birth (*Eddius*, c. 1). The miraculous hand may possibly be a reminiscence of the Hand of God, often seen in the art of the West from the fourth century onward. Two interesting Pre-Conquest English examples are the Rood at Romsey (A. W. Clapham, *English Romanesque Architecture before the Conquest*, Oxford, 1930, pl. 61) and St Cuthbert's Stole in which the hand appears from a cloud and is surrounded with the inscription, 'Dextera Dei'. Cf. Cabrol et Leclercq, *Dictionnaire d'archéologie chrétienne*, x, col. 1205 *s.v.* 'main'.

CHAPTER X (p. 76)

Guthlacingas. See Introduction, p. 3.

CHAPTER XI (p. 78)

Baptism. In the early church, infants were baptized on the eighth day, the day on which circumcision, which foreshadowed infant baptism, was administered by the Jews. Cf. Luke i. 59, Phil. iii. 5. Cf. also Cyprian (*Corp. script. eccl. Lat.* ed. Hartel, Vienna, 1872, vol. III, pt. II, Ep. 64, p. 718). Cyprian here lays it down as a custom 'that infants are baptized on or before the eighth day'.

CHAPTERS XII–XV (pp. 78–80)

Guthlac's youthful virtues. Like Antony, whom Felix clearly had in mind, Guthlac was an obedient and virtuous child. Cuthbert on the other hand had to be warned to avoid foolish games by a three-year-old child (cf. *Vit. Ant.* c. 1; *V.pr.* c. 1). It serves as one of the many examples of how Bede, though working on the Antonine model, nevertheless succeeds in giving a more personal and realistic touch to the Life of Cuthbert.

CHAPTER XVI (p. 80)

Valiant deeds of heroes of old. There is little doubt that Guthlac would be familiar with the deeds of the great men of his race through the heroic songs and poetry recited by the minstrel at court or elsewhere. We gather from c. xviii that the heroic deeds he heard of were partly at any rate concerned with the heroes of his own ancestry, the royal race of Mercia, though on the other hand, one of the features of the heroic poetry which has come down to us is its international character, e.g. *Beowulf*, which is concerned almost entirely with Scandinavian heroes. Cf. Chadwick, *H.A.* pp. 77–90.

Guthlac's warfare. This was presumably against the Britons, judging by c. xxxiv, though our knowledge of Mercian history in the latter part of the seventh century is so limited that it is not possible to say if he fought elsewhere.

CHAPTER XIX (p. 82)

Twenty-fourth year. If Guthlac were born in 674 this would make the year 698 or 699. Benedict Biscop who had also been a soldier became a monk at the age of twenty-five (*H.ab.* 1; Plummer, II, p. 364).

CHAPTER XX (p. 84)

Repton. According to Giraldus Cambrensis (*De vita S. Davidis*, R.S. III, p. 386), St David founded a monastery at Repton in the sixth century. This is, however, a late tradition for which there is no other evidence. The passage in Felix is in fact the first mention of it. As it is ruled over by a woman it is clearly a double monastery of monks and nuns such as were to be found in the seventh century at Hartlepool, Whitby, Coldingham, Barking, Ely, Bardney, as well as at Wimborne Minster (Thanet) and Wenlock. Cf. P. Stephanus Hilpisch, 'Die Doppelklöster: Entstehung und Organisation' in *Beiträge zur Geschichte des alten Mönchtums und des Benediktinerordens herausgegeben von Ildefons Herwegen*, xv (Münster in Westf., 1928), pp. 44 ff. See also *Two Lives*, p. 318. It was at Repton that Æthelbald was buried in

755 (*T.S.C. s.a.* 755). Here too, according to the 'Resting places of English Saints', St Wigstan was buried (*Die Heiligen Englands*, p. 12). It was destroyed by the Danes about 870 (*V.C.H. Derby*, II, p. 58).

Tonsure. Felix is careful to explain that he received the Roman form of the tonsure and not the Celtic form. The latter was a shaving of the front of the head from ear to ear. The shape of the tonsure, the difference in the rite of baptism (possibly the formula of administration) and above all the date of Easter were the main points of difference between the Roman and the Celtic Churches. It is pretty certain, therefore, that the monastery at Repton, whatever its past history had been, had now accepted the Roman obedience (cf. Plummer, II, pp. 353-4 and *Two Lives*, p. 316). The tonsure is being performed by a bishop in the third picture on the Guthlac Roll (Warner, pl. 3) though no reference is made to this in Felix.

Ælfthryth. This was a fairly common woman's name in Anglo-Saxon times. She is therefore not very likely to be the same as the Ælfthryth mentioned in the Durham *Liber Vitae* under the heading of 'Reginarum et abbatissarum' (fo. 14). In the Guthlac Roll (Warner, pl. 3) the name of the abbess is given as Ebba. There was an abbess of that name at the end of the seventh century in the Isle of Thanet, but this is doubtless a mere slip on the part of the artist, to be compared with his slip in making Headda bishop of Winchester (see below); see Birch, p. xxxix, Searle, *On. Sax.* pp. 4, 23-4.

Intoxicating drink. The Irish monks like the Eastern monks were divided in the matter of the use of intoxicating drinks (Ryan, *Monast.* pp. 388 ff.). But it is probably the fact that Bede describes Cuthbert as abstaining from all intoxicants (*V.pr.* c. 6) which leads Felix to attribute the same abstemiousness to Guthlac (*Two Lives*, pp. 175, 345). It was the custom in the English and Irish monasteries at this time for the monks to receive at Holy Communion under both species. This was in fact the custom in the West as well as the East right down to the twelfth century (Cabrol et Leclercq, III, col. 2463 *s.v.* 'communion'; cf. *H.ecc.* IV, 23 and Plummer, II, p. 247).

CHAPTER XXI (p. 84)

The hostility of his fellow monks. St Benedict of Nursia in the same way incurred the hostility of his fellow monks owing to the austerity of his life so that they even attempted to poison him (*Greg. dial.* II, c. 3, pp. 80 ff.). Macarius of Alexandria also offended the monks of Tabennisi so much by his ascetic feats that they desired Pachomius to send him away (*The Lausiac History of Palladius*, II, ed. D. Cuthbert Butler, Texts and Studies, VI, Cambridge, 1904, pp. 52 ff.).

Guthlac's virtues. Felix borrows a considerable amount of this passage from the anonymous *Vita Fursei* (ed. Krusch, *Script. rer. Merov.* IV, pp. 434 ff.). Felix had before him a MS. of the Life, of a kind which Krusch calls B i, for the word 'divinae' at the end of c. XXI occurs only in MSS. of this type.

St Fursey was an Irish monk who founded a monastery in Ireland, then emigrating to England he established a monastery at Burgh Castle in E. Anglia. He later went on to Gaul where he founded another monastery at Lagny-sur-Marne and was buried about 650 at Péronne in Picardy. *Peronna Scottorum*, as it was called, became a great centre of pilgrimage for Irishmen. Bede gives a summary of his life in *H.ecc.* III, 19, basing it on the *Vita Fursei*. Felix would be familiar with the work, both because of its East Anglian associations and further because of Fursey's remarkable visions of the unseen world which the writer describes and which Bede retells. This Life has its importance in that it 'may have been the starting point of an important branch of Irish literature' (Gougaud, *C.C.L.* p. 147). But the stories of visions of the other world which were to play so large a part in medieval didactic literature owed something to classical literature, particularly to Virgil's Sixth Book of the *Aeneid* but more to the Dialogues of Gregory the Great (cf. for example, *Greg. dial.* IV, cc. 13–18) and the *Visio Sancti Pauli* (ed. Th. Silverstein, in *Studies and Documents*, ed. by K. and S. Lake, London, vol. IV, 1935). Both of these exercised a great influence on medieval literature. Bede, in his account of Fursey's experiences of the after-life, was obviously writing with Gregory in mind. Boniface writing to the Abbess Eadburh, giving an account of the vision of the next world seen by a monk at Much Wenlock, also has verbal echoes of Gregory (*Ep.* 10, ed. Tangl, pp. 8 ff.). Dante's vision is the greatest but by no means the last of this very distinctive literary genre. See also St John D. Seymour, *Irish Visions of the Other World* (London, 1930).

CHAPTER XXIV (p. 86)

The solitary life. It is clear that at this time the life of the hermit or anchorite, the life of divine contemplation, was considered more advanced than the cenobitic life, not only in Egypt or Ireland as we should probably expect, but over most of Western Europe. Bede in the *V.pr.* (c. 17) praises a hermit's life highly, but makes it quite clear that, when Cuthbert sought Farne, he had obtained the consent of the abbot of Lindisfarne and his brethren (*Two Lives*, pp. 325, 349). In the same way Guthlac gains the permission of his elders. The Rule of St Benedict (c. 1) recognizes the anchorite as a kind of monk but stresses that this solitary life is not for the beginner but only to be adopted after long trial in the monastery.

Rivigarum. This strange word is glossed in C₂ and N as 'ubi congregatur aqua'. It is most probably a misreading of the Vulgate, Isaiah xix. 6: 'attenuabuntur et siccabuntur rivi aggerum.' I owe this explanation to Father P. Grosjean.

CHAPTER XXV (p. 88)

Tatwine. A fairly common Old English name. The name of an arch-bishop of Canterbury (731–4) and of an abbot of Fritzlar to whom Boniface writes (737–8); cf. *Ep.* 40, ed. Tangl, p. 65. The name occurs no less than nine times in the *Liber Vitae* of Durham. Thanks to the Pseudo-Ingulf his name appears in some calendars, his feast being 3 July.

He appears in the fourth roundel of the Guthlac Roll (Warner, pl. 4) wearing a hooded cloak and a hat with a knob at the top. He appears there to be a comparatively old man. He is seated in the stern and is steering the boat with a crutched paddle. He is called 'Tadwinus'. The same subject can still be seen sculpted in a quatrefoil over the west doorway of Crowland Abbey (Warner, frontis., p. 12, and pl. 4).

Aliam insulam. The use of *alius* in the sense of *aliquis* is a common feature of Irish Latin. It is found in the *Vita* in several places (cf. cc. XXXVII, XLI, XLIII, L, etc.).

Crowland. The explanation of the name as given by Ordericus (IV, 22) is presumably the traditional one, 'Crulandia enim crudam, id est coenosam terram significat'; Ekwall (*Oxford Dictionary of Place-names*, p. 127) explains the first element as an otherwise unknown word *cruw* (*crug*), perhaps cognate with Norw. *kryl*, 'a hump'. He takes it to mean a bend, referring to the bend of the Welland at Crowland. Though this is not marked now, it may well have been more obvious before the draining of the fens. Interchange of *g* and *w* is sometimes found in Old English after *u* as *muga, muwa*. The form *Croy-* goes back to at least the end of the twelfth century. But the earlier forms were doubtless the *crug, cruw* forms. No *Croi-* forms appear in any of the MSS., but in the fourth of the roundels in which Tatwine is conducting the saint to the spot, the name appears as 'Croiland'.

The description of the place as given here was quoted by Camden in his *Britannia* (ed. 1586, p. 276).

The statement that none had been able to live there before the saint is borrowed from the *V.pr.* There it refers to Farne Island which was the scene of Cuthbert's hermitage (*Two Lives*, p. 214). But in spite of the fact, neither of the writers of these Lives of St Cuthbert lays emphasis on the devils. In the saints' lives written more strictly on the Antonian model, the fights with devils form a very important part of the warfare carried on by the Christian warrior (cf. Kurtz, pp. 108 ff.). Felix of course also lays much emphasis on the same devil combats.

St Bartholomew's feast. It is strange that Guthlac should be said to have reached Crowland on his first visit on a feast of St Bartholomew. This must have been three or four months before his permanent settlement which in c. XXVII is stated to have been on Aug. 25th. But so far as I am aware there never has been a feast of St Bartholomew in April or May. The Bollandists were so conscious of this difficulty that they omitted the sentence 'contigit... coeperat' from their edition of the Life. But the sentence occurs in all the MSS. See further Cabrol et Leclerq, II, col. 500, s.v. 'Barthélemy (Saint).'

CHAPTER XXVII (p. 90)

St Bartholomew's day.   The present date of St Bartholomew's feast is 24 August, but in the earlier calendars, up to the end of the eleventh century, his feast is always 25 August. The only exception is the Wells calendar dated 1061–88 (*English Kalendars before 1100*, p. 107). All the MSS. have 'viii kal. Sept.' (25 August) but in D a glossator has added 'ix' above. All the calendars so far published by Professor Wormald after 1100 have the feast on the 24th.

The close association of the saint with St Guthlac has been preserved in the dedication of the abbey at Crowland. It was dedicated to St Mary, St Bartholomew and St Guthlac.

CHAPTER XXVIII (p. 92)

Second part of the Life.   At this point the second part of the Life begins. Chapter headings are more uniform in the MSS. (except in D which has its special variants), and once more Felix quotes his authorities, Wilfrid and Cissa. In fact it is pretty clear that Felix regarded the part preceding as a kind of prologue to the *Vita* proper which only begins with the establishment of the saint on the island which is to be the seat of his warfare.

Guthlac's asceticism.   This is in the true tradition of Egyptian and Celtic monasticism. Felix was probably influenced in his description of it by the Lives of St Antony and St Paul. The description of St Cuthbert's asceticism also had its influence, though Bede does not overemphasize this side of Cuthbert's habits (cf. *Two Lives*, pp. 74, 315–16).

Guthlac's fasting is less prolonged than Antony's, for though the former takes only small quantities of bread and water, yet he seems to have fed regularly after sundown. Antony on the other hand sometimes fasted completely for two days, sometimes even for four (*Vit. Ant.* c. 6). It was also the custom under the Columban rule not to break the fast until sunset (Ryan, *Monast.* p. 386). In the poem of Henry of Avranches, the latter describes a temptation not related by Felix in which the devil appeared in the form of his sister Pega and urged him to break his vow by taking food before sunset. (See Introduction, p. 24.)

Cuthbert wore woollen clothes though totally unadorned (*V.pr.* c. 16). Presumably Guthlac wore goatskins like the monks of Tabennisi. But they wore a sleeveless linen tunic underneath, reaching to the knees (Ryan, *Monast.* p. 383). Felix says that the saint wore no linen.

Guthlac's dwelling-place.   The site of Guthlac's cell, judging by the description, sounds like a chambered long barrow. Another example of a chambered long barrow used as a dwelling-place is the *hoga* at Cutteslowe, now part of Wolvercote, north of Oxford (Helen M. Cam, 'The *hoga* of Cutteslowe', *Antiquity*, IX, 1935, pp. 96ff.); but as Dr G. E. Daniel has pointed out (*Prehistoric Chamber Tombs of England and Wales*, pp. 22-3 and notes) Guthlac's cell was hardly a prehistoric barrow unless it was a chance one, very much out of the normal area for such a type of earthwork. But it may well have been a Roman barrow or it may even have been a bronze age cist. Dr Daniel adds further in a letter, 'It could of course be an ordinary round barrow with a stone cist in it. It would not be difficult to build a house using a cist or chamber as a basis.'

Such barrows were regularly broken into throughout the Middle Ages, but the barrow-robbing here mentioned is the first historically attested grave-robbing in England. Several of the barrows at Sutton Hoo had been robbed, and an opening had even been made in the mound containing the great treasure ship, but by a happy accident the robbers missed the treasure (*The Sutton Hoo Ship Burial*, British Museum, 1947, p. 36).

The site of the cell was traditionally associated with a site called Anchorite or Anchor Church hill, about a quarter of a mile north-east of the present abbey. In the year 1708, Dr Stukely says he saw the remnant of a chapel there, which was then turned into a dwelling house or cottage (*Palæographia Britannica*, Stamford, 1746, II, p. 35). It was called Anchorage House. He associates the cell with Pega, Guthlac's sister. Canon E. Moore ('St Guthlac and Croyland', *Journal of the British Archaeological Association*, XXXV, 1879, pp. 133ff.) relates that up to 1866 the property belonged to a family called Hickling (see note to c. II, p. 177). After it went out of their possession, the foundations were exposed by the new owner in order to get stone. He carted away 200 tons of Barnack rag, but before this operation had been fully carried out, Canon Moore and Mr A. S. Canham were able to make a plan of and describe the foundations (for Canham's plan, see Birch, p. xlii). Canon Moore thus describes the plan: 'The foundations consisted of two parallel walls running east and west, about 14 feet apart and 84 feet in length. On either side, towards the western end, was a room, making the whole width of the western end 42 feet. These foundations consisted of concrete walls, nearly three feet thick, with, at intervals, substantial bases of unhewn stone, more than 8 feet square, three on each side, opposite to each other, about 12 feet apart, with an intermediate base (half the size of the other bases) between the two easternmost bases on the south side.' What this building was, it is difficult to say. The plan seems to be like a medieval chapel. What precisely Canon Moore meant by 'concrete' is not clear, but certainly the unhewn stone of the access passages gives a prehistoric air to the building, though one must remember Dr Daniel's statement already quoted that the site is away from the main centres of prehistoric monuments. In a letter, my colleague, Professor Ian Richmond, says: 'The evidence suggests that we have a rectangular structure which might be either Roman or mediaeval, associated with a "passage" or access which has structural features very suggestive of the prehistoric, but which lies off the recognized areas of distribution of comparable prehistoric monuments.' It may be that the foundations represent Guthlac's seventh-century adaptation of his prehistoric or Roman barrow, with medieval additions.

CHAPTER XXIX (p. 94)

Guthlac's first temptation. Chapters XXIX–XXXVI are devoted to his various fights with devils after the Antonian model. Guthlac is quickly introduced to the warfare to which, at any rate in his early hermit life, he is to be subjected. The first temptation is that of despair, based upon a sense of his unworthiness and his inability to support the life he had undertaken. It is the trouble which haunts all beginners in the monastic and mystical life—the sin of 'accidia' in the form of despair. Cf. Chaucer, *The Parson's Tale*, 'De accidia': 'Now comth wanhope, that is despeir of the mercy of God, that comth somtyme of to muche outrageous sorwe, and somtyme of to muche drede ymaginynge that he hath doon so much synne that it wol not availen hym, though he wolde repenten hym and forsake synne; thurgh which despeir or drede he abaundoneth al his herte to every maner synne' (Chaucer, ed. F. N. Robinson, p. 297). There is also a reminiscence of Antony's sermon and his warning against allowing the devil to overwhelm the hermit with memories of past sins. (See next note.)

CHAPTER XXX (p. 98)

The temptation to fast to excess. This is a temptation to which the Celts, following in the footsteps of the Egyptian Fathers, were particularly prone (Ryan, *Monast.* pp. 393–4). It is probable that Felix is thinking of Antony's warning against this very evil. The latter warns his hearers (c. XVI) against devils who in the habit of monks blame their victims with past sins and urge them on to fastings and prayers; they urge impossible tasks so that the beginner, when he sees how difficult is the life he has undertaken, loses heart and gives up in despair. Cassian found it necessary to mitigate the Egyptian practices while Benedict in his Rule, like St Basil, placed ascetical exercises under the control of a Superior (*Sancti Benedicti Regula Monasteriorum*, ed. D. Cuthbert Butler, editio altera, Freiburg, 1927, c. 49, pp. 93–4).

CHAPTER XXXI (p. 100)

Guthlac's visit to hell. See note to chapter XXI, p. 180 above. It was a widespread conception that one of the punishments of hell consisted of extremes of alternate heat and cold. Many examples of this are collected by Plummer (*H.ecc.* II, p. 296). It is possible that the idea many have been based upon an interpretation of St Luke xiii. 28, 'ibi erit fletus et stridor dentium'. Cf. Bede (ed. Giles), *Opp.* XI, p. 191, 'Fletus de ardore, stridor dentium solet excitari de frigore ubi duplex ostenditur gehenna: id est nimii frigoris, et intolerabilis esse fervoris, cui beati Job sententia consentit dicentis (xxiv. 19) ad calorem nimium transibunt ab aquis nivium'. For further details see Bede, *L.T.W.* p. 215; and Sir Edmund Craster, 'The Miracles of St Cuthbert at Farne', *An. Boll.* lxx (1952), p. 12, n. 1.

Seed of Cain. Dr Whitelock has called attention (in *The Audience of Beowulf*, Oxford, 1951, p. 80) to the fact that in the O.E. poem *Beowulf*, the monsters who haunt the 'misty moorlands' are also described as 'the seed of Cain' (*Beowulf*, ll. 103-10, 1261-6). The other likenesses between *Beowulf* and the Life to which she calls attention (*ut supra*) are, as she herself suggests, merely accidental and are indeed commonplaces in saints' lives on the Antonian model, with some of which the poet may well have been familiar. So the reference in both to monsters as 'the seed of Cain' is simply due to the fact that this tradition, based upon an early interpretation of certain passages in Genesis, was widely known and is often referred to in early writings.

CHAPTER XXXIII (p. 106)

Caelo demoverat umbras. This is one of many Virgilian echoes in Felix. On the basis of it he has invented a series of similar descriptions of dawn. Cf. 'Sol igneum demoverat ortum' (c. xix); 'lux crastina demoverat ortum' (c. xxvi); 'Sol aureum caelo demoverat ortum' (c. xli).

The weeping spirits. Here, as in chapter xxxi, the evil spirits complain of their inability to overcome the saint and are reduced to tears. So in the Life of Antony (c. iv) a devil in the form of a black boy appears to the saint and laments his failure to make any impression on him.

CHAPTER XXXIV (p. 108)

Cœnred. See Introduction, p. 5.

British hosts. This famous account of the attack on Guthlac by the hosts of the Britons has sometimes been taken too literally by historians (see Introduction, p. 2 n. 1). Though there is little doubt that the Welsh border was the scene of much fighting during the late seventh and early eighth century, yet we cannot safely associate the appearance of the Britons here with the survival of people of that nation in the fens. It is clear from this chapter that a Welsh attack on Mercia, which would seem to have been particularly heavy, must have taken place some time in Coenred's reign (704-9) though we have no information about it from any other source (cf. Whitelock, *The Audience of Beowulf*, Oxford, 1951, p. 86). But we must take the story as one of Guthlac's 'unquiet dreams', as Dr Whitelock terms them. These Britons are obviously devils in disguise. The story forms one of a series (cc. xxix–xxxvi) intended to show Guthlac's power over devils.

The burning of his buildings and the tossing on spears are clearly demonic illusions. A verse from the Psalms (with which Antony also dispels his demon visitors, *Vit. Ant.* c. 12) puts the Britons to flight and 'all the hosts of demons vanished like smoke from his presence'. It is therefore clear that no hypothesis as to British survivors in the fens can be based on this passage.

CHAPTER XXXV (p. 110)

Beccel. The form of the name in D and on the Guthlac Roll is Beccelmus. This was misread by Mabillon or by some earlier writer (see below) as Beccelinus. The Acta adopted the same form and it has been copied by later writers (e.g. Gonser, p. 196, etc.). The name is perhaps a form of Becca (cf. Redin, p. 85), a name which occurs twice in the O.E. poem *Widsith*, probably belonging to two different people (*Widsith*, ed. Kemp Malone, London, 1936, pp. 68, 91, 127–8). Another form, probably West Saxon, is Beocca. Redin suggests that it may be derived, either from Celtic *bekko-s*, little, or perhaps be a hypocoristic form of compounds with *Beorn- Beorht-* (Redin, p. 84). The Vita of a Bertellinus or Beccelinus was drawn up based mostly on Felix (*B.h.L.* 1263) by an anonymous author some time in the fifteenth century and added to Wynkyn de Worde's 1516 edition of the *Nova Legenda Angliae* (*Nova Legenda Angliae*, ed. C. Horstmann, Oxford, 1901, I, p. xvii).

He is said to have been a son of a 'king of Stafford'. He returned after the death of Guthlac according to this Life to the 'eremum Staffordiensem' and there he died on 9 September. The connexion with Stafford is probably due to a confusion on the part of the fifteenth-century editor with another hermit whose name was similar. His Life is printed in *AA.SS.* September, III, pp. 446 ff. See also A. Oswald, *Excavation Report of the Church of St Bertelin* (Birmingham, 1955).

Beccel's attempt on the saint's life. This extraordinary incident is reminiscent of two incidents in the Life of St Benedict (*Greg. dial.* pp. 81 and 91) in the first of which the monks of the monastery over which Benedict had been invited to rule rebel against his strict way of life and offer him a poisoned cup of wine. The other, which more closely resembles the story here, is that of a priest of a neighbouring church, whose name was Florentius, who, being envious of the fame of Benedict, gave him a piece of poisoned bread. Needless to say, the saint was aware of the machinations of the priest and bade a raven remove the deadly morsel.

CHAPTER XXXVI (p. 114)

Evil spirits appear as beasts. This chapter, as the verbal echoes show, is based on a similar incident in the Life of Antony (*Vit. Ant.* c. 8). Guthlac shows the same contempt for the creatures as Antony does; Guthlac mocks at Satan because, though he once tried, before the fall of the angels, to make himself equal to God, he now has to assume the form of 'miserable beasts'. Antony, on the other hand, jeers at their weakness because though they have come in vast numbers to terrify him, yet they are unable to touch him. This incident ends the series of demonic attacks upon Guthlac.

CHAPTER XXXVII (p. 116)

Guthlac's power over birds and animals. The story of the attack by devils in the form of wild beasts leads on naturally to a series of miracles intended to show the saint's power over birds and animals, and their instant obedience to his command. Stories of this kind are very frequently found in the lives of the saints (cf. *Two Lives*, p. 320) and particularly in the models used by Felix, the Lives of St Antony, St Paul and St Cuthbert as well as the Dialogues of Sulpicius Severus (I, cc. 13, 14; Halm, pp. 164 ff.) and of Gregory (cf. note to c. xxxv above). In c. xxxviii Felix quotes Bede's statement to the effect that if a man wholeheartedly serves the Maker of all created things, all creation will minister to his commands and wishes. In the lives of Irish saints, stories about animals and birds are particularly common (cf. *V.S.H.* I, pp. cxlii ff.).

Jackdaws. The Latin word *corvi* normally means ravens, but the mischievous tricks of the birds in this story are more usually associated with jackdaws than ravens. The jackdaw, of course, belongs to the raven family.

CHAPTER XXXIX (p. 120)

Swallows. This story illustrates well the kindness and longsuffering towards animals mentioned in c. xxxviii. The same feature is to be found in most of the Egyptian and Irish stories of the same type. It is particularly noticeable in the Lives of St Cuthbert. The *corvi* pull the thatch from the saint's guest house, and other birds rob him of his crops, but he is always patient with them (*Two Lives*, pp. 221, 223).

Ventinula. This word is an invention of Felix. Though the meaning is quite uncertain, I have taken it to be a latinization of O.E. *windel*, a basket. If this is so, Felix has of course misinterpreted the derivation of the word, for it has nothing to do with 'wind' (*ventus*), but with O.E. *windan*, to wind, referring to the wickerwork of which baskets were made.

Angelic ministrations. Stories of angelic ministrations go back to the fathers of the Egyptian desert. In Sulpicius Severus (*Dial.* II, 13; Halm, p. 196), in the Life of Antony and in the Lives of St Cuthbert, angels also play an important part. In the Irish Lives they almost seem to have taken the place of the fairies of the Irish legends (cf. *L.I.S.* II, p. 300; *V.H.S.* I, p. clxxxi). Guthlac received consolation from angels every morning and every evening from his second year in Crowland, as he explained to Beccel on his deathbed (c. L).

CHAPTER XL (p. 124)

Æthelbald.   See Introduction, pp. 6 ff.

Gloves.   These were probably mittens. The use of finger gloves first appears in early Christian times as part of a bishop's robes. But little information can be gained either from MS. illustrations or from literary references as to the use of gloves in the Pre-Conquest period (cf. J. Hoops, *Reallexikon der Germanischen Altertumskunde*, Strassburg, 1913–15, II, p. 445, *s.v.* 'Handschuh'). Jonas in his Life of St Columban tells the story of how a thieving crow ran off with Columban's gloves ('tegumenta manuum quos Galli wantos vocant'), but repented and returned them (Jonas, *Vita Columbani, Script. rerum Merov.* IV, p. 81).

CHAPTER XLI (p. 126)

Hwætred.   This name, which is not uncommon in Anglo-Saxon times, occurs in the runic inscription on the west face of the Bewcastle cross as the name of one of those who set it up (*A.E.E.* v, fig. 18 (1)). It occurs no less than five times in the *Liber Vitae* of Durham. St Antony, in the same way, heals violent lunatics (*Vit. Ant.* cc. 29, 35, 36).

limali.   Another good example of Felix's invented words, based on *lima*, a file. Cf. Old English *feol-heard*. See Bosworth-Toller, *s.v.*

Double-winged axe.   This is the double-edged axe known from antiquity, and in classical times called *bipennis*, and in medieval Latin *bisacuta* (cf. Smith, *Dictionary of Greek and Roman Antiquities*, London, 1891, II, p. 616, *s.v.* 'securis'). In the Old English translation of the *Vita*, the word used to translate it is *twibil*, a word found frequently in O.E. vocabularies, usually glossing *bipennis*. The *twibil* was a kind of axe with two cutting edges used for cutting mortises. The word also meant a double-headed battle-axe or bill. It was used throughout the Middle Ages but is now obsolete in both these senses. See *N.E.D. s.v.* 'twibill'.

Holy places of the saints.   There is a widespread type of miracle found in the lives of saints, in which when other relics are unsuccessful, those of a particular saint prove successful. In this case, as in a similar story told of St Benedict by St Gregory, it is the saint himself who effects the cure which the relics of other saints could not perform (*Greg. dial.* II, 16, pp. 103 ff.).

Breathed on his face.   The ancient custom of *exsufflatio* to drive out the devil is still practised in the Roman rite of baptism (cf. *Cath. Enc.* v, p. 711, *s.v.* 'exorcism'). The account seems to suggest that Guthlac did in fact baptize the boy in order to drive out the evil spirit. The story implies that the boy had already been baptized before on several occasions. But as the evil spirit had not been driven out, presumably the baptism was not considered valid. His parents may well have been heathen, or recent converts, who still looked upon the rite of baptism as a form of magic.

CHAPTER XLII (p. 130)

Comes. This word is perhaps best translated by the Old English word *gesith* though the O.E. translation always uses *gefera* as the equivalent, which simply means companion. *Gesith*, which also meant companion, came to mean companion of the king, and so a member of the upper classes. In the Old English translation of Bede's *Ecclesiastical History*, *comes* is nearly always rendered by *gesith* (H. M. Chadwick, *Studies in Anglo-Saxon Institutions*, Cambridge, 1905, pp. 325 ff.; Stenton, pp. 298 ff.).

Ecga. A hypocoristic or weak form of some name beginning with 'Ecg-' such as Ecgfrith, Ecgberht, etc. Like Ofa (c. XLV), Ecga accompanies his lord into exile (cf. Dorothy Whitelock, *The Beginnings of English Society*, London, 1952, p. 31).

Girdle. The miracle is reminiscent of, and perhaps based on, a story told by Bede about how Ælfflæd was cured of an illness by Cuthbert's girdle (*V.pr.* c. 24).

CHAPTER XLIII (p. 132)

Guthlac's spirit of prophecy. The same quotation is used about Benedict in *Greg. dial.* II, 12, and is followed in each case by a series of stories to illustrate the gift. The story which follows in Gregory is about certain brethren who ate outside the monastery in the house of a religious woman, thus disobeying their rule; it is clearly this story on which Felix's story of the erring clerics is based, only the religious woman has become a widow of luxurious habits.

CHAPTER XLIV (p. 136)

The hidden flasks. This story is based on a very similar story told by Gregory (*Greg. dial.* II, 11; Moricca, p. 108) of a boy sent to St Benedict with two flasks of wine, one of which he kept back and hid by the roadside. The saint warns the astonished youth not to drink from it until he has ascertained the contents. The boy, on returning to the spot where he had hidden it, turned the flask upside down and a serpent came out. Here the concealment of the flasks of beer is of a less reprehensible nature and the incident is treated very lightly by the saint. Presumably the brethren's fault was a too anxious care for their creature comforts.

CHAPTER XLV (p. 138)

Guthlac's popularity. The passage is based, with considerable borrowings, on Bede's descriptions of the crowds who flock to St Cuthbert. Both are ultimately based on the *Vit. Ant.* (c. 28) and both Bede and Felix are clearly writing with Evagrius's translation of the Life before them (Kurtz, pp. 119 ff. and *Two Lives*, p. 351).

Sincelli. A glance at the variant readings will show how much difficulty the scribes had over Felix's strange word. It may well be that Felix found the word *syncellus* in a glossary bearing the meaning 'familiar friend'. Du Cange explains 'syncellus' as a man appointed to live with a great ecclesiastical dignitary so that he could witness the intimate details of the great man's private life. So it comes to mean an intimate companion or familiar friend.

Ofa. The subject of the miracle survived into Æthelbald's prosperous days and witnesses some of his charters (cf. Stenton, p. 299). The name occurs twice in the Durham *Liber Vitae* but it is obviously not the same man.

CHAPTER XLVI (p. 142)

Bishop Headda. This is Headda, bishop of Lichfield and Leicester, who was consecrated bishop of Lichfield in 691 and became bishop of Leicester in 709, dying somewhere between the years 716 and 727. It is only natural that he should have been confused with Hæddi, bishop of Winchester, his contemporary. In fact this became afterwards the traditional story at Crowland, for one of the roundels (Warner, pl. 11) shows Guthlac being ordained by 'Hedda episcopo Wintoniensi'. In Crowland calendars of the mid eleventh and fifteenth centuries the name of Hedda occurs under 7 July, doubtless as a result of the same tradition, for this Hedda is also the bishop of Winchester (*English Kalendars before 1100*, p. 260; *English Kalendars after 1100*, I, pp. 114, 123).

The fact that it was the bishop of Lichfield who ordained Guthlac and dedicated the church, definitely connects Crowland with Mercia (cf. Stenton, p. 49 and n. 3).

Wigfrith. A common Old English name occurring frequently in charters and elsewhere and four times in the *Liber Vitae* of Durham.

Librarius. In Archbishop Ælfric's tenth-century vocabulary (T. Wright, *Anglo-Saxon and Old English Vocabularies*, London, 1884, I, col. 146) occurs 'librarius vel bibliopola vel antiquarius vel scriba vel fenestella, wrytere'.

Ireland. Bede (*H.ecc.* III, 27 and notes) speaks of the large number of scholars who in the time of Colman (about 664) went to Ireland to study. Aldhelm, about 690, writes to a certain Ehfrid who had just returned from six years' study in Ireland, complaining that the number of scholars resorting to Ireland was like a swarm of bees (Aldhelm, pp. 486 ff.). See also E. S. Duckett, *Anglo-Saxon Saints and Scholars* (New York, 1947), pp. 65 ff.

False hermits. Wigfrith's account of the mixed state of religion in Ireland may reflect reports received from the Continent about some of the Irish 'peregrini' who 'were a source of constant scandal among foreign churchmen' (Gougaud, *C.C.L.* p. 164). Boniface encountered two of these Irish heretics and obtained condemnation of them from the councils of the Holy See (Boniface, ed. Tangl, *Epp.* 57, 60).

CHAPTER XLVII (p. 144)

The church. This was clearly the same building as the saint's oratory in which he would now say mass as a priest. We learn from the account of his death in c. L that it had an altar. It was here too that Guthlac was buried. It was in accordance with custom that the church should be consecrated before the sacred rite of ordination took place in it. It is to be presumed from the text that the ordination took place on the same day as the consecration. In the fifteenth century, the consecration of Crowland Abbey was clearly not associated with this event. The feast of the dedication of the church is entered in a Crowland calendar of that period under Nov. 3 (*English Kalendars after 1100*, I, p. 127). Felix has nothing to say about the building of this oratory, though he mentions it several times (cc. XXXVII, XLII, L, LIII). But in one of the roundels (Warner, pl. 5) the saint is represented building a 'capella' of a somewhat elaborate kind, with the help of two companions who wear close-fitting caps.

Consecration of the island. This was presumably equivalent to the consecration of the ground immediately surrounding the church.

Date of consecration. As St Bartholomew's Day was 25 August, it follows that the consecration took place on 21 August. In the Crowland calendar mentioned above there is a feast for the ordination of St Guthlac under that date.

CHAPTER XLVIII (p. 146)

Ecgburh's gifts. Nothing is known of the royal abbess daughter of King Aldwulf (see p. 16 above). She has sometimes been confused, in spite of the different names, with Eadburh, abbess of Thanet and correspondent of Boniface, or the Eadburg whose body rested at Southwell (*Die Heiligen Englands*, p. 18). There is also a lady called Egburg who writes to Boniface in about 718, telling him her troubles (Boniface, ed. Tangl, *Ep.* 13, p. 18) but it is not at all likely that she is this Ecgburh. It is more likely that she is the Ecgburh mentioned in the *Liber Vitae* of Durham (fo. 14b) under the heading of 'reginarum et abbatissarum'.

The leaden coffin and linen cloth correspond closely with the gift of a linen cloth to Cuthbert by the Abbess Verca and the gift of a stone coffin by Cudda (*V.pr.* c. 37).

Ad patibulum dominicae crucis. This obscure phrase seems to refer to an attitude of prayer common especially among the Irish. The arms were stretched out in the form of a cross (Gougaud, *C.C.L.* p. 93).

Cissa. See Introduction, p. 19 and notes to the prologue, p. 175. The abbess's questions about Cissa are very reminiscent of Abbess Ælfflæd's questions to Cuthbert about King Ecgfrith's successor to the Northumbrian throne (*V.pr.* c. 24; *Two Lives*, p. 239).

CHAPTER XLIX (p. 148)

Æthelbald's visit. The later tradition (see Introduction, p. 8) was that Æthelbald visited Guthlac after he had succeeded to the throne. This chapter proves conclusively that this tradition was incorrect and was of course invented to support the forged charter which Æthelbald is supposed to have given to the abbey shortly afterwards. Felix seems to have no doubts as to the unworthy character of Ceolred (see pp. 5 ff. above). The latter was a grandson of Penda, king of Mercia from 632? to 654. Æthelbald was the grandson of Penda's brother Eowa. On Ceolred's death in 716, Æthelbald came to the throne peacefully as Guthlac had promised. It may have been that the ability and strength of character of the latter were already known and so he was accepted as king without a struggle.

Quando humanum consilium defecisset. A phrase similar to this is quoted by Gildas as from Philo (Gildas, *De excidio et conquestu Britanniae, Mon. Germ. Hist.*, Auct. Antiquiss., XIII, t. I, 1894, p. 36, l. 10). An almost identical phrase is also quoted as from Philo in Eginhard's letters (Plummer, II, 27). It is possible that Felix may have found the phrase either in Gildas or in Rufinus (*Historia Ecclesiastica*, II, 5, 5, edd. T. Mommsen and E. Schwartz, Leipzig, 1908, p. 119).

CHAPTER L (p. 150)

Guthlac's death. The whole story of Guthlac's death is closely modelled on that of St Cuthbert as related by Bede (*V.pr.* cc. 37–9). Instead of Herefrith it is Beccel who tells the story of the last days. Phrase after phrase is borrowed and the general effect is to deprive the story of much of that reality and poignancy which Cuthbert's death-scene possesses. The more confused but also more vivid description of Cuthbert's death, gives an air of verisimilitude and credibility which Felix's account entirely fails to convey. (But see Kurtz, p. 121, who holds the opposite view about the dramatic qualities of Felix's account as compared with that of Bede.)

Guthlac's foreknowledge of his death. This foreknowledge of the exact time of one's death was constantly granted to the saints and there are many examples of it in Bede and elsewhere (cf. *Two Lives*, p. 335). Bede makes no mention of this foreknowledge in the actual death-scene of Cuthbert, though it is made clear elsewhere in the story that Cuthbert had this knowledge.

Pega. This is the first mention of Guthlac's sister though she plays a leading part during the rest of the Life. For further details about her see Introduction, pp. 13–14, 24. Her day was 8 January, under which date she appears in the mid eleventh- and fifteenth-century Crowland calendars already mentioned (*English Kalendars before 1100*, p. 254; *English Kalendars after 1100*, I, p. 117). She has no separate Acta, but the Bollandist account of her

(*AA.SS.* Jan. 1, pp. 532–3) is based on Felix, Ordericus and the Pseudo-Ingulf. She was supposed to have lived at Peakirk (i.e. Pega's church) and to have died in Rome. The Pseudo-Ingulf has an extravagant story of how, on her arrival in Rome, all the church bells rang for an hour to indicate to the citizens the merits of her holiness (*Historia Ingulphi*, p. 5).

Tell to no one. It was extremely common for a saint to forbid those who had witnessed a miracle to make any mention of it until after his death. The prohibition probably derives from our Lord's command to His disciples on the Mount of Transfiguration (Matt. xvii. 9). For a further discussion of this injunction see *Two Lives*, pp. 319–20.

Ecgberht. This is the first mention of the name of this anchorite. It would seem from the saint's words that he was in close contact with Guthlac though not in his immediate neighbourhood. In the next chapter, Ecgberht is said to have sent the shroud which in c. xlviii is described as the gift of Ecgburh (see note, p. 191). The Pseudo-Ingulf names him as one of the four anchorites living in cells near Guthlac's oratory at the time of the alleged foundation of the monastery in 716 (*Historia Ingulphi*, p. 5). Ecgberht 'alone' knew of the angelic ministrations enjoyed by the saint. But apparently he only knew of them vaguely; it is their full import which Beccel is to reveal to him.

Stretching his hands towards the altar. The saint had said his last mass on the previous Easter Sunday and had doubtless 'reserved' the Sacrament on the altar for this his last moment, which he knew to be at hand.

Marvels associated with the death of the saint. The sweet odour associated with the death of a saint is less common than the sweet odour associated with the elevation of the relics and especially when, as not infrequently happened, the saint's body was discovered incorrupt. The same is true also of the heavenly light. These two marvels are the typical authentication of the relics of a saint (cf. H. Gunter, *Legenden-Studien*, Cologne, 1906, p. 32; *Bede, L.T.W.* p. 219). The only miracle associated with the death of Cuthbert is the healing of the man suffering from dysentery (*V.pr.* c. 38). The very absence of these marvels makes Bede's account of Cuthbert's death more impressive and dramatic.

Date of death. Guthlac died on 11 April which in 714 was the Wednesday of Easter week.

Three days. The deposition of St Cuthbert and that of most saints was on the same day as the death (Plummer, ii, p. 240; *Two Lives*, p. 358). Guthlac's sister did not arrive at the earliest until the day after his death. But even then his obsequies occupied three days. It is difficult to explain the reason for these prolonged obsequies. Perhaps it was in order to pay the saint special honour, just as in later times abbots were buried after three days while monks were buried on the same or the following day (E. Martène, *De antiquis ecclesiae ritibus*, Bassani, 1788, ii, p. 370).

CHAPTER LI (p. 160)

The incorrupt body. This account of the elevation of the relics and the discovery of the incorrupt body is again based upon the corresponding chapter in the *V.pr*. The main difference is that Cuthbert's body remained eleven years in its stone coffin before it was raised from the grave, while Guthlac's body was raised twelve months afterwards. In each case the elevation took place on the anniversary of the deposition. Pega, like Cuthbert's fellow monks, is astonished at the state of the body and the clothes. The very words describing her discovery are borrowed at large from Bede's account. In each case the body is placed in a shrine above the ground. This shrine was elaborated by Æthelbald as we are told in the chapter. But there is no reference to the establishment of a monastery as there certainly would have been if the story of the Pseudo-Ingulf had been true.

At this point in the *V.pr*. Bede inserts a poem in praise of the incorrupt saint; but Felix contents himself with a paean of praise in prose. No later references are found to the incorruptibility of the body of the saint (see Introduction, p. 10). It would therefore seem as if the claim, if ever seriously made, was soon forgotten. A story preserved in a MS. now in Trinity College, Dublin (T.C.D. B.2.7), and written in an early thirteenth-century hand, tells how some of Guthlac's bones were carried round the country in the middle of the twelfth century in order to obtain subscriptions for the rebuilding of the monastery after the great fire which destroyed the monastic buildings of Crowland in 1147 (Bertram Colgrave, 'St Guthlac of Crowland: a Durham incident', *Durham University Journal*, N.S., vol. xv, 1954, pp. 93 ff.). Further at the translation of the saint in 1136, the account refers explicitly to his bones though the sweet odour testifies to his sainthood (see above, p. 40 and *AA.SS*. Aprilis, II, p. 55). Cf. also p. 9 n. 4.

Ecgberht's gift. It is curious that the gift of the 'sindo' attributed in c. XLVIII to Ecgburh seems here to have been attributed to the anchorite Ecgberht. Of course it is possible that the gift of Ecgberht may have been a different garment, but it does not seem likely. Perhaps the names have been confused; and yet there is no MS. evidence of such confusion, so that such confusion, if confusion there be, goes back to a very early stage in the history of the transmission of the Life.

CHAPTER LII (p. 164)

Æthelbald's visit. It seems probable that Æthelbald's visit to the saint took place after the elevation of the relics. He is promised that he shall come to the throne within twelve months, which agrees with the accepted date for the beginning of Æthelbald's reign in 716. The miracle is a good example of a very common type in which the suppliant visits the shrine of some saint or other holy place and is granted either healing or knowledge of the future. It was known in classical times under the name of *incubatio*, in which the consultant obtained direct communion with the god or departed spirit, by laying himself down in some holy place to await a vision. The practice passed over to the Christian Church and is still found in churches, especially in Eastern Europe (cf. *E.R.E. s.v.* 'incubation', vol. VII, p. 206. For a series of Neapolitan examples see D. Mallardo, 'L'Incubazione nella Cristianità medievale Napoletana', *An. Boll.* LXVII, 1949, pp. 465–98).

CHAPTER LIII (p. 166)

Wissa. This is the name of the 'provincia' or group of peoples who, in the eighth century, probably dwelt along the lower reaches of the River Wissey and the River Nene (Stenton, p. 291 and O. K. Schram, 'Fenland Place Names', *The Early Cultures of North-west Europe*, H. M. Chadwick Memorial Studies, Cambridge, 1950, p. 436). The people would take their name from the river.

Healing of the blind man. The method of healing by infusion in water is well known in miraculous healings. There are many examples of the same thing in Bede (e.g. *V.pr.* c. 41; *H.ecc.* III, 17, IV, 3; and see *Bede, L.T.W.* pp. 219–20).

Orfanitatem. Felix may well have found this or a similar word in a glossary, glossed as *orbus parentibus* (cf. Virg. *Aen.* II, 216). Taking the first word as equivalent to the lemma, he used the word in the sense of 'deprivation' (cf. A. Campbell, 'Some linguistic features of early Anglo-Latin verse', *Transactions of the Philological Society*, 1953, pp. 1–20).

Salt. The importance of salt as a necessary ingredient in food has given it a religious significance which is reflected in both the Old and the New Testaments. It has also been used in ritual since the early days of the Church. It may be that the salt here mentioned had been exorcized and blessed by the saint in the preparation of holy water perhaps for baptism. Having been once blessed it might be used again without a new benediction (*Cath. Enc. s.v.* 'salt', XIII, p. 403). The incident happened some time after the saint's death and so the salt was in a glutinous state.

Offertoriam. An invention of Felix, perhaps based on the word *oblaticus* normally used of something offered at the altar. So Felix uses his word loosely in the sense of something consecrated.

INDEX